Mystery Accomplished

The Hope of the World

by

Jim Reeves

Mystery Accomplished, The Hope of the World

ISBN 978-1506-912-31-8 PBK
ISBN 978-1506-902-51-7 EBK

May 2016

Library of Congress Control Number: 2016945541

Published and Distributed by
First Edition Design Publishing, Inc.
P.O. Box 20217, Sarasota, FL 34276-3217
www.firsteditiondesignpublishing.com

To my mother, Ruth Reeves (1910-1996), whose unending quest for God's truth shaped my future more than she would ever know. She not only gave me the ancient prayer below, but lived it in her daily life. Her expressed desire in her later years was to write down for her children and grandchildren, "Why we are not living in the last days." She passed away, leaving that task for another. It is my prayer that this book, although less eloquent than she would have written, will express God's truth and will honor both her Lord and her memory.

From the cowardice that shrinks from new truth,

From the laziness that is content with half-truth,

From the arrogance that thinks it knows all truth,

O God of Truth, deliver us!

~ Ancient Prayer

In Appreciation

I am deeply grateful to my wife, Donna, whose constant love, support, and unwavering faith in God have been my strength to carry on when I wanted to quit.

~

Special thanks to my good friend, Sharon McDaniel, who not only spent hours reading, correcting, and contributing to the contents of this book, but has also been an inspiration as a "fellow seeker" of God's truth for many years.

~

Most of all, I am thankful to Jesus for willingly bearing my sin and shame to accomplish the mystery of God and make it possible for me to be what I am, a sinner saved by grace!

INTRODUCTION

The Breath of Life

A New York-based human resources company recently compiled a ranking of cities that qualify as hardship posts based on a set of criteria that includes levels of pollution, disease, political violence, and availability of goods and services. The worst of the worst is located in an oil-rich country in the tropical region of Africa. The weather is sweltering hot and humid. The vast majority of the fifteen million people who live in this city have no electricity, running water, or toilet facilities. Trash is piled in the streets and on back roads, drainage ditches and gutters are filled with raw sewage and debris, and disease-carrying mosquitoes and rats are constant, daily companions. Over 24% of all children die of malaria before the age of five. Including adults, there are more than 25,000 malaria deaths every month, and that is only one of dozens of major health risks.

Then there is the smell. From the smoke of millions of charcoal fires over which meager rations are cooked and the diesel exhaust from power generators, mixed with the odor of rotting trash and open sewers, there is no place to catch a breath of fresh air. At the end of my first ten weeks there, I boarded an airplane for the thirteen-hour flight from Africa to Atlanta, Georgia. Exhausted from the long flight, I made my way to the tram which would take me to my connecting flight to Houston. As I exited the tram and ascended the escalator to the main floor of the Atlanta terminal, I was immediately rejuvenated by the aroma of freshly brewed

Starbucks coffee and the sweet, mouth-watering smell of freshly baked cinnamon rolls. Then it hit me…I COULD BREATHE! For the first time in ten weeks I could take a breath and not smell the sewer. I stopped for a couple of minutes, took a few deep breaths, and silently thanked God for fresh air!

Almighty God wants to give us far more than just fresh air. He wants to breathe into us everlasting life. In the account of creation, the Bible says in Genesis 2:7, *"The Lord God formed the man from the dust of the ground and breathed into his nostrils the breath of life, and the man became a living being."* **God breathes life!** The Bible is the divinely inspired Word of God. *"All Scripture is God-breathed and is useful for doctrine (teaching), rebuking, correcting and training in righteousness, so that the man of God may be thoroughly equipped for every good work"* (2 Timothy 3:16-17). Far worse than malaria or yellow fever, all of us are terminally afflicted with the disease of sin. The Scriptures are the breath of heaven through which we learn of the curative, atoning blood of Jesus. We have all smelled the stench of Satan's sewer long enough. It is time for a breath of fresh air!

Because the Scriptures are God-breathed, they alone are the deciding criteria for everything we believe and practice as Christians. When some of the Jews decided to leave Jesus because they could not accept his teachings, he asked his disciples if they would also leave. Peter replied, *"Lord, to whom shall we go? You have the words of eternal life"* (John 6:68). It matters not what any man, including this author, thinks or says about a particular subject; God's Word is the final authority. In Galatians 1:8, the apostle Paul said, *"But even if we or an angel from heaven should preach a gospel other than the one we preached to you, let him be eternally condemned!"* This was such an important point in Paul's life and teaching he repeated it again in the very next verse, *"As we have already said, so now I say again: If anybody is preaching to you a gospel other than what you accepted, let him be eternally condemned!"*

This is strong language and, like today, some people who listened to Paul and the other apostles were careful about what they accepted as truth, yet others were not. In Acts 17:10-11 the Bible says, *"As soon as it was night, the brothers sent Paul and Silas away to Berea. On arriving there, they went to the Jewish synagogue. Now the Bereans were of more noble character than the Thessalonians, for they received the message with great eagerness and examined the Scriptures every day to see if what Paul said was true."* The church today desperately needs a new crop of "Bereans."

There are many teachings prevalent today that need to be examined in light of the Scriptures to see if they are true. These doctrines have permeated the modern-day Christian church, have changed its world view and the focus of its mission, and have negated the positive impact it should be having in the world. In short, much of what people hear at church and on "Christian" television is "stinking thinking" that smells more like the sewer than the fresh aroma of good news. It is my earnest prayer that all who read this book will "*Search the Scriptures to see if these things are true.*"

Can we know what the Bible says…and means? Absolutely! The God who created the world and loves us so much he sent his only Son to be crucified for our sin is able to write a book we can understand. How foolish of us to think otherwise. The problem with misunderstanding God's Word lies not with the Scriptures, but with our lack of study and willingness to accept what God says, especially if it means we must change our own thinking or our lives. There is more effort by many today to make the Bible say what they want it to say, to approve their own opinions and beliefs, than simply to learn and live what God says.

The Bible is not a collection of short stories about many different topics. It is a collection of the writings of many different inspired authors over centuries of time, all telling the same story. There is one overall theme in the entire Bible; the redemption of man from the consequences of sin. The Old Testament contains prophesies of God's plan for redemption as well as physical examples showing how this great mystery would be accomplished. The New Testament is the fulfillment of the Old in which we see the reality of what was promised. This redemptive plan of the Creator of the Universe was the mystery of the ages. The mystery is revealed in his Word. God wants, more than anything else, to breathe life back into his most beloved creation. Take a deep breath!

There are three fundamental principles of Bible study:

1. **Let the Bible interpret itself.**
2. **Keep Scripture in its context.**
3. **Understand the historical time frame.**

These fundamentals are critical to the proper understanding of any communication, written or oral. Although very simple and just plain common sense, the basic standards of Biblical interpretation are being largely ignored today, resulting in much confusion. The application of these three principles opens God's will in clear and understandable terms. The Psalmist said, *"The unfolding of your words gives light; it gives understanding to the simple"* (Psalm 119:130). In Ephesians 5:17 Paul wrote, *"Therefore do not be foolish, but understand what the Lord's will is."* Remember, the Bible is God's *revelation* to enlighten us. We can understand it!

Let's look at a few examples of how these principles help us understand what the Lord's will is. The Old Testament ends with a prophecy that the prophet Elijah would come before the great day of the Lord (Malachi 4:5). Who was this "Elijah" and when would he come? The Bible tells us. Jesus said in Matthew 11:14 that John the Baptist was this Elijah who was to come. If it were not for this verse in Matthew, one can only imagine what modern-day "prophets" would be saying about a coming of Elijah! Other obvious examples of how the Bible interprets itself are seen in what we call parallel passages. This is especially helpful in reading the Gospels. Comparing how different writers recorded the exact same teachings and events can answer a lot of questions. The Bible is a self-interpreting book. Our job is to study.

The second principle of proper Bible study is context. A statement in any language or setting means little without knowing the context. In 1 Corinthians 7, Paul says it is better if one does not get married. In verse 27 he says if one is not married, *"Don't look for a wife."* Does the Bible teach that marriage is not a good thing...even though in the beginning God created Eve for Adam and said, *"It is not good for man to live alone?"* If we study the context of the apostle's teaching to the Corinthians his message will become clear. They were living in some terrible times that were only going to get worse. Paul knew this because it was revealed to him by the Holy Spirit. In verse 26 of that same chapter he plainly says, "*Because of this present crisis...*" it is better not to marry. Without the context the Bible seems to contradict itself. Read in context it all makes perfect sense, and, once again, the Bible properly interprets itself.

The third principle critical to a proper understanding of Scripture is recognizing the historical time in which it was written and the Biblical time in which we are living. With all the evil in the world today, why is nobody building a boat? We properly understand that Noah's ark was a one-time event, and we are not living in the days of Noah. No boat is needed. Why do we not offer animal sacrifices today? Because, taking the Bible's message as one entire story, allowing God's Word to interpret itself, and keeping sacrifices in their proper context, we correctly understand we are not living in the days of Moses and the Old Law. Jesus was the once and for all, perfect sacrifice. Thus, no more animal sacrifices are needed.

Failing to apply these fundamental principles of Bible study will only lead to confusion and a myriad of Biblical "interpretations" that are simply false doctrines. Many Christians today have fallen victim to modern philosophies based on erroneous explanations of certain passages resulting from the failure to understand the historical time frame for many of the events described in the Bible. By taking Scriptures out of context and not allowing the Bible to interpret itself, preachers today are confusing people about the times in which we are living and proclaiming messages that are far from the truth.

As important as studying and understanding the Bible is, it should be stressed that teaching one particular issue should not become an obsession, nor should it detract from the primary mission of the church. Certain subjects, particularly those that are difficult to grasp and likely to have widely differing viewpoints, should be handled carefully and in situations where everyone has an opportunity to ask questions and express a different understanding. Only through open discussions in a non-threatening atmosphere can we hope to reach a more common understanding. If Christians are to move from the milk of the Word to meat, churches must provide opportunities for such open discussions, and all viewpoints should be evaluated in light of Scripture.

While we wrestle with a better understanding of the more difficult issues in Scripture, we must never take our attention off the primary mission of the church, which is the proclamation of the gospel to save lost souls. Jesus explained his second coming to his apostles in a private session, not during the Sermon on the Mount to the multitude. Even though the Apostle Peter quoted the Prophet Joel in his first gospel sermon (Acts 2), he did not make Joel's predictions of the coming wrath and judgment of the last days the subject of his message. He had a more urgent message that day, "*Repent and be baptized, every one of you, for the remission of sins...*" His message that day was to the lost. Several years later he wrote two letters explaining what Jesus had taught concerning his coming and judgment.

All of the apostles followed this same pattern of teaching. Their primary mission was to proclaim the gospel to the world, and they never lost sight of that. Paul said, *"I am not ashamed of the gospel, because it is the power of God for the salvation of everyone who believes: first for the Jew, then for the Gentile"* (Romans 1:16). Later, in personal visits and letters, he and the others explained more difficult concepts. We are fortunate to have both their example of evangelism, particularly in the Acts of the Apostles, as the primary mission and their letters of instruction on the "weightier matters." As we in the church today discuss and learn the latter, let us never forget the primary mission.

It is precisely because the focus of many churches has been misdirected that the issue of eschatology needs to be studied. "Jesus is coming soon" has virtually replaced "Repent and be baptized" as the current proclamation of Christianity. Because the world has witnessed hundreds of failed prophesies concerning Jesus' coming and the end of the world, this message has undermined the primary mission as well as the message and credibility of the church. All Christians need to remember that the most essential message to a lost and dying world is the death, burial, and resurrection of Jesus Christ. Other issues belong in Christian study groups in which we can move from infants to maturity in our knowledge of God's will.

The "good news" of the Gospel and the Revelation of Jesus Christ is not about an angry, jealous God who is fed up with the world and is soon going to "rapture" a few holy people and destroy everyone else, along with the entire universe, with fire. Rather it is that, *"God so loved the world that he gave his only begotten Son that whoever believes in him should not perish, but have everlasting life."* Salvation, not destruction, is the hope of the world.

My fellow Bereans, join with me in searching the Scriptures anew to see if these things are true. Each section of this book will contain many Scripture references and quotations. Please take the time to look them up for yourself, study the context, do searches to find other passages where these concepts are explained, and learn for yourself what God is actually saying. While it is often wise to consider what various authors and scholars have said concerning the Scriptures, the best source of information will always be the Bible itself. The purpose of this study is to learn what God says. His view is the one that matters. As you study his Word, breathe deeply and savor the fresh air!

Section One

Setting the Stage

CHAPTER 1

And God Said…

Human beings possess a seemingly unquenchable desire for knowledge while at the same time confidently accepting everything we now understand and believe as being "right." Many things believed to be true are actually false. For centuries people believed the earth was the center of the universe and the sun and other heavenly bodies revolved around it. Galileo (1564–1642), working on a theory first introduced by another scientist named Nicolaus Copernicus, proved this long-held belief to be wrong. His teachings were extremely radical at the time and went against the accepted beliefs of other scientists and the Roman Catholic Church. Although his theory of heliocentrism was true, he was eventually forced to recant his teaching and *he spent* the last years of his life under house arrest on orders of the Roman Inquisition. However, opposition from the scientific community and the church did not change the truth. Galileo was right.

Although we have learned a lot of truth through the centuries, we still only comprehend a small portion of Almighty God's creation. As the prophet said in Isaiah 40:28, *"The Lord is the everlasting God, the Creator of the ends of the earth. He will not grow tired or weary, and his understanding no one can fathom."* Our concern here is not to understand the scientific laws of the universe, but to understand the will of God for our lives. How do we know his will for us today?

How does God communicate with us? We often hear someone

say, "God told me..." and they proceed to tell of something they believe the Lord said to them. Claiming personal communication with the Almighty is becoming the accepted way of expressing God's will for Christians today. "The Lord told me to do this." "The Lord told me to tell you..." "The Lord gave me this message." "He (or she) is a Holy Spirit-inspired instrument of God." "The words of the song were given to me by God." Not everyone who uses this language means God personally speaks to them, although an increasing number do. Any non-believer who is not familiar with Scripture or the Christian faith would assume these people are claiming divine inspiration, or at least a very real, personal message direct from the Almighty.

False claims regarding messages supposedly from God by prominent men and women have done irreparable damage to the cause of Christ and brought immense reproach on him and his church. Despite the popularity of these self-proclaimed "prophets of God," the Scriptures do not hold them in such high regard. Jeremiah 23:16 says, *"This is what the Lord Almighty says: 'Do not listen to what the prophets are prophesying to you; they fill you with false hopes. They speak visions from their own minds, not from the mouth of the Lord.' "*

Again the Bible says in Ezekiel 13:1-7, *"The word of the Lord came to me: Say to those who prophesy out of their own imagination: 'Hear the word of the Lord! This is what the Sovereign Lord says: Woe to the foolish prophets who follow their own spirit and have seen nothing! Their visions are false and their divinations a lie. They say, 'The Lord declares,' when the Lord has not sent them; yet they expect their words to be fulfilled. Have you not seen false visions and uttered lying divinations when you say, 'The Lord declares,' though I have not spoken?"*

Do Christian evangelists today follow their own spirits and declare things in God's name when the Lord has not sent them? According to the Bible, the test would be to examine their "prophesies" and see if they come true. If they claim to receive a message from the Lord, yet that prophecy does not happen, both they and their message are to be totally rejected.

Certain so-called Christian television programs, books, and universities have become distribution points for the modern health-and-wealth gospel. The promotion of the now-famous "seed faith" doctrine has brought in untold millions of dollars to these organizations. In 1977 the major proponent of this "gospel" claimed that he received a vision and revelation from God. In the vision he claimed that God told him to build a medical center. He also claimed that he saw a 900-foot-tall Jesus, who said that the medical center would be successful. Four years later, in 1981, the facility was opened. In 1983 this same evangelist claimed that Jesus Christ appeared to him in person (not a vision) and told him to find a cure for cancer. So far, he has not found that cure. In 1986 he said that God told him to raise $8 million for the school or he would be "called home." In April of 1987 the school reported having received $9.1 million, which was $1.1 million more than was supposedly required by God.

Then in November 1987, just seven months after claiming to receive the money God had required to make the medical center a success, an announcement was made that it would be closing down. In September 1989, apparently no longer afraid that God was going to call him home, the evangelist closed the medical center. Obviously his vision from God and the 900-foot-tall Jesus had been false. Explaining the colossal failure of the medical center, instead of admitting that his so-called "revelations" and "prophesies" were all from his own imagination, he claimed to have received yet another revelation! In this new vision God said he had changed his mind about the medical center and that he (God) had precipitated its failure and closing.

Another popular "prophet of God" and "healer" falsely predicted that all the homosexuals in America would die by fire in the late 1990's. He stated on TBN, after a crusade in South America in 2002, that he would return from his next foreign mission with video footage of Jesus appearing on stage during the crusades, because Jesus had told him this was going to happen. This man also stated that very soon people would no longer need to take their deceased loved ones to the morgue. Instead they should be placed in front of the television during the airing of TBN, and they would rise from the dead. He claims to receive messages from God, yet all his prophesies have been proven false.

These, and countless other modern-day "prophets of God", teach that they have healed many people and continue to do so. Yet they have never caused a missing arm or leg to appear, caused a congenitally deformed individual to become whole, healed a Down 's syndrome child, caused a quadriplegic to walk, or raised a dead person. All of their claimed healings cannot be seen or verified, i.e., diseases inside the body, headaches and other ailments that cannot be proven to exist. The supposed healings that occur during their crusades are paraded across the platforms, while those with debilitating conditions, the blind, the terminally ill, and those with missing body parts, never see these great men performing miracles on them.

Decade after decade of false claims, yet the Christian world still holds such men in high esteem, considering them great men of faith. Hundreds, if not thousands, of examples could be given of evangelists today who claim to receive messages from God and who also claim miraculous powers of the Holy Spirit. Seeing the millions of dollars collected in the name of Jesus by their predecessors, countless preachers on every continent have followed suit.

Another constant message heard among modern-day prophets concerns the second coming of Jesus. Over the past few decades, primarily because of strife in the Middle East, we have heard countless predictions of the end of the world, not only from the charismatic television evangelists but also from pulpits in mainstream churches throughout the land. Not one of these prophesies has come true. False prophecies of the end of the world and bogus claims of healing have become a favorite topic of national news media reporters when they want to display the ignorance and gullibility of those who claim to be Christians. The result of such stories causes non-believers to see all of Christianity as a hoax. Who can blame them?

What does God say about a prophet whose prophesies do not come true? Deuteronomy 18:20-22, *"But a prophet who presumes to speak in my name anything I have not commanded him to say, or a prophet who speaks in the name of other gods, must be put to death. You may say to yourselves, 'How can we know when a message has not been spoken by the Lord?' If what a prophet proclaims in the name of the Lord does not take place or come true, that is a message the Lord has not spoken. That prophet has spoken presumptuously. Do not be afraid of him."* The church of Jesus Christ desperately needs to turn its back on the false prophets who are hindering its mission and return to the Word of Almighty God.

God has spoken to mankind. The Scripture says God spoke to many people throughout history. He spoke to Adam and Eve in the Garden of Eden. He spoke to Noah and told him to build a boat. He spoke to Moses in a burning bush and through Moses to the Israelites and Pharaoh to deliver his people from Egyptian bondage. He spoke to Moses on Mt. Sinai. He spoke to the prophets. He spoke through the angel to Mary concerning the birth of Jesus. He spoke through Jesus in the flesh. He spoke by the miraculous power of the Holy Spirit to the apostles and writers of the New Testament.

Does he still personally speak to people today? Our answer to this question has everything to do with how we view the Bible and how much time we spend in Bible study. God spent centuries revealing, confirming, and recording his Word. Is that revelation complete? In 2 Timothy 3:15-17 the Apostle Paul told Timothy, *"From infancy you have known the holy Scriptures, which are able to make you wise for salvation through faith in Christ Jesus. All Scripture is God-breathed and is useful for teaching, rebuking, correcting and training in righteousness, so that the man of God may be thoroughly equipped for every good work."*

Jesus, when tempted by the Devil in the wilderness, did not tell the Devil, "God told me to tell you..." Three times he answered Satan with Scripture. This was a pattern he followed throughout his personal ministry. He went to the synagogue in Nazareth and, instead of simply telling them who he was, he read from the scroll of Isaiah. Then he said to them, *"Today this Scripture is fulfilled in your hearing"* (Luke 4:16-19). Speaking to the Emmaus disciples in Luke 24:27-45, *"And beginning with Moses and all the Prophets, he explained to them what was said in all the Scriptures concerning himself... They asked each other, 'Were not our hearts burning within us while he talked with us on the road and opened the Scriptures to us?'* ***Then he opened their minds so they could understand the Scriptures."***

The apostles and early disciples learned well this lesson from the Master Teacher. Commissioned by him to preach the Gospel to the entire world, they did not go tell folks, "God told us to tell you..." In Acts 17:2, *"As his custom was, Paul went into the synagogue, and on three Sabbath days he reasoned with them* ***from the Scriptures."*** Again in Acts 18:28 Paul *"...vigorously refuted the Jews in public debate,* ***proving from the Scriptures*** *that Jesus was the Christ."* Again in 1 Corinthians 15:3 Paul said, *"For what I received I passed on to you as of first importance: that Christ died for our sins* ***according to the Scriptures."***

Phillip teaching the eunuch in Acts 8:32-35, *"The eunuch was reading this passage of Scripture: he was led like a sheep to the slaughter, and as a lamb before the shearer is silent, so he did not open his mouth...Then* ***Philip began with that very passage of Scripture*** *and told him the good news about Jesus."*

The Apostle Peter in 2 Peter 1:20-21 said, *"Above all, you must understand that* ***no prophecy of Scripture came about by the prophet's own interpretation****. For prophecy never had its origin in the will of man, but men spoke from God as they were carried along by the Holy Spirit."*

These men, although divinely inspired by the Holy Spirit, used none of the language we hear so often today. Instead, they were very careful to always use Scripture as the basis for God's message. They understood something missed by too many Christians today, including many preachers. The coming of Jesus Christ and subsequent revealing of the new covenant of grace was not a new message. Rather it was the fulfillment of thousands of years of Old Testament prophecies.

Miss this point and the Bible becomes a collection of unrelated writings, the meaning of which is open to a myriad of varying interpretations with no hope of knowing which one is correct. **There is nothing "new" in the New Testament.** God spent centuries foretelling, through the Old Testament Scriptures, a carefully orchestrated divine "mystery" about the ultimate redemption of mankind. Virtually every word in every book of the New Testament is directly related to the revealing of these prophecies.

John the Baptist was the promised "Elijah" who was to come (Malachi 4:5, Matthew 11:10). Jesus was the "promised Messiah." He said in Luke 24:44, *"Everything must be fulfilled that is written about me in the Law of Moses, the Prophets and the Psalms."* Every minute detail of his birth, life, and death on the cross, down to the disposal of his clothes, was *"...so that the Scriptures might be fulfilled."*

The New Testament is the consummate exposition on the Old. Each book reveals more details about the mystery of God and how it was being brought to fruition. The final book is entitled The

Revelation of Jesus Christ and is the grand summation of all that had been said before. In Revelation 10:7 John said, *"But in the days when the seventh angel is about to sound his trumpet,* ***the mystery of God will be accomplished, just as he announced to his servants the prophets.****"*

When people today say, "God told me...' a red flag should immediately go up and they should be asked for the chapter and verse where God said what they claim he said. There are some legitimate questions for those who claim to have a message from God other than the Bible. When did God tell you? How did he tell you? Did you physically hear his voice? Did anyone else hear it? Was it confirmed by a miraculous sign that others could see so people would know it was from God? Do you believe you are divinely inspired by the Holy Spirit to receive God's revelation? And if the Bible is the complete, inspired Word of God, what possible explanation can there be for additional messages from God?

Consider this seriously. Every word spoken from God was by the divine inspiration of the Holy Spirit. How can anyone today claim to hear the voice of God and not have this same divine inspiration? Most people today will admit they did not actually *hear* God's voice or see a burning bush. Rather they "...felt the presence of the Lord" and "...these thoughts came to my mind so clearly it had to be from God." Some simply claim, "God laid this on my heart."

Attributing one's thoughts and feelings to God speaking is a very convenient interpretation of how God communicates with man. It is also an extremely dangerous false doctrine. It makes our human thoughts become God's will! How can one possibly refute a word or teaching if it "came from God"? If that doesn't bother us just a little, something is woefully wrong.

How does the Bible say God speaks to us? Through the Scripture...the Bible. Hebrews 2:3-4 says, *"This salvation, which was first announced by the Lord, was confirmed to us by those who heard him. God also testified to it by signs, wonders and various miracles, and gifts of the Holy Spirit distributed according to his will."* We can know there is a God and know a great deal about God from created things (Romans 1). But when it comes to his Word and his promises, we should demand Scripture. One can see God's promise in the rainbow, but if it were not for the written Word you would not know a rainbow was a promise from God. When God spoke to people he also testified to it. Absent the testimony, we should not believe the message is from God.

The belief that somehow God personally explains his will to us on a daily basis as we go through life relieves us of the need to study the Bible. It is a very convenient and conscience-soothing doctrine for Christians who are too busy to devote hours to learning his will. Why study when he is going to tell me everything I need to know as I go along? If Jesus and the apostles were careful to use Scripture for everything they taught, should we be any less?

It should be noted that a majority of Christians today who speak about what "God told me" are not claiming to have seen a 900-foot-tall Jesus, a burning bush, or literally heard the voice of God. It is a figure of speech by which they mean through their understanding of God's Word they believe this is what God wants them to do. The problem with the language is not what they mean by it; rather what others understand them to be saying. One should choose words carefully when expressing how God reveals his will to us today. Only through a proper understanding of Scripture can we know his will. Paul said, *"Faith comes by hearing, and hearing by the Word of God"* (Romans 10:17).

How then do we gain an understanding of Scripture that will sustain us in life? While we cannot know everything, we can know what he has chosen to reveal to us in his Holy Word, the Bible. As we study, let's remember the lesson learned from Galileo and search for truth, not just information to support a preconceived view. Truth will ultimately prevail.

When it comes to studying the Bible, it is also important to know that not all truth is revealed to us by God and not all that is revealed is of the same importance. There are fundamental truths without a knowledge and acceptance of which one cannot be saved. Jesus said in John 14:6, *"I am the way and the truth and the life. No one comes to the Father except through me."* Without faith in Jesus Christ as the Son of God there is no salvation. The majority of God's word brings us to a better understanding of his will for our lives, but it is not necessary to fully understand all Biblical truth to receive his grace and forgiveness. As we begin to unpack the Scriptures to discover the great mystery of God, we will see the following:

1. **There are secret things**
2. **There are disputable things**
3. **There are elementary things**
4. **There are things that require deep, thorough study**

Some things God simply does not reveal to us. In Deuteronomy 29:29 the Bible says, *"The secret things belong to the Lord our God, but the things revealed belong to us and to our children forever, that we may follow all the words of the law."* We do not know what Jesus wrote in the sand (John 8:1-11) or what the seven thunders said (Revelation 10:3-4) because they were not revealed. It is a waste of time to speculate on secret things that are not revealed in his Word.

There are also some things which are "disputable matters" discussed in the Scriptures. Romans chapter 14 explains what disputable matters are and how to handle them. In verse one Paul says, *"Accept him whose faith is weak, without passing judgment on disputable matters."* He is very clear in this chapter about not allowing disputable matters to destroy the church and God's work on earth. But exactly what are these "disputable" matters?

First, Paul speaks about food choices. One person eats meat and another is a vegetarian. This is a disputable matter…it doesn't matter one way or the other. Both are right, so do not condemn somebody who eats differently than you. Second, in verses 5-8, he talks about some who consider one day more sacred than another. Again Paul says both are right, neither is wrong. If you consider Sunday a "holy day" to the Lord, that's great. If you consider every day as holy to the Lord, that is okay as well. Don't judge one another because of days.

A few verses later he explains how we should handle these things when he says, *"Therefore let us stop passing judgment on one another. Instead, make up your mind not to put any stumbling block or obstacle in your brother's way. As one who is in the Lord Jesus, I am fully convinced that no food is unclean in itself. But if anyone regards something as unclean, then for him it is unclean. If your brother is distressed because of what you eat, you are no longer acting in love. Do not by your eating destroy your brother for whom Christ died. Do not allow what you consider good to be spoken of as evil. For the kingdom of God is not a matter of eating and drinking, but of righteousness, peace and joy in the Holy Spirit, because anyone who serves Christ in this way is pleasing to God and approved by men."* (Romans 14:13-18) And in verse 22, *"So whatever you believe about these things keep between yourself and God."* He concludes his remarks by saying we should live in keeping with our own conscience with regard to these disputable matters.

But what makes something a "disputable matter?" From these and other Scriptures we learn some principles that should help us know the difference between what is "disputable" and what is not. First, for something to be disputable in the Biblical sense, there must be at least two options, both of them must be true, and both of them must be right in God's sight. Two people disagree about eating meat. Either possibility is true; one can eat meat or eat only vegetables. According to Paul, either option is right in God's eyes.

Galileo created quite a "dispute" with his heliocentric view of the universe. That does not mean it was a "disputable matter" because both views could not be right. Two people may sit in a dark room and argue about whether or not the sun is shining outside. Both cannot be right. They can either stay in their dark room and argue, or go outside and look! Sometimes we prefer to stay in the dark and label our differences as "disputable matters" for fear the light of truth will prove us wrong.

Disputable matters are only those beliefs or practices which can have opposing viewpoints that can simultaneously be right and about which the Bible does not give specific teachings or instructions one way or the other. Just because people may hold differing views on certain subjects does not make them "disputable matters" in the Biblical sense. Ignorance of Scripture about a particular subject does not make that subject a disputable matter. If the Bible contains specific teachings about an issue or practice, it is not disputable. We may not understand it; however, it does not fall into the category of "disputable matters."

Finally Paul says if a matter is truly disputable, *"Keep it between yourself and God."* One's personal feelings about these things might be quite strong, but in reality either opinion or practice is right in God's eyes. Because they are matters of opinion, they are not things that relate to one's salvation, nor should they ever become a divisive point in the fellowship of the church. If that happens, they then become sinful. And if one encourages another Christian to violate his or her conscience by insisting on one of these practices, that is also sin. Neither side of a truly disputable matter has any place in the public teaching or worship of the church.

It should be noted that there are some issues about which there are various opinions as to whether or not they are disputable based on honest differences of understanding. There are two fundamental principles in Romans 14 which should determine our attitude and actions regarding such matters. The first is to understand that God is the judge, not man. In verse 4 Paul wrote, *"Who are you to judge someone else's servant? To his own master he stands or falls. And he will stand, for the Lord is able to make him stand."* We are responsible before God, not each other, to act in keeping with our own comprehension and conscience. We should never stand in God's place and pass judgment on a fellow believer. Since we are not perfect, we are all wrong to one degree or another. God judges a person's heart. God is able to make us stand! Second, in verse 19 the apostle wrote, *"Let us therefore make every effort to do what leads to peace and to mutual edification."* We should always be willing to listen, with an open mind, to a different viewpoint. Only by study and discussion can we edify each other and perhaps come to agreement. Even if there is still no agreement, we should do whatever leads to peace in the body of Christ. There must be room in the church for differences. We are not all at the same level of maturity in the faith or in our understanding of the Bible.

Then there are things in Scripture that are elementary. These make up the fundamental tenets of the Christian faith. They are not the sum total of Christian doctrine and practice, but they are the foundation on which our overall understanding of God's Word is built. In 1 Corinthians 15:3-8 the Apostle Paul said, *"For what I received I passed on to you as of first importance: that Christ died for our sins according to the Scriptures, that he was buried, that he was raised on the third day according to the Scriptures, and that he appeared to Peter, and then to the Twelve. After that, he appeared to more than five hundred of the brothers at the same time, most of whom are still living, though some have fallen asleep. Then he appeared to James, then to all the apostles, and last of all he appeared to me also, as to one abnormally born."* Here Paul says the elementary truths of the Gospel are the death, burial, resurrection, and appearance (not second coming) of Jesus Christ.

These are things one must understand and believe to be saved. Christian baptism is the reenactment of these very truths and a symbol by which we proclaim to the world our belief in Jesus' sacrifice for our sins and our belief in his resurrection, based on the undeniable witness of those to whom he appeared. Since we have now been made free from sin, we also share in his resurrection and will live forever with him.

The Hebrew writer, attempting to explain our atonement by Jesus as our High Priest, described these same elementary truths when he said in chapter 5:11-14, *"We have much to say about this, but it is hard to explain because you are slow to learn. In fact, though by this time you ought to be teachers, you need someone to teach you the elementary truths of God's word all over again. You need milk, not solid food! Anyone who lives on milk, being still an infant, is not acquainted with the teaching about righteousness. But solid food is for the mature, who by constant use have trained themselves to distinguish good from evil."* He begins chapter six with these words, *"Therefore let us leave the elementary teachings about Christ and go on to maturity, not laying again the foundation of repentance from acts that lead to death, and of faith in God, instruction about baptisms, the laying on of hands, the resurrection of the dead and eternal judgment. And God permitting, we will do so."*

This passage in Hebrews describes these elementary truths as the "milk" of the word, the diet of infants. Milk is the starter food for life. As critical as milk is for infants, it is not the only food on the menu for life. Like some to whom this letter was addressed, many Christians today choose to live their entire Christian lives on the milk of God's Word. As a result, they remain spiritual infants.

There are secret things, disputable things, elementary things, and then there is the meat of God's revelation. As the writer of Hebrews said, solid food is for the mature. There are Biblical subjects and concepts that require deep, thoughtful, time-consuming study. These things may not be readily or easily understood, but they are neither secret nor disputable. There is truth to be learned if we are willing to chew.

This understanding is not acquired by surveying all the preachers or seminaries in the area to see what the prevailing opinion is. If we learned anything from Galileo, it should be the majority opinion is not always right. It does not come by osmosis from our parents or grandparents. The only source of absolute truth is God. Jesus said, *"I am the truth."* He did not say he knew the truth...but that he IS the truth. To know the truth, one must first know Jesus. To understand truth one must understand his Will, the Bible.

Bible study takes time. As technology advances, the world continues to become smaller and faster. What used to take weeks or months now takes hours or even minutes. Everyone is in a hurry, and we want everything to be available in an instant. We can be in constant contact with people around the world and are even able to travel to and work in outer space. This generation has seen astounding inventions and discoveries. It has also often allowed the demands of the immediate to distract us from the important.

Families spend little time together, fooling themselves into believing that "...it's not the quantity of time spent together that matters...it's the quality." As the first generation of "institutionally raised children" face the world with little concept of family and spiritual values, we are getting a dose of reality that two hours per day of "quality time" is not nearly enough to properly *"...train up a child in the way he should go."* Some things still take time...lots of time. However, it's worth every minute invested. If it means sacrificing some material things, it's well worth the price.

The same problem has plagued the church as Christians have spent less and less time studying the Scriptures. For several decades we have increasingly allowed the fast pace of the world to dictate almost everything related to church. There is no time for Bible study today. Most churches still try to have an hour on Sunday morning, but fewer than half of the members attend. Sunday night and Wednesday night services have been cancelled...no time for those any more. Home Bible studies have to be planned as a series of one-time lessons because most who actually express a desire to attend will not attend regularly. There are just too many other things that interfere.

As a result there can be no in-depth study. Such is no longer necessary. All one has to know is that Jesus is God's Son, he died on the cross for our sin, and he wants us to live forever with him in heaven after we die...which is a good thing because we don't have time for him NOW. As a whole, Christians have an extremely shallow view of Scripture with little or no concept of context or historical setting. They mistakenly believe their pastor or preacher understands the Bible in depth and will tell them what they need to know. The lack of any depth of knowledge among preachers and teachers is evidenced by their messages, which are little more than positive motivational speeches, a kind of psychological pep talk.

Another development that is directly related to this fast-paced culture and that has had a profound impact on the modern church is the emergence of the "mega churches." Their size and multi-million dollar budgets give them access to international media and their leaders are viewed as great men of God because of the huge organizations they have built. They conduct seminars, sell millions of books, headline lectureships and conferences, and are in constant demand to share their "method of success" with the less gifted among us.

This is not to be critical of all large churches. There are many churches in the world that have seen their numbers grow precisely because they have boldly and persuasively proclaimed the

Scriptures. People who are seeking a relationship with God have a deep hunger for his Word. The admonition to preachers today is the same as when Paul told Timothy *to "...preach the Word; be prepared in season and out of season; correct, rebuke and encourage—with great patience and careful instruction"* (2 Timothy 4:2).

The basic mission of the church is to go and make disciples. Who can possibly question the importance of growth? As a matter of principle, anyone who is not interested in church growth does not fully comprehend the gospel message. The church in Jerusalem was not only the first Christian church; it was also the first mega church. There were over three thousand people baptized the first day, and thousands more were converted during the next three-and-one-half years. Their number probably exceeded 20,000 before severe persecution forced most of these first Christians to leave the city. However, there is a very deceptive element to the current mega-church mentality.

There is a frequently repeated refrain among modern church growth "experts" that "God does not bless a church that is not aligned with his will." While this sounds very holy and Biblical on the surface, it is actually used to support a very dangerous false doctrine. According to this belief, since God does not bless a church that is not aligned with his will, churches that have experienced tremendous growth must be properly aligned with God's will. Conversely, churches that do not experience numerical growth are either not aligned with Scripture or simply do not have the necessary skills or employ the correct methods to grow.

First, this concept of growth is the exact opposite of what the Bible actually teaches. Church growth is not our responsibility; it is God's. The Apostle Paul said in 1 Corinthians 3:6, *"I planted the seed, Apollos watered it, but God made it grow."* The KJV says, *"God gives the increase."* This is exactly what happened in Jerusalem. Peter and the other apostles preached the gospel message, and God gave the increase. Acts 2:47 says, *"The Lord added to their number daily those who were being saved."*

The church's mission is to teach and preach the gospel. If the gospel message convicts people of sin and leads to their conversion, the Lord will add them to his church. God will indeed give the increase if we proclaim the truth. The problem with many mega churches today is they have decided a better way to "grow the church" is to do whatever is necessary to attract people to the building and make sure they have a wonderful time while they are present. The so-called "gospel message" cannot contain anything that would be offensive. We must be "seeker sensitive."

There are times when the truth is offensive, but still must be preached. Stephen concluded his sermon in Acts 7 with these words: *"You stiff-necked people, with uncircumcised hearts and ears! You are just like your fathers: You always resist the Holy Spirit! Was there ever a prophet your fathers did not persecute? They even killed those who predicted the coming of the Righteous One. And now you have betrayed and murdered him—you who have received the law that was put into effect through angels but have not obeyed it."* If only Stephen had attended a church growth workshop and learned to be seeker sensitive, he might not have been stoned.

It is not the mission of the church, by modifying the message to suit the world, to ensure growth. While every Christian should be keenly interested in saving lost souls, which will result in church growth, growth itself is not our task. Our job is to proclaim God's truth. God found Noah to be a righteous man and extended him his grace. But after more than one hundred years of preaching the truth and being correctly aligned with God's will, Noah did not win a single convert. There are times, for reasons only God knows, when people simply do not respond to his message. That does not mean we should change the message or invent new ways to grow the church other than the proclamation of the gospel. Jesus attracted thousands of followers during his personal ministry as long as he was healing and feeding them. When it came time for commitment and sacrifice, all but a few deserted him. Does that mean he ceased to be aligned with God's will? Would anyone dare say Jesus was not "seeker sensitive"? Proclaiming the unchanging message of God's Word to lost souls is our challenge. Churches should not be judged by their growth rate or size but by the emphasis they place on the Word of God and the truth of their preaching and teaching.

Although giving lip service to God's Word, modern church growth workshops and books speak mostly about marketing methods. The church is viewed in much the same as any other collective organization. Do what the people like and they will come. Church services in these mega churches have turned into entertainment extravaganzas that would rival any rock concert. This approach is extremely successful and, following the "blessings equals alignment" theology, validates their feel-good message. These churches actually depend on a Biblically illiterate population for their success.

Second, if growth means that a religious body is enjoying God's blessings because they are properly aligned with his will, how does one explain that, according to the World Christian Database, during the period of 2000-2005 the five fastest growing religions are Islam (1.84%), Bahai Faith (1.70%), Sikhism (1.62%), Hinduism (1.57%), and Christianity (1.32%)? If the mega-church growth theology is correct, that would mean Islam, Bahai Faith, Sikhism, and Hinduism are all more aligned with God's will than Christianity. And among those churches that are considered "Christian," the Catholic Church must be more closely aligned with his will than most others since they are the largest. According to this belief, if they were not aligned with God's will, he would not have blessed them so much.

A third problem with the mega-church theology that God blesses those who are properly aligned with his will is the pressure that is brought to bear on the entire Christian community to accept the most ridiculous and false doctrines simply because their proponent has built a mega church. Since he has obviously been blessed by God, who dares to question his teachings? This is one reason we see preachers teaching every doctrine known to man, many of which certainly do not align with Holy Scripture, on the same stage at the same seminar. It has become a mega-church fraternity. The message is that doctrine is not important. It really does not matter what one believes or teaches because God is obviously blessing them all.

Church growth is important. Growth is one way to measure the success of a church, but ONLY if doctrine has not been compromised. Growth is not nearly as important to the church of Jesus Christ as our commitment to truth. Jesus said, *"I am the way, the truth, and the life. Nobody comes to the Father except by me."* Whatever else we do to foster growth, we must preach the Word. Watered down preaching will build a watered down church.

The test of a Biblically aligned church is its message, not its size.

The words of Hosea 4:6 seem particularly appropriate for our generation. *"My people are destroyed from lack of knowledge."* We have a choice. We can either *"...study to be approved of God...handling correctly the word of truth"* (2 Timothy 2:15), or we can live on milk and remain spiritual infants. The prayerful intent of this book is the former. As we go forward, we will attempt to examine the Scriptures to learn what God has revealed concerning some of the pressing issues facing Christians today.

As we study some of these Biblical subjects, some will wonder why it matters. It is a well-known fact some people in the church become so caught up in "issues" they lose track of the mission. They become more interested in winning an argument than winning souls for Jesus. It is precisely for the mission of the church that these issues need to be studied, not to settle arguments or set doctrinal policies for the church, but to send the clear message to a dying world of a loving God whose Son died for their sins and wants them to be saved.

Focusing on the mission demands a logical, believable explanation of Scripture so that a non-believer can come to the knowledge of truth and accept Jesus Christ as Savior. Endless speculation and false predictions about the end of the world have led to nothing but skepticism and ridicule for the church. The attempt to apply Revelation and other Biblical prophesies to every event in modern history, especially the violence in the Middle East, is seen in the media and in the world at large, as the foolishness it is and has maligned the church and crippled the impact Christians should be having in the world. Likewise, a television evangelist selling a prayer cloth that will cure cancer does nothing but bring reproach on the name of Christ.

Paul addressed the concern Christians should have about the reputation of the church as it relates to evangelism in 1 Corinthians 14:23-25, *"So if the whole church comes together and everyone speaks in tongues, and some who do not understand or some unbelievers come in, will they not say that you are out of your mind? But if an unbeliever or someone who does not understand comes in while everybody is teaching, he will be convinced by all that he is a sinner and will be judged by all, and the secrets of his heart will be laid bare. So he will fall down and worship God, exclaiming, 'God is really among you!' "*

The church's obsession over miraculous gifts of the Holy Spirit, the second coming of Jesus and the end of the world, and similar issues has taken our focus off the gospel message and our mission to the lost. It is interesting that, while these issues have become a major part of the message of most churches, there is very strong resistance to comprehensive Bible study to examine the message for its true consistency with Scripture. These issues desperately need to be studied so we can come to a proper understanding of the truth and get back to the heart of God's message to the world.

The Apostle Paul said, *"I am not ashamed of the gospel, because it is the power of God for the salvation of everyone who believes: first for the Jew, then for the Gentile"* (Romans 1:16). Jesus said, *"I am the way and the truth and the life. No one comes to the Father except through me"* (John 14:6).

The stakes could not be higher for both Christians and non-believers today. The primary mission of the church is the proclamation of the good news that Jesus Christ, God's only Son, died on the cross for our sins. We have a choice between life and death, between heaven and hell. The eternal destiny of every soul is at stake.

The message we proclaim to the world must be a consistent one. It must be simple, understandable, and come from hearts filled with love. But it must be unmistakably clear. As Moses, standing before the Israelites as they were about to cross over the Jordan, said, *"This day I call heaven and earth as witnesses against you that I have set before you life and death, blessings and curses. Now choose life, so that you and your children may live and that you may love the Lord your God, listen to his voice, and hold fast to him"* (Deuteronomy 30:19-20).

But the promises of life and prosperity on the other side of the Jordan were conditional. You will be blessed only *"...if you obey the Lord your God and keep his commands and decrees that are written in this Book of the Law and turn to the Lord your God with all your heart and with all your soul"* (vs. 10). The Book of the Law, given by God to Moses, was taken seriously. Everything in it was important. In those days, doctrine mattered...every word in the Law was sacred.

It is sometimes difficult today to find any doctrine in many churches. The prevailing thought among most Christians is that it really doesn't matter much what the Bible says as long as you believe in God. Imagine...believing in an eternal, all powerful, all knowing, all loving God and not taking his every Word as something that matters.

It is imperative that we teach the truth. Secret things and disputable things need to be sidelined, and the church needs to understand and preach the fundamental doctrine of God's Holy Word. Did doctrine matter to the Holy Spirit and the apostles? Here is a sampling of what Paul told Timothy about doctrine.

> 1 Timothy 2:3-4, *"As I urged you when I went into Macedonia, stay there in Ephesus so that you may* **command certain men not to teach false doctrines** *any longer nor to devote themselves to myths and endless genealogies. These promote controversies rather than God's work—which is by faith."*

> 1 Timothy 1:8-11, *"We know that the law is good if one uses it properly. We also know that law is made not for the righteous but for lawbreakers and rebels, the ungodly and sinful, the unholy and irreligious; for those who kill their fathers or mothers, for murderers, for adulterers and perverts, for slave traders and liars and perjurers—***and for whatever else is contrary to the sound doctrine** *that conforms to the glorious gospel of the blessed God, which he entrusted to me."*

> 1 Timothy 4:13-16, *"Until I come, devote yourself to the public reading of Scripture, to preaching and to teaching. Do not neglect your gift, which was given you through a prophetic message when the body of elders laid their hands on you. Be diligent in these matters; give yourself wholly to them, so that everyone may see your progress.* **Watch your life and doctrine closely.** *Persevere in them, because if you do, you will save both yourself and your hearers."*

1 Timothy 6:3-4, *"If anyone teaches* ***false doctrines*** *and does not agree to the sound instruction of our Lord Jesus Christ and to godly teaching, he is conceited and understands nothing. He has an unhealthy interest in controversies and quarrels about words that result in envy, strife, malicious talk, evil suspicions...."*

2 Timothy 1:13, *"What you heard from me,* ***keep as the pattern of sound teaching,*** *with faith and love in Christ Jesus."*

2 Timothy 4:2-4, *"Preach the Word; be prepared in season and out of season; correct, rebuke and encourage—with great patience and careful instruction.* ***For the time will come when men will not put up with sound doctrine.*** *Instead, to suit their own desires, they will gather around them a great number of teachers to say what their itching ears want to hear. They will turn their ears away from the truth and turn aside to myths."*

We have a mission with a message. Like Moses, we set before the world a life and death choice. It is a message of hope because one can choose life. But it is also a choice based on reason and understanding. This challenge was the conclusion of Moses' message. At the beginning of the previous chapter we read, *"Your eyes have seen all that the Lord did in Egypt to Pharaoh, to all his officials and to all his land. With your own eyes you saw those great trials, those miraculous signs and great wonders. But to this day the Lord has not given you a mind that understands or eyes that see or ears that hear. During the forty years that I led you through the desert, your clothes did not wear out, nor did the sandals on your feet. You ate no bread and drank no wine or other fermented drink. I did this so that you might know that I am the Lord your God"* (Deuteronomy 29:1-6). He goes on to tell them of one thing after another they had witnessed proving the goodness and faithfulness of God. Then, based on all the evidence, he tells them to choose between this faithful God who had led them from Egypt and through the wilderness for the past forty years, or the gods in the land they would soon enter.

What if Moses had promised them God was going to part the Red Sea, but it had never happened? What if Moses had promised them God would send meat in the wilderness, but it had never come. Suppose Moses kept trying to explain to them God was going to do what he promised...SOME DAY? Now suppose those promises had not come to pass after thousands of years? How much credibility would Moses or his God have? Would there be any reason to "choose life" when everything else that had been promised never came to pass?

That is precisely what is happening in the world today with the message of the gospel of Christ. Rather than hearing the simple truth of the Gospel and a reasonable, understandable and consistent explanation of Scripture, the world has witnessed decades of confused doctrine and failed prophecies. Moses based his plea for people to choose life on the faithfulness of God to keep his Word. If people today, listening to television evangelists and a growing list of other preachers and teachers who make endless promises and prophecies that never come true, use the same criteria to judge the message of the modern church, how can anyone reasonably expect them to choose life? Only by getting back to the Bible and presenting God's complete, understandable message can there be any hope of fulfilling our mission.

2 Corinthians 5:17-21, *"Therefore, if anyone is in Christ, he is a new creation; the old has gone, the new has come! All this is from God, who reconciled us to himself through Christ and gave us the ministry of reconciliation: that God was reconciling the world to*

himself in Christ, not counting men's sins against them. And he has committed to us the message of reconciliation. We are therefore Christ's ambassadors, as though God were making his appeal through us. We implore you on Christ's behalf: Be reconciled to God. God made him who had no sin to be sin for us, so that in him we might become the righteousness of God." We will not reconcile the world to God until we reconcile our own beliefs and doctrine with his Word.

CHAPTER 2

Are We Living in the Last Days?

"Do you believe in God?" "I used to…I used to be very religious, but I'm not so sure any more," was the hesitant response. Tunde is a single man in his mid-thirties with a graduate degree from the state university. He has a good job and a promising future…as promising as the future can be in one of the most difficult places on earth. I asked him why he had doubts about God and religion. His answer was haunting, but not surprising to one who has been there. "If God exists, why does he not do something about the suffering and disease in my country?"

This was not the usual question about how a loving God could allow people to suffer. His doubts were not rooted in the human suffering, but in the failure of God to respond to praying people. He lives in what is statistically the most religious country on earth. According to the census, over 98% of the population consider themselves to be religious, more than 92% very religious. It is not only the home of the largest weekly gathering of Christians for a single Sunday worship service (over 50,000) in the world, there are thousands of similar gatherings of various size churches everywhere. Religion is not limited to church buildings. Most professional employees keep a Bible at their desk and read it every morning before beginning their daily job. Many companies periodically set aside a "day of prayer" for the employees and management to come together and pray for the success of the company and its employees. Religion is a huge part of the fabric of this society.

Attending a Sunday worship service at a local church is a life-changing experience. Never will one encounter a more zealous people, a more earnest and complete immersion in the worship of the Almighty, or more fervent prayers. So why are many people beginning to doubt God? Almost all Christian churches in this culture are Pentecostal. Every week hundreds of thousands of faithful believers congregate to hear their pastors proclaim healing for every disease, deliverance from every trial, and prosperity for every household. According to them, Jesus will grant their every prayer because he promised in Mark 11:24, *"Therefore I tell you, whatever you ask for in prayer, believe that you have received it, and it will be yours."*

So, Sunday after Sunday, people come to receive their healing, their deliverance from poverty, and their divine blessing. And week after week they all return to the same squalor, disease and poverty that have gripped this nation for decades. The cause of Tunde's doubt, and that of millions of other honest seekers around the world, is not a non-caring God. It is the pervasive, faith-destroying result of unfulfilled hope. As Solomon said, *"Hope deferred makes the heart sick."* Thirty years of being emotionally pumped up every week to expect God's miraculous intervention, only to be disappointed by another non-occurrence, creates a lot of doubt. The failure of pastors to properly understand and teach the Biblical truths about the last days, the kingdom of heaven, the consummation of the ages, and the miraculous gifts of the Holy Spirit is causing irreparable harm to the faith of millions of Christians.

An oft repeated statement among Christians today is that we are living in the "last days." This should evoke one obvious question - the last days of *what*? The Scriptures have a lot to say about events that will happen during the "last days." In order for something to have last days, it must have an end. If we keep the

Scripture in its context and allow the Bible to interpret itself, and if we understand the historical time frame to which it is referring, we will be able to determine that which was coming to an end and, therefore, have "last days." We will also be able to understand whether or not we are currently living during those days.

Let us begin by examining some other time-related concepts that are sometimes confusing. There are three different "heavens and earth" discussed in Scripture. There are also different "worlds" or "ages." To understand whether or not we are living in the Biblical "last days," we need to first understand these very different creations, worlds, and ages.

The first heaven and earth is obviously recorded in Genesis 1:1, *"In the beginning God created the heavens and the earth."* This was the creation of the physical universe. The Bible, in a few instances, refers to the physical creation as the world. The Apostle Paul in Romans 1:20 wrote, *"For since the creation of the world God's invisible qualities—his eternal power and divine nature—have been clearly seen, being understood from what has been made, so that men are without excuse."* However, most references in the Bible to the world (often translated "age") refer either to the human population at a given time or a specific nation of people; not the physical creation.

In Genesis 11:1 the text reads, *"Now the whole world had one language and a common speech."* This was prior to God's confusing the people with multiple languages at the building of the tower of Babel so they would scatter out into other regions of the planet. In the Gospel of John 1:29, when Jesus was coming to John the Baptist to be baptized, John said, *"Look, the Lamb of God, who takes away the sin of the world!"* In both of these instances the Bible is obviously referring to the people of the world, not the planet.

The differing uses of the terms "world" and "age" are familiar to most people today since we use the same terminology in our own language. It is also important to understand that in the ancient Hebrew language in which the Old Testament was written, the term "heavens and earth" was used in exactly the same way. A close examination of Isaiah 51 clearly illustrates this.

In this passage the prophet is exhorting Israel to be faithful to God who not only created the heavens and earth (physical universe) but also created *their* heavens and earth (kingdom of Israel). In Isaiah 51:13 he says, *"And you forget the Lord your Maker, who stretched out the heavens and laid the foundations of the earth…"* In this verse the prophet is referring to the physical creation of the universe. Then in verses 15-16 he says, *"But I am the Lord your God, who divided the sea whose waves roared— The Lord of hosts is his name. And I have put My words in your mouth; I have covered you with the shadow of My hand, that I may plant the heavens, lay the foundations of the earth, and say to Zion, 'You are My people' "* (NKJV). In these verses he is speaking of how God brought them out of Egypt through the Red Sea so he could establish them as his own people. This establishment of the nation of Israel as God's people, his kingdom, was called "planting the heavens" and "laying the foundations of the earth." Do not forget, as we move forward into our study, that the physical creation is called the "heavens and earth" and the kingdom of Israel is also referred to in Scripture as the "heavens and earth." We should not be surprised to see later in Scripture the destruction of that kingdom described as the destruction of the "heavens and earth." (NIV improperly translates verb tenses in Isaiah 51:16)

In the Apostle Peter's second letter he was explaining the soon approaching destruction of Jerusalem and its temple and compared it to the flood of Noah's day. 2 Peter 3:5-7 says, *"But they deliberately forget that long ago by God's word the heavens existed and the earth was formed out of water and by water. By these waters also the world of that time was deluged and destroyed. By the same word the present heavens and earth are reserved for fire, being kept for the day of judgment and destruction of ungodly men."*

Read the above passage from 2 Peter over several times and think through what he said. He then said the "world" (heavens and earth) at that time was deluged and destroyed by the flood. This obviously does not refer to the physical universe, as it was not destroyed. He is referring to the "world" of human beings that lived prior to the flood. The physical creation was not destroyed, but the world (heavens and earth) was. He then says the "*present* heavens and earth" are reserved for fire. Since the first "destruction of the world" (heavens and earth) was not the physical destruction of the universe, why would we assume the second "heavens and earth," which he compared to the flood, would be such? Peter was using the language of Isaiah when he called the present kingdom of Israel, which was soon to be destroyed, the "present heavens and earth." Since Peter was explaining what had been spoken by the prophets, he used the same prophetic language.

So far we see, in addition to the creation of the physical universe, there was a world (heavens and earth) age prior to the flood, which was destroyed by that event. We also see another world (heavens and earth) age of the kingdom of Israel, which came into being following the flood and was still in existence when Jesus and his apostles lived and taught. This is the "present age" referred to in the New Testament. In 1 Corinthians 2:8 the Apostle Paul, speaking of the gospel of Christ said, *"None of the rulers of this age understood it, for if they had, they would not have crucified the Lord of glory."* It was the rulers of "this age" (the Jews) who crucified Jesus.

This age in which Jesus and the apostles lived was going to end. In Matthew 24, Mark 13 and Luke 21 Jesus explained that Jerusalem and its temple would soon be destroyed. In Matthew 24:3 the disciples asked Jesus about this coming event. *"As Jesus was sitting on the Mount of Olives, the disciples came to him privately. 'Tell us,' they said, 'when will this happen, and what will be the sign of your coming and of the end of the age?' "* The end of the Jewish age did coincide with the destruction of the temple and we know from history this prophecy was fulfilled in A.D. 70.

But there was also an "age to come." This coming age would also see the creation of a "new heaven and earth." As Isaiah 65:17-18 foretold, *"Behold, I will create new heavens and a new earth. The former things will not be remembered, nor will they come to mind. But be glad and rejoice forever in what I will create, for I will create Jerusalem to be a delight and its people a joy."* Again, following a description of God's judgment on the nation, he promises in Isaiah 66:22, *"As the new heavens and the new earth that I make will endure before me, declares the Lord, so will your name and descendants endure."* The present "heavens and earth" would end but the new "heavens and earth" would never end.

And the Hebrew writer tells us this prophecy would be fulfilled in the church. In Hebrews 12:22-24 he says, *"But you have come to Mount Zion, to the heavenly Jerusalem, the city of the living God. You have come to thousands upon thousands of angels in joyful assembly, to the church of the firstborn, whose names are written in heaven. You have come to God, the judge of all men, to the spirits of righteous men made perfect, to Jesus the mediator of a new covenant, and to the sprinkled blood that speaks a better word than the blood of Abel."* And in Revelation 21:1, *"Then I saw a new heaven and a new earth, for the first heaven and the first earth had passed away, and there was no longer any sea."* The first heaven and earth was the physical nation or kingdom of Israel which was a prototype of the new heaven and earth, the spiritual kingdom of God, the church.

We can see in Scripture there was the age of Noah, the age of the kingdom of Israel and a coming age of the new Jerusalem, or the church. In addition to these broad ages that cover thousands of years of human history, the Bible also speaks of a specific time period known as the "last days." Does this time period relate to one of these ages and, if so, which one? Are we living in the Biblical "last days"?

The Bible speaks of certain periods of time as "the days" of someone or something. A few examples are:

1. The days of Saul (1 Samuel 14:52)
2. The days of Solomon (2 Chronicles 30:26)
3. The days of the judges who led Israel (2 Kings 23:22)
4. The days of the prophet Samuel (2 Chronicles 35:18)
5. The days of our forefathers (Ezra 9:7, Joel 1:2, Matthew 23:30)
6. The days of Noah (Isaiah 54:9, Matthew 24:37, 1 Peter 3:20)
7. The days of Moses and his people (Isaiah 63:11)
8. The days of Jesus' life on earth (Hebrews 5:7)

There is also a specific time period identified in Scripture as the "last days." The Bible is very clear about this time and what events would occur during these last days. The modern church is inundated with prophecies concerning these events and their "very soon" fulfillment. Books and movies fill the shelves at Christian bookstores telling in graphic detail what is about to happen, and it is not a very comforting picture.

These doomsday prophets are certainly not without Scripture. There are some pretty scary things mentioned in the Bible concerning the "coming of the Lord," when there will be great calamity and destruction. In 2 Timothy 3:1 it says, *"But mark this: There will be terrible times in the last days."* In Matthew 24:21 Jesus said, *"There will be great distress, unequaled from the beginning of the world until now—and never to be equaled again."* Paul, in 1 Corinthians 7:31, *"For this world in its present form is passing away."* The Apostle Peter warned in 1 Peter 4:7, *"The end of all things is near."* And again in 2 Peter 3:10-11, *"But the day of the*

Lord will come like a thief. The heavens will disappear with a roar; the elements will be destroyed by fire, and the earth and everything in it will be laid bare. Since everything will be destroyed in this way, what kind of people ought you to be?" Again, the Apostle Paul in 1 Thessalonians 4:16 said, *"For the Lord himself will come down from heaven, with a loud command, with the voice of the archangel and with the trumpet call of God, and the dead in Christ will rise first. After that, we who are still alive and are left will be caught up together with them in the clouds to meet the Lord in the air. And so we will be with the Lord forever."*

Are all the present-day predictions about the end of the world true? Are we indeed about to witness the end of creation as we know it? There are numerous interpretations about exactly how these events will unfold, but one thing every preacher and teacher who subscribes to this world view agree upon is that all these things will definitely occur during the "last days." The Bible also agrees. The real question is, are we living in the "last days"?

Understanding the Biblical time period known as the last days is critical to a proper interpretation of many confusing doctrines challenging the church today. In order to understand where we fit into God's plan we need to know the Scriptural time frame in which we are presently living. Using the basic principles of Bible study discussed in the introduction, let's *"...examine the Scriptures and see if these things are true."*

We know from Scripture a lot of things were to happen during the "last days" leading up to the "great day of the Lord."

1. Israel would be ruled by foreigners. (Daniel 2:44, 7:25)
2. "Elijah" would come. (Malachi 4:5, Matthew 11:14)
3. The Messiah would be born in Bethlehem. (Daniel 9:25-27, Micah 5:2, John 7:42)
4. ALL prophecy would be fulfilled. (Luke 21:22)

5. The Holy Spirit would be poured out on all flesh. (Joel 2, Acts 2)
6. Miraculous signs and wonders would confirm the word. (Daniel 9:27, Mark 16:20, Acts 2, Acts 14:13, Hebrews 2:2-4)
7. The church would be established in Jerusalem. (Isaiah 2:1-3, Daniel 2:44, Acts 2)
8. The gospel would be preached to all the world, beginning at Jerusalem. (Daniel 9:27, Matthew 24:14, Mark 13:10)
9. The physical kingdom of Israel would be replaced by the true, spiritual kingdom. (Daniel 7-12, Matthew 24, Revelation 11:15)
10. Israel would reject the truth and the Messiah (Luke 9:22, 17:25
11. Terrible times of suffering would exist, like nothing before or after. (Daniel 12:1, Matthew 24:19-22, Mark 13:17-19)
12. The Lord would come in judgment upon Israel and the nations. (Isaiah 66:15-16, Daniel 12:1-4, John 5:24-30, 12:31, Revelation 14:7)
13. The Lord would "shake the earth". (Isaiah 2:20-22, Haggai 2:6, Hebrews 12:25-28)
14. Armies would surround Jerusalem. (Daniel 12:9-12, Luke 21:20-21)
15. The temple would be desecrated. (Daniel 9:27, 11:31, 12:11, Matthew 24:15, Mark 13:14)
16. The dead would be raised. (Daniel 12:1-4, John 5:24-30)
17. Forgiveness of sins would finally be a reality. (Daniel 9:24, Joel 3, Hebrews 10:15-39)
18. The power of death would be forever destroyed. (Isaiah 28:17-19, Hosea 13:14, 1

Corinthians 15:55-57, Hebrews 2:13-15)

19. The city of Jerusalem and the physical temple would be totally destroyed. (Daniel 9:25-27, 11:16, Matthew 24:2, Mark 13:2, Luke 21:6, Revelation 18)
20. The new Jerusalem (spiritual nation of Israel, promised to Abraham) would be an everlasting kingdom. (Daniel 2:44-45, Hebrews 12:22-29, Revelation 21:1-5)
21. The dwelling of God would, once again, be with men. (Revelation 21:1-5)

Can we know for sure the historical time frame of these Biblical "last days"? Yes! The concept of "the last days" and the events that would happen during those times begin in Old Testament prophecies. This time period is first mentioned in Isaiah 2 where the Bible says, *"This is what Isaiah son of Amoz saw concerning Judah and Jerusalem: In the last days the mountain of the Lord's temple will be established...and all nations will stream to it."* Isaiah clearly identifies the "last days" with Judah and Jerusalem. A closer examination of the entire chapter reveals several significant things about those last days that we will see again and again as we study further.

First, he says it will be during these "last days" of Judah and Jerusalem that *"...the mountain of the Lord's temple will be established as chief among the mountains."* What is this mountain that the Lord will establish in these last days? We read in Exodus where God gave the Law of Moses and confirmed his covenant with the kingdom of Israel on Mt. Sinai. Mt. Sinai was often referred to in Old Testament Scriptures as the Holy Mountain or the Mountain of the Lord.

After David became king of Israel, he conquered a Jebusite fortress located on Mt. Zion and built a city around that area. It was called the City of David and later, Jerusalem. Zion came to designate the entire area of Jerusalem and later became a metonym for Solomon's temple, the city of Jerusalem, and the entire concept of God's presence among his people.

There are many Old Testament prophesies which foretold of the salvation of the Lord going out from Zion. In Zechariah 8:3, *"This is what the Lord says: 'I will return to Zion and dwell in Jerusalem. Then Jerusalem will be called the City of Truth, and the mountain of the Lord Almighty will be called the Holy Mountain.' "* We see from this, and a host of other Scriptures, that it was Zion, not Sinai, which would eventually represent the Holy Mountain of the Lord Almighty.

The writer of Hebrews makes this abundantly clear in chapter 12:18-29 when he compares the covenant that was represented by Sinai to the new covenant in Jesus Christ represented by Mt. Zion.

> *"You have not come to a mountain (Sinai) that can be touched and that is burning with fire; to darkness, gloom and storm; to a trumpet blast or to such a voice speaking words that those who heard it begged that no further word be spoken to them, because they could not bear what was commanded: 'If even an animal touches the mountain, it must be stoned.' The sight was so terrifying that Moses said, 'I am trembling with fear.' But you have come to* ***Mount Zion****, to* ***the heavenly Jerusalem, the city of the living God****. You have come to thousands upon thousands of angels in joyful assembly, to* ***the church*** *of the firstborn, whose names are written in heaven. You have come to* ***God****, the judge of all men, to the spirits of righteous men made perfect, to* ***Jesus*** *the mediator of* ***a new covenant****, and to the sprinkled blood that speaks a better word than the blood of Abel."*

We can clearly understand from Scripture that the church (also figuratively called Mt. Zion, The heavenly Jerusalem, The City of God) was the "mountain of the Lord's temple" that was to be established during the "last days" of Judah and Jerusalem. And we know Jesus lived and died during these same "last days," as did his apostles. We also know the church was established during these same "last days," and the word of the Lord went out from Jerusalem, just as Isaiah predicted.

We also see in the remainder of Isaiah 2 some additional things which the prophet saw would happen during the "last days of Judah and Jerusalem." Verses 12-17 say, *"The Lord has a day in store"* when *"...the arrogance of man will be brought low and the pride of men humbled; the Lord alone will be exalted in that day."* Verse 19 says, *"Men will flee to caves in the rocks and to holes in the ground from dread of the Lord and the splendor of his majesty, when he rises to shake the earth."*

These events are of particular interest because they are quoted by Jesus and other New Testament writers as the time of their fulfillment neared. One cannot understand Isaiah and apply Jesus' (and others) quotation of these same passages to some future ending of the universe. These were things that were to happen during the "last days" of Judah and Jerusalem. They have nothing to do with the end of the physical creation or the time in which we are living today.

God demonstrated for Hosea in chapter three how, just as he had been estranged from his wife Gomer and was now to be reconciled, Israel would also return to the Lord in their last days. *"For the Israelites will live many days without king or prince, without sacrifice or sacred stones, without ephod or idol. Afterward the Israelites will return and seek the Lord their God and David their king. They will come trembling to the Lord and to his blessings in the last days"* (Hosea 3:4-5). These "last days" are the same as Isaiah's...the last days of Israel...not the last days of the physical earth.

A third description of the "last days" comes from Micah 4. The end of chapter three says, *"...Zion will be plowed like a field, and Jerusalem will become a heap of rubble, the temple hill a mound overgrown with thickets."* He follows this description of Jerusalem's destruction with, *"In the last days the mountain of the Lord's temple will be established...and people will stream to it."* Again, nobody can understand these prophetic "last days" to be anything other than the last days of Judah and Jerusalem, or the physical nation of Israel.

That the "last days" do not pertain to the present is also logical. The physical nation of Israel was God's prototype of the church. She had a specific purpose and time and would be replaced by the "true kingdom" identified in Scripture as the church. The kingdom of Israel indeed had "last days" and came to an end in A.D. 70. The kingdom of God has NO END, therefore, can have no last days. The term "last days" cannot apply to the church, or the "church dispensation," since, according to the Bible, it will never end.

One of the clearest and easiest to understand books of prophecy concerning the "end times" is the book of Joel. Although Joel did not specifically use the phrase, "the last days," Peter, referring to his prophecy, did. In Acts 2, speaking of the strange events that were happening on the day of Pentecost, Peter said, *"This is that which was spoken by the prophet Joel;* ***in the last days*** *God will pour out his Spirit..."* Peter had no doubt that what was happening was the fulfillment of prophecies concerning the "last days of Israel" spoken of by Joel (Acts 2:17-21). Old Testament prophecies continually contrasted the physical nation of Israel, which would be destroyed, with the eternal kingdom that was Israel's true inheritance. The "world" of the Jews (physical Israel) would be destroyed, have "last days," "end times," and would one day cease to exist.

To understand the teachings in the New Testament concerning the "last days," the "day of the Lord," and the "time of the end," one must consider that these events all came from the Old Testament prophesies and the first-century writers used the same language and imagery as was used by the prophets. In Isaiah 13 there is a prophecy against Babylon (vs. 1). Verse 4 says, *"The Lord Almighty is mustering an army of war."* Verse 6 says, *"Wail for the day of the Lord is near; it will come like destruction from the Almighty."* In verses 10 and 13 we read, *"The stars of heaven and their constellations will not show their light. The rising sun will be darkened and the moon will not give its light... Therefore I will make the heavens tremble; and the earth will shake from its place at the wrath of the Lord Almighty, in the day of his burning anger."* Verses 17-19 tell how God is going to accomplish this. *"See, I will stir up the Medes... Babylon, the jewel of kingdoms, the glory of the Babylonians pride, will be overthrown by God like Sodom and Gomorrah."*

The Medes did overthrow the Babylonian Empire just as Isaiah predicted. Isaiah was speaking of the end of the Babylonian kingdom, not the end of the world. This apocalyptic language is typical throughout the Old Testament prophesies concerning God's judgment against nations. Descriptive terms like *the day of the Lord, the coming of the Lord,* the heavens and earth being destroyed, the stars falling, the sun and moon turning to blood or not giving their light...all these were used dozens of times throughout the prophesies and in every case were describing God's coming judgment on one or more nations. It should not surprise anyone with knowledge of Old Testament Scriptures to find this same language used to describe the destruction of Jerusalem and its temple and the end of the kingdom of Israel. Neither the Old nor New Testament Scriptures ever speak of the destruction of the universe and the end of time as taught by many today.

As we examine the New Testament passages which refer to the

"last days," we quickly see they refer to the same time frame originally defined by the prophets. Hebrews begins, *"In the past God spoke to our forefathers through the prophets at many times and in various ways, but in these last days he has spoken to us by his Son..."* Jesus lived, taught, and died during the "last days" of Israel. Since the church was not established until after his death and resurrection, the "last days" could not refer to the present time often referred to as the "church dispensation." And to apply the term in this passage to the end of the universe makes absolutely no sense at all. Jesus spoke during Isaiah's "last days of Judah and Jerusalem." The Hebrew writer knew the Old Testament Scriptures.

In 2 Timothy 3:1-5, Paul wrote of *"...terrible times in the last days."* These were the same "last days" and "terrible times" spoken of by Daniel and Isaiah. Paul was not making up some new "last days" which have no Scriptural basis. He was speaking of the same time Jesus discussed in Matthew 24 when he quoted from Daniel stating that *"...there would be terrible times unequaled from the beginning of the world until now...and never to be equaled again."* Jesus, in Matthew 24, was speaking of the destruction of Jerusalem. In Luke's vivid description of these same events for the Gentile audience he said, *"When you see Jerusalem surrounded by armies, you will know that its desolation is near. Then let those who are in Judea flee to the mountains, let those in the city get out, and let those in the country not enter the city.* ***For this is the time of punishment in fulfillment of all that has been written****"* (Luke 21:20-22).

Peter also spoke of the "last days" in his writings. In 1 Peter 1:20 he said, *"He* (Jesus) *was chosen before the creation of the world, but was revealed in these last times for your sake."* Jesus was revealed (born) in the "last days" of Israel, not the last days of the physical universe. Again in 2 Peter 3 he said, *"I want you to recall the words spoken in the past by the holy prophets and the command given by our*

Lord and Savior through your apostles. First of all, you must understand that in the last days scoffers will come...they will say 'where is this coming he promised?' " Comparing this passage with the "holy prophets" and the words spoken by Jesus in Matthew, Mark, and Luke describing these very times, Peter's message is clear. He was speaking of the exact same "last days" as all the rest. He could not have been speaking of different "last days" unless one can find them in the "holy prophets" and in the words of Jesus.

Jude 18 mentioned the same thing as did Peter when he said, *"...remember what the apostles of our Lord Jesus Christ foretold. They said to you, 'in the last times there will be scoffers who will follow their own ungodly desires' "* Again, Jude was discussing the same "last times" as everyone else in Scripture.

Finally, the Apostle John in 1 John 2:18 said, *"Dear children, this is the last hour; and as you have heard that the antichrist is coming, even now many antichrists have come. This is how we know it is the last hour..."* John clearly identifies the time in which he was living as the "last hour." Why are modern-day "prophets" still predicting some future coming of the "antichrists" when John clearly said they had already come in his day? He knew from Jesus' teachings they were coming in that generation and would precede the coming of the Son of Man. In Matthew 16:27-28 Jesus said, *"For the Son of Man is going to come in his Father's glory with his angels, and then he will reward each person according to what he has done. I tell you the truth, some who are standing here will not taste death before they see the Son of Man coming in his kingdom."* In Matthew 24:30-35 and Luke 21:25-33, describing the events that would take place when the temple was destroyed, Jesus said, *"At that time they will see the Son of Man coming in a cloud with power and great glory. When these things begin to take place, stand up and lift up your heads, because your redemption is drawing near."* When would these things take place? In those same passages Jesus told them to watch for the signs and said, *"I tell you the truth, this generation will certainly not pass away until all these things have happened."* One of the many signs they were to watch for was false (anti) christs. John believed Jesus and was watching. He said they had come, which is how he knew it was the "last hour."

John and Peter also had the explicit statement from Jesus that John would be one of those who would live to see Jesus' return. In John 21:15-23, when Peter was told how he was going to die, he asked, *"Lord, what about John?"* Jesus answered, *"If I want him to remain alive until I return, what is that to you? You must follow me."* Many dismiss this statement of Jesus as just an expression to make a point to Peter. We know that is clearly not the case because some listening misunderstood and thought Jesus meant John would not die. In explaining the misunderstanding, the Scripture continues, *"Jesus did not say he (John) would not die; he only said 'if I want him to remain alive until I return, what is that to you?' "* Jesus never used false or misleading statements to illustrate a point. If it were not possible for John to remain alive until his return, Jesus would certainly have never said so. The fact is, Jesus did want John to remain alive until he returned because he was the one selected to write the final chapter in God's REVELATION! And so he did.

Some might contend that the last days began in the first century but will continue until the end of the world. The Bible does contain several references to the "end of the world." Like everything else, we must apply the same principles to this concept as to all other Scriptural passages. Rather than jumping to our own conclusion about the meaning, let's let the Bible interpret itself, keep all Scripture in context, and understand the time to which it is referring. In Genesis 9:11 God told Noah, *"...neither shall there anymore be a flood to destroy the earth."* We all know the earth (dirt) was not destroyed in the flood. The term "earth" was used to denote all living animals, including mankind.

As has already been briefly discussed and will be seen again and again as we continue our study, the term "world" is used throughout Scripture to refer to a particular society, an age, a dispensation, etc. In Hebrews 9:26 the Scripture says, *"But now he* (Christ) *has appeared once for all at the end of the ages to do away with sin by the sacrifice of himself."* The King James Version renders this, *"But now once in the* ***end of the world*** *hath he appeared to put away sin by the sacrifice of himself."* In the New American Standard Version we find perhaps the best translation of the phrase, *"But now once at the* ***consummation of the ages*** *he has been manifested to put away sin by the sacrifice of Himself."* Young's Literal Translation says, *"At the full end of the ages."* Regardless of translation, the verse clearly says that Jesus appeared at the "end of the world." This is consistent with Jesus' own statement in Matthew 24:3 that he would come at the end of the age (world). And, citing examples from Israel's history, Paul explains in 1 Corinthians 10:11, *"These things happened to them as examples and were written down as warnings for us, on whom the fulfillment of the ages has come."* We know that the coming of the Messiah, his crucifixion as the ultimate Passover Lamb, his victory over death, and the establishment of the eternal kingdom (church) was the promised fulfillment of the ages. That happened, just as promised, during the "last days" of that age…the age or days (or world) of physical Israel.

In a careful examination of Scripture it becomes vividly apparent that one's understanding of the Biblical concept of the "last days" is paramount in properly interpreting the timing and events associated with the "coming of the Lord" and all other eschatological events. All the New Testament writers spoke of the fulfillment of the prophetical, Biblical "last days" of Judah and Jerusalem. There is not one single Scripture that speaks of some future "coming of Jesus" to destroy the physical creation. There are many other passages that have not been mentioned here...and some of them require diligent study. Even Peter said Paul wrote some things that were difficult to understand. Whatever we teach must be consistent with what we do understand, and we can know from Scripture that the "last days" were the last days of Israel.

Summary points:

1. The Bible defines the "last days" to be the last days of Israel.
2. Jesus and the apostles lived during the "last days" of Israel.
3. The church was established during the "last days" of Israel.
4. An eternal kingdom cannot have "last days."
5. The "abomination of desolation" that preceded the destruction of the Jerusalem temple was accompanied by terrible times in the "last days" that would never be equaled again.
6. Jerusalem and its temple were destroyed in A.D. 70 exactly as Jesus predicted.
7. Some, including John, of that generation lived to see the "coming of the Son of Man" during the "last days."

Since we know from Daniel, Joel, and Jesus there would be *"...terrible times unequaled from the beginning of the world until now...and never to be equaled again,"* and from Jesus that the destruction of the temple would be this *"...time of punishment in fulfillment of all that has been written,"* the only way one can believe that a future "more terrible time" is still coming in the "last days" is to subscribe to the notion that we are still living in the "last days," dismiss the events of A.D. 70 as irrelevant, and the scoffers Peter wrote about were right...Jesus lied. Jesus clearly said,

"This generation will certainly not pass away until all these things have happened" (Matthew 24:34, Mark 13:30, Luke 21:32). In Matthew 16:27-28 Jesus also said, *"For the Son of Man is going to come in his Father's glory with his angels, and then he will reward each person according to what he has done. I tell you the truth, some who are standing here will not taste death before they see the Son of Man coming in his kingdom."* The scoffers of Peter's day, and the doomsday prophets of today, were and are wrong. As Paul said, *"Let God be true, and every man a liar"* (Romans 3:4).

Some people object to the destruction of Jerusalem being the fulfillment of Daniel's and Jesus' prophesies by questioning whether that event could have possibly been the worst calamity to ever occur on earth, past, present or future. Would not the flood of Noah's day been more devastating since there were only eight people left on the earth? And even applied to the Jewish world, did not the holocaust of WW2 claim far more lives than the Roman invasion of Jerusalem in A.D. 70?

While it may seem plausible, this objection fails to recognize the spiritual significance of what happened in A.D. 70. Daniel's prophecy, which Jesus quoted, specifically concerned the Jewish nation. The kingdom of Israel was not just another nation in the world. They were called by God to be his chosen people for the express purpose of bringing the Messiah into the world. They were a special people, a Holy Nation. No other kingdom in the world ever had, or ever will have, that distinction. When Jerusalem and its temple were destroyed, that Holy Nation was completely obliterated from the earth, never to exist again. Nothing in the history of the human race had, or ever will have, the same eternal implications as that one event. The only possible way for this prophecy to still be in our future would be for the kingdom of Israel to be reestablished as God's chosen people and the temple rebuilt. This would mean that Jesus was not the promised Messiah and Christianity is a false religion. The reestablishment of a Jewish state in 1948 did not reinstate their position with Almighty God as his chosen people. That distinction now belongs to the new Jerusalem, the church. Jesus was, and is, the Son of God, the promised Messiah.

It is vital to the mission of the church that we understand the times in which we are living. The current preoccupation with the end of the world has taken us off message and off our mission. Christians are confused, not knowing whether to *"go into all the world"* or *"run to the hills"!* If the modern futurist message is true, the latter is the advice of Jesus. If it is not, we have a mission before us and an exciting message the world is dying to hear! We are not living in the "last days." May God help us get back on message.

CHAPTER 3

The Kingdom of Heaven

It was a hot afternoon with unusually heavy traffic. The ride home from church was not only slow, but unusually quiet. After about thirty minutes, Alex broke the silence. "I'm not going to church anymore." His matter-of-fact statement took me by surprise. "Why not?" I inquired. Then he asked, "Do you believe what that preacher said?" We had just listened to a self-proclaimed "prophet of God" deliver a "message he had received from God" that the Holy Spirit was going to work mighty miracles that morning during the worship service.

After an hour of emotional frenzy, countless prayers, and declarations of healing and deliverance that would be more appropriately described as a "religious séance" than a worship service, nothing miraculous happened. It was the same message heard every Sunday in churches around the world and on religious television programs every day of the week. Why did it trouble Alex so much this time? His mother died of cancer when he was only ten years old. He had heard the same empty promises of miraculous cures countless times before and after his personal tragedy. Why had he just now decided to leave the church? Perhaps it was because I was with him and he was embarrassed by the obviously false claims made by the preacher. Perhaps he had finally heard enough empty promises from "men of God" to come to the realization that everything said and done "in the name of Jesus" is not from God. Whatever the reason, it was one more example of how false prophets and fake "healers" today are *"...using Godliness as a means to financial gain,"* making a mockery of Christianity, and turning honest, truth-seeking people away from the church. Alex was not expressing a desire to leave God. He, and countless others like him, are simply not finding him at church.

The solution, however, is not to leave the church, but to rediscover its true meaning and purpose, as described in Scripture. What is called "church" today is a far cry from what Jesus died to build. The church is the kingdom of heaven. When the disciples of Jesus asked him to teach them to pray, one line in his model prayer was, *"Thy kingdom come."* For what were they supposed to pray? Did they understand what Jesus was telling them? How would they know if God answered this prayer? Is this still to be the prayer of Christians today? If one does not properly understand the Biblical concept of the "last days," it will be difficult indeed to determine the nature and establishment of the kingdom of heaven and whether or not God ever answered this prayer. This kingdom is the subject of the Scriptures from beginning to end because it is the dwelling place of all the redeemed. It is important that we understand what the Bible teaches about it.

When Adam and Eve sinned in the Garden of Eden, God told the Devil that day that someone who would come through the woman's offspring would crush Satan's head. In Genesis 3:15 the Lord said, *"And I will put enmity between you and the woman, and between your offspring and hers; he will crush your head, and you will strike his heel."* Nobody at that time knew what, but something was coming.

As we follow the history of successive generations from Adam and Eve we see just how pervasive sin became. Finally God sent a worldwide flood that destroyed everyone except Noah and his family. Following that event man continued to sin, and it became abundantly clear Satan would not be crushed by destroying those who fell for his deceptive schemes. In Genesis 12:1-2, *"The Lord had said to Abram, 'Leave your country, your people and your father's household and go to the land I will show you. I will make you into a great nation and I will bless you; I will make your name great, and you will be a blessing.' "* Abraham understood his descendants would become a nation. But somehow he also knew there was more to God's promise than just physical cities in a physical country. Hebrews 11:10 says, *"For he (Abraham) was looking forward to the city with foundations, whose architect and builder is God."* Abraham did not know exactly what, but something great was coming.

A few centuries passed, and Abraham's descendants ended up as slaves in Egypt. To the people living under the cruel taskmasters of the Pharaohs it must have felt like God had forgotten his promise to their ancestors. Yet all the while they were living in Egypt, God was blessing them with children, and their numbers were steadily growing. By the time they were finally led through the Red Sea to freedom, over a million people had become the independent nation of Israel. They had not yet come to their promised land, but they were the beginning of a great nation.

Exodus 19:3-6 tells us that when they reached Mt. Sinai the Lord called Moses up to meet with him and said, *"This is what you are to say to the house of Jacob and what you are to tell the people of Israel: 'You yourselves have seen what I did to Egypt, and how I carried you on eagles' wings and brought you to myself. Now if you obey me fully and keep my covenant, then out of all nations you will be my treasured possession. Although the whole earth is mine, you will be for me a kingdom of priests and a holy nation.' These are the words you are to speak to the Israelites."* For the first time we see this nation promised to Abraham was to become the kingdom of God. This was going to be no ordinary kingdom, but a kingdom of priests, a holy nation. Something special was coming.

In 1 Samuel 16 we read about the Lord sending the prophet

Samuel to anoint David as king over Israel. David was the first king to reign over Israel by God's own choosing. (Saul was made king because of the people's demand to be like the other nations. This was a sin against God, and none of his descendants succeeded him on the throne.) With David, the throne of Israel was now aligned with God's will, and it was established as an everlasting kingdom. David reigned seven years in Hebron, but after conquering the Jebusites who were living in Jerusalem, he made that the permanent capitol of the kingdom. 2 Samuel 5:9 tells us, *"David then took up residence in the fortress and called it the City of David."* He had the Ark of the Covenant brought to Jerusalem and placed in the tent tabernacle that was erected on what would be the future temple site.

With the tabernacle, the Holy of Holies, and the Ark of the Covenant now present, Jerusalem became not only the City of David, but also the City of God. It was in this tabernacle that God's presence dwelled. In spite of all the incredible things that had happened to David during his lifetime, he still knew there was more to come. In Psalm 16:9-10 he wrote, *"Therefore my heart is glad and my tongue rejoices; my body also will rest secure, because you will not abandon me to the grave, nor will you let your Holy One see decay."* The Apostle Peter said of David's words in Acts 2:29-31, *"Brothers, I can tell you confidently that the patriarch David died and was buried, and his tomb is here to this day. But he was a prophet and knew that God had promised him on oath that he would place one of his descendants on his throne. Seeing what was ahead, he spoke of the resurrection of the Christ, that he was not abandoned to the grave, nor did his body see decay."* David sat on his throne in the kingdom of God, but he knew something better was coming.

The prophet Nathan was sent to tell David about the throne and the kingdom in 2 Samuel 7:8-16. *"Now then, tell my servant David, 'This is what the Lord Almighty says: I took you from the pasture and from following the flock to be ruler over my people Israel.*

I have been with you wherever you have gone, and I have cut off all your enemies from before you. Now I will make your name great, like the names of the greatest men of the earth. And I will provide a place for my people Israel and will plant them so that they can have a home of their own and no longer be disturbed...The Lord declares to you that the Lord himself will establish a house for you: When your days are over and you rest with your fathers, I will raise up your offspring to succeed you, who will come from your own body, and I will establish his kingdom. He is the one who will build a house for my Name, and I will establish the throne of his kingdom forever...Your house and your kingdom will endure forever before me; ***your throne will be established forever.****' "*

As we continue to follow the story, we know that David's son Solomon did build the temple for the Lord in Jerusalem. The temple was more than just a beautiful house of worship. It was built exactly as God had instructed Moses to build the tabernacle in the wilderness as a sanctuary for the Lord. This magnificent structure became the permanent tabernacle where God's presence would dwell in his kingdom on earth.

One can read about the building and dedication of the temple in 2 Chronicles chapters 1-9. It was this temple, not Solomon's palace, which became the symbol for the entire kingdom of Israel. Israel had indeed become the kingdom of God, and Jerusalem had become the place that bore his name, just as he had told the Jews in the wilderness when he gave them instructions about keeping the Passover Feast (Deuteronomy 16:5-8). With the building of the temple, Jerusalem was forever established as the City of God, and his kingdom would be everlasting, just as he had promised. Psalm 145:13, *"Your kingdom is an everlasting kingdom, and your dominion endures through all generations. The Lord is faithful to all his promises and loving toward all he has made."* But there was more coming...much more.

During the succeeding reign of the various kings in Jerusalem, the prophets were foretelling of a future king that would sit on David's throne in a new Jerusalem. Isaiah 9:6-7, *"For to us a child is born, to us a son is given, and the government will be on his shoulders. And he will be called Wonderful Counselor, Mighty God, Everlasting Father, Prince of Peace. Of the increase of his government and peace there will be no end. He will reign on David's throne and over his kingdom, establishing and upholding it with justice and righteousness from that time on and forever. The zeal of the Lord Almighty will accomplish this."*

Isaiah clearly identifies Jesus as the ultimate successor to David's throne and David's kingdom. David's throne and the kingdom of Israel had been set up by the God of heaven as a prototype of a future kingdom who would encompass the entire earth and endure forever. Daniel 2:44 says, *"In the time of those kings* (Roman Empire)*, the God of heaven will set up a kingdom that will never be destroyed, nor will it be left to another people. It will crush all those kingdoms and bring them to an end, but it will itself endure forever."*

However, following Solomon's reign the physical kingdom of Israel was divided and went through immense struggle. By the time Jesus arrived on the scene, it must have appeared to a lot of Jews that God had abandoned his promise about their kingdom and David's throne lasting forever. Not since the death of Zedekiah in 586 B.C. had there been a descendant of David on the throne in Jerusalem.

After hundreds of years of silence, God sent his angel to a young virgin in Judea to tell her she was going to have a baby. In Luke 1:32-34 the angel said, *"He will be great and will be called the Son of the Most High. The Lord God will give him the throne of his father David, and he will reign over the house of Jacob forever; his kingdom will never end."* God had not forgotten his promise. Everything was now in place for him to restore the kingdom and throne of David.

Almost thirty years following the announcement by the angel to Mary, John the Baptist began proclaiming, *"Repent, for the kingdom of heaven is near"* (Matthew 3:2). Being very familiar with the Old Testament prophesies concerning a coming Messiah who would sit on David's throne and *"...restore the fortunes of Judah and Jerusalem"* (Isaiah 9:6-7, Joel 3:1). John's preaching caused no small stir in Israel. Folks began to get excited about what was coming.

When Jesus was baptized by John, the Spirit of God descended on him and proclaimed him to be the Son of God. From that time on Jesus began to preach, *"Repent, for the kingdom of heaven is near"* (Matthew 4:17). Later Jesus sent his apostles out to preach the same message. In Matthew 10:5-7 we read where he sent them out with the following instructions: *"Do not go among the Gentiles or enter any town of the Samaritans. Go rather to the lost sheep of Israel. As you go, preach this message: 'The kingdom of heaven is near.' "* Why would they not go to the Gentiles with that message? It was to Abraham and his descendants that the promise was made. It was David's throne that was to be restored to last forever. The "good news" of the kingdom (Matthew 24:14) was first to be proclaimed to those to whom it had been promised. Just as Daniel had prophesied, *"He will confirm a covenant with many for one 'seven.' In the middle of the 'seven' he will put an end to sacrifice and offering. And on a wing of the temple he will set up an abomination that causes desolation, until the end that is decreed is poured out on him"* (Daniel 9:27). This promise was given specifically to the Jews. God was going to confirm his covenant with them first, after which the gospel would be preached to the Gentiles.

The kingdom of heaven was the subject of almost all of Jesus' parables and most of his other teachings. In Matthew 11:11-13 he said, *"I tell you the truth: Among those born of women there has not risen anyone greater than John the Baptist; yet he who is least in the kingdom of heaven is greater than he. From the days of John the Baptist until now, the kingdom of heaven has been forcefully advancing, and forceful men lay hold of it. For all the Prophets and the Law prophesied until John."* About what had all the Prophets and the Law before John prophesied? Obviously the coming kingdom of heaven, which was now near. In Luke 4:43 Jesus said the reason he was sent was to *"...preach the good news of the kingdom of God."*

As Jesus entered Jerusalem for the last time we read in Mark 11:9-10 that those who went ahead of him and those who followed shouted, *"Hosanna!" "Blessed is he who comes in the name of the Lord!" "Blessed is the coming kingdom of our father David!" "Hosanna in the highest!"* This coming kingdom of God would also be the restored kingdom of David. Jesus was born into the world through the tribe of Judah and thus was a descendant of David. He could rightfully claim the throne of David and fulfill all the promises of the Old Testament concerning the everlasting nature of the kingdom of Israel.

Not only was the "good news" message of John, Jesus, and the apostles about a coming kingdom to fulfill the prophesies and "restore the fortunes of Judah and Jerusalem," but the time was "at hand." It was going to happen soon! In Matthew 16:28 Jesus said, *"I tell you the truth, some who are standing here will not taste death before they see the Son of Man coming in his kingdom."* Mark records this in Mark 9:1, *"I tell you the truth, some who are standing here will not taste death before they see the kingdom of God come with power."*

Jesus added a new twist to the story in Matthew 16:18-20. After asking his disciples who they thought he was, Peter replied that he was the Christ, the Son of God. Jesus said to him, *"And I tell you that you are Peter, and on this rock I will build* **my church***, and the gates of Hades will not overcome it. I will give you the keys of* **the kingdom of heaven***; whatever you bind on earth will be bound* *in heaven, and whatever you loose on earth will be loosed in heaven."* Here Jesus identified the kingdom of heaven as the church which he was going to build. In his parable about the sheep and goats in Matthew 25:34 Jesus said the king would say, *"Come, you who are blessed by my Father; take your inheritance, the kingdom prepared for you since the creation of the world."* According to Jesus the inheritance of the righteous was this coming kingdom, the church, which had been prepared since creation.

The message was clear. The kingdom of God was coming, and some of them were even going to live to see it. The crowds grew, excitement was building, hope was at an all-time high. Then something seemed to go terribly wrong. Jesus was falsely accused, arrested, tried, sentenced, and crucified outside Jerusalem. All the hopes of his disciples, all their excitement, all their dreams died and were buried with him in that borrowed tomb.

Joseph must have had a heavy heart when he approached Pilate for Jesus' body. Mark 15:43 tells us, *"Joseph of Arimathea, a prominent member of the Council,* ***who was himself waiting for the kingdom of God****, went boldly to Pilate and asked for Jesus' body."* He had been waiting for the kingdom and fully believed this was the time. Now he was asking for the body of the person he had thought was the one.

The apostles and other disciples scattered. Peter, James and John went back to fishing. Perhaps the utter disappointment was best expressed by the ones going home to Emmaus. *"We had hoped that he was the one who was going to redeem Israel."* (Luke 24:21). One can feel the sadness in those words. They were living examples of one of King Solomon's proverbs, *"Hope deferred makes the heart sick"* (Proverbs 13:12).

But as soon as those heavy words were spoken, Jesus said to them, *"How foolish you are, and how slow of heart to believe all that the prophets have spoken! Did not the Christ have to suffer these things and then enter his glory? And beginning with Moses and all the*

Prophets, he explained to them what was said in all the Scriptures concerning himself" (Luke 24:25-27). As soon as they realized he had really come back from the grave, they hurried back to Jerusalem to tell the other disciples. By this time the news was spreading like wild fire. HE IS ALIVE!

Hope was reborn. The story was far from over. Something wonderful was still coming. Jesus had tried to explain all this to them prior to his death, but they just could not believe it. After all, David died and was still dead. So were all his successors. Why would the next king to sit on his throne be any different?

John 18:36-37, when Jesus was standing trial before Pilate, tells how Jesus explained the true nature of his kingdom. *"My kingdom is not of this world. If it were, my servants would fight to prevent my arrest by the Jews. But now my kingdom is from another place." "You are a king, then!" said Pilate. Jesus answered, "You are right in saying I am a king. In fact, for this reason I was born, and for this I came into the world..."* Jesus had come to be the king of the Jews, but it was the nature of his kingdom people did not understand. *"Once, having been asked by the Pharisees when the kingdom of God would come, Jesus replied, The kingdom of God does not come with your careful observation, nor will people say, 'Here it is,' or 'There it is,' because the kingdom of God is within you"* (Luke 17:20-21). Jesus' kingdom was going to be a spiritual kingdom, not a physical one. The ultimate fulfillment of God's promise to the patriarchs was this new spiritual kingdom. The real tragedy of sin is spiritual death, the victory we have through Jesus Christ is spiritual life. The physical was only a prototype of the coming spiritual. They didn't get it...neither do the majority of Christians today.

With the resurrection of Jesus came a renewed excitement and hope for the future. Now would the kingdom be restored? That was what the apostles wanted to know. We read in Acts 1:1-8:

> *"In my former book, Theophilus, I wrote about all that Jesus began to do and to teach until the day he*

was taken up to heaven, after giving instructions through the Holy Spirit to the apostles he had chosen. After his suffering, he showed himself to these men and gave many convincing proofs that he was alive. He appeared to them over a period of forty days and spoke about the kingdom of God. On one occasion, while he was eating with them, he gave them this command: 'Do not leave Jerusalem, but wait for the gift my Father promised, which you have heard me speak about. For John baptized with water, but in a few days you will be baptized with the Holy Spirit.'

So when they met together, they asked him, **'Lord, are you at this time going to restore the kingdom to Israel?'** *He said to them: 'It is not for you to know the times or dates the Father has set by his own authority. But you will receive power when the Holy Spirit comes on you; and you will be my witnesses in Jerusalem, and in all Judea and Samaria, and to the ends of the earth.' "*

His resurrection convinced his disciples he was the one to restore the kingdom. However, they still did not understand when or how, although he had explained this to them prior to his death. Most Jews believed the Messiah would come, raise an army, defeat the Romans, set up an earthly kingdom and physically reign on David's throne. Many Jews tragically missed their own Messiah because they could not understand and accept the spiritual nature of his kingdom. They wanted a physical kingdom, a physical king, so they refused to believe Jesus. It is even more amazing that a majority of Christians today have believed the same false doctrine concerning the coming king and his kingdom. They have been told Jesus will physically return to the earth to establish his kingdom and reign on David's physical throne in a rebuilt city of

Jerusalem for a thousand years. If that is the case, where does that leave Christians today? If the church and the kingdom are one and the same, as Jesus taught, how is this possible? Has the church not yet been established? The theology of this teaching is completely foreign to Scripture.

Jesus taught otherwise during his earthly ministry. He plainly said his kingdom was *"not of this world"* and it *"would not come visibly."* He also taught when it would come. In his instructions to the apostles recorded in Matthew 24-25, Mark 13, and Luke 21, he told them his kingdom would come at the same time the old physical one was removed from the earth. That is how they would know when it was completed. Luke 21:20 Jesus said, *"When you see Jerusalem being surrounded by armies, you will know that its desolation is near."* A few verses later in that same discussion he said, *"Even so, when you see these things happening, you know that* ***the kingdom of God is near.*** *I tell you the truth, this generation will certainly not pass away until all these things have happened"* (Luke 21:31-32).

In his parable of the talents Jesus taught the same thing. Matthew's account of this parable begins, *"Again, it will be like a man going on a journey, who called his servants and entrusted his property to them…"* (Matthew 25:14). Keeping Matthew in its context, we see Jesus was still speaking of the day of the Lord when the temple and its buildings would be destroyed.

Luke 19:11-13 clearly links this parable with the coming kingdom. *"While they were listening to this, he went on to tell them a parable, because he was near Jerusalem and the people thought that the kingdom of God was going to appear at once. He said: A man of noble birth went to a distant country to have himself appointed king and then to return. So he called ten of his servants and gave them ten minas. Put this money to work, he said, until I come back."*

What were the people expecting? Jesus was going to Jerusalem and they thought the kingdom of God was going to come immediately when he got there. The story of the parable is about *"...a man of noble birth who was going away to have himself appointed king and then return."* Jesus was the noble man who was going to become the King of Kings. We know the kingdom had not come prior to his death, and we know it had still not come following his resurrection. If it had his disciples would not have asked in Acts 1 when it was coming. In the parable Jesus said when the man of noble birth first has to go away to be anointed king, then he would return. The instruction to his disciples was for them to be good stewards until he returned as king. When did that happen? When did the kingdom come?

As we continue through the Acts of the Apostles and the letters in the New Testament we find the Holy Spirit guided the first century disciples and writers to continue teaching about the coming kingdom. In 2 Timothy 4:1 the Apostle Paul tells young Timothy, *"In the presence of God and of Christ Jesus, who will judge the living and the dead, and* ***in view of his appearing and his kingdom,*** *I give you this charge: Preach the word..."* Evidently the appearing of Jesus and his kingdom were still in Paul's and Timothy's future. They were also inextricably linked together.

The writer of Hebrews discussed in great length the change from the Old Law to the new covenant in Christ, from the physical kingdom of the Jews to the spiritual kingdom of Jesus. He also clearly recognized this change was still in progress and would be completed when the Lord returned **during their lifetime**. In chapter 10:36-37 he said, *"You need to persevere so that when you have done the will of God, you will receive what he has promised. For in just a very little while, he who is coming will come and will not delay."* Then in chapter 12:26-29, he spoke of the removal of the old and the coming of the new when he said, *"At that time (giving of the Old Law on Mt. Sinai) his voice shook the earth, but now he has promised, 'Once more I will shake not only the earth but also the heavens.' The words 'once more' indicate the* *removing of what can be shaken—that is, created things—so that what cannot be shaken may remain. Therefore,* ***since we are receiving a kingdom*** *that cannot be shaken, let us be thankful, and so worship God acceptably with reverence and awe, for our God is a consuming fire."*

The giving of the old Law of Moses on Mt. Sinai led to the eventual building of the temple in Jerusalem where God's presence dwelled during the days of the physical nation of Israel. All these physical (created) things could be "shaken" or removed from the earth. The physical nation had been shaken in the past and even the sacred furnishings of that physical temple had been carried off into foreign countries. God was replacing the physical kingdom with a spiritual one that could not be shaken. According to Hebrews, that spiritual kingdom was still coming at the time of his writing and would be complete when Jesus returned. He said we *are receiving* (not *have received*) a kingdom.

So when did the kingdom come, or is it still coming? If the parable is true and Jesus has not yet been crowned king, the kingdom cannot be a reality. You cannot have a kingdom without a king. Since the kingdom and the church are one and the same, that would mean the church has not yet been established. Another possibility is that the church was established on the Day of Pentecost (Acts 2) and since the church and the kingdom are the same, that is when the kingdom came. This explanation cannot be correct since the passages in Timothy and Hebrews, written three decades after Pentecost, clearly state that the kingdom, as well as Jesus' appearing, were still to occur in the future.

If the coming of Jesus is to be at the "end of time," that would mean neither the kingdom nor the church will ever exist in this world. The only possibility that makes any sense is to simply believe what Jesus said. He said he was going away to become king, and he would return in his kingdom. He also taught the new spiritual kingdom will replace the old physical one and fulfill all the prophesies of Old Testament Scripture. Further, he said when the armies came and destroyed the temple in Jerusalem, that would be the sign that all these things had been completed. To make sure we didn't miss it, he said, *"This generation will not pass away until all these things have happened."*

Jesus ascended to the Father. He went away to be anointed king. During the time he was away he sent the Holy Spirit to reveal to the apostles (and others) the new covenant of the spiritual kingdom. Once that revelation was complete, he returned, destroyed the physical temple and Jerusalem (what could be shaken), thus fulfilling the final prophesies concerning the consummation of the ages. The kingdom of God and David's throne were now fully established in the Heavens where they can never again be shaken.

The Apostle John was privileged to witness the events of that great "day of the Lord" when the physical kingdom of Israel (the prototype) became the kingdom of God (the reality). Revelation 11:15 says, *"The seventh angel sounded his trumpet, and there were loud voices in heaven, which said: 'The kingdom of the world has become the kingdom of our Lord and of his Christ, and he will reign for ever and ever.' "* The book of Revelation is about this consummation of God's plan to complete his eternal plan for redemption and establish the eternal kingdom. It is the Revelation of Jesus Christ, not the revelation of some imagined end of the world.

And what about God's promise to the devil in Genesis? Revelation 12:10, *"Then I heard a loud voice in heaven say: 'Now have come the salvation and the power and the kingdom of our God, and the authority of his Christ. For the accuser of our brothers, who accuses them before our God day and night, has been hurled down.' "* The Apostle Paul had written about this just a few years earlier in Romans 16:20. *"The God of peace will soon crush Satan under your feet." In 1 John 3:8 Jesus said, "He who does what is sinful is of the devil, because the devil has been sinning from the beginning. The reason the Son of God appeared was to destroy the devil's work."*

Remember, God had told Satan one of the woman's descendants would crush his head. Jesus did!

Remember, God had promised Abraham that his "seed" would bless the whole world? Jesus did!

Remember, God had promised David one of his descendants would reign on his throne forever? Jesus does!

Remember, God promised the kingdom of Israel would become an eternal kingdom that would never end, and Jesus said this promised kingdom of heaven was his church. That kingdom has come, the prayer was answered. JESUS REIGNS!

The church was never intended to be some magical place where one can go on Sunday to experience a connection with the "spirit world" and, through a mystical séance of "prayers" and divinations by the "spirit filled" speaker, receive healing from every physical ailment or release from the "demons" that plague our lives. It is the gathering of the redeemed, where we go to worship the Almighty and praise him for our deliverance from sin and thank him for the grace he has given us, regardless of the various conditions of our present circumstances. It is the fellowship of believers who all belong to the family of God because of the kinship we share in Jesus Christ.

CHAPTER 4

The Consummation of the Ages

What do the majority of Christians today have in common with Henny Penny, Ducky Lucky, Goosey Loosey, and Turkey Lurkey? In the more modern version of the ancient fable, an acorn falls on the head of Chicken Little. Terrified by the experience, she mistakenly assumes the sky is falling and runs to tell the king. Along the way she encounters each of the other characters to whom she excitedly relates her belief that the sky is falling. She tells them, "I saw it with my own eyes, and heard it with my own ears, and part of it fell on my head!" They all believe her story and join the frenzy. After all, how could they question her personal experience? Foxy Loxy, being the cunning fellow he is, seizes the opportunity for a meal of banquet proportions and offers to "show them the way to the king." With the wise Foxy Loxy now leading the way, they are all proclaiming the most important and urgent message the world has ever heard; "The sky is falling!" Foxy Loxy is not about to tell them otherwise.

In 1970 Hal Lindsey wrote the bestselling book of the century entitled The Late Great Planet Earth. Based on the reestablishment of the nation of Israel in 1948 he claimed Bible prophesies indicated the world was on its final countdown to the end of time. It immediately caught the attention of many in the Christian world and today it has sold over 40 million copies worldwide. Without a doubt he was the greatest influence of the twentieth century on the modern church in molding its doctrine of eschatology. He has often been referred to as the "dean of prophecy."

Although Lindsey did not claim to know the exact dates of future events with certainty, he suggested that Jesus' return would be within "one generation" of the rebirth of the state of Israel. Lindsey asserted that "in the Bible" one generation is forty years, indicating that the Tribulation or the Rapture would occur no later than 1988. In his 1980 work, The 1980s: Countdown to Armageddon, which was essentially an updated version of his former book, Lindsey predicted that "…the decade of the 1980s could very well be the last decade of history as we know it."

Countless preachers and authors jumped on this doomsday bandwagon. Despite the fact that every prediction Lindsey made proved to be false, this philosophy continues to be the primary eschatological doctrine among Christian churches. Beginning in 1995 authors Tim LaHaye and Jerry B. Jenkins launched the Left Behind series of books that have eclipsed Lindsey's record, having now sold over fifty million copies. Even though these books are officially classified as fiction, their end-time scenario has been embraced by virtually the entire Christian community on almost the same level as inspired Scripture. Sadly, the vast majority of Christians know more about the Left Behind philosophy than they do about the Bible version of these events.

To promote their completely fictional view of the end of the world, these men continue to misapply and even misquote what the Bible says. In a recent article on their web site entitled "Three Signs of the End," they say, "Jesus' disciples asked him a classic question 2000 years ago: 'What shall be the sign of your coming, and of the end of the age?' That remains one of the most prominent questions to this day. The fact is that the signs of the times are all around us. Many are asking, 'How long can it be until the end of history, the end of life as we know it?' " (leftbehind.com/02_end_times) These prominent authors completely ignore the context of the apostles' question, conveniently choose Matthew's account, and quote only part of it.

In the Biblical record, the apostles were asking Jesus questions following his statement that the temple in Jerusalem would be completely destroyed. *"'Tell us,' they said, '**when will this happen**, and what will be the sign of your coming and of the end of the age' "* (Matthew 24:3)? In Mark 13:4 we have another account of the exact same question, *"Tell us, when will these things happen? And what will be the sign that they are all about to be fulfilled?"* A third account of the very same question is found in Luke 21:7. *" 'Teacher,' they asked, 'when will these things happen? And what will be the sign that they are about to take place?' "* The apostles were asking when the temple would be destroyed and what would be the signs of its impending destruction. In all three of the gospel accounts of this conversation Jesus went on to explain to these men that *"...this generation will not pass away until all these things have happened."* There is nothing in their question or in Jesus' answer about the end of the world. However, correctly quoting the Bible in its context would not have supported LaHaye's and Jenkins' fictional story, so they changed it to suit their "Left Behind" theology.

Proponents of this doctrine, which include some of the most prominent names in religion today, still believe and teach that the temple in Jerusalem will be rebuilt, the "abomination of desolation" spoken of by Daniel is still future, that we are living in the "last days" of the "end times," the "great tribulation" is just around the corner, and Jesus is coming...SOON! This doctrine has allowed "men of God" to bilk hundreds of millions of dollars out of innocent believers who have not been taught the truth about Biblical eschatology. In his nationally televised *Spring '94 Praise-A-Thon*, televangelist Paul Crouch declared, "We are in the last moments of grace before the wrath of God is revealed. We don't have much time left. If Jesus hasn't come back by the year

2000 A.D., then we (he and his guest preachers) have misread the Scriptures." Of course this was followed by an urgent plea for money in the face of impending doom.

Televangelist Pat Robertson said on *CBN's The 700 Club*, "All signs point to the end of the world and the end of life as we have known it. What this means is we are coming up on the time of the end. Now the time is urgent to bolster the resources of CBN. Your dollars may not do any good in five years or so." (1995 CBN fundraising telethon) As we now know, all the predictions leading up to the year 2000, over which they had the Christian world in a frenzy, proved to be totally false. They had, however, successfully proven just how financially profitable this emotionally charged doomsday philosophy can be.

The Apostle Paul said in 1 Timothy 6:3-5, *"If anyone teaches false doctrines and does not agree to the sound instruction of our Lord Jesus Christ and to godly teaching, he is conceited and understands nothing. He has an unhealthy interest in controversies and quarrels about words that result in envy, strife, malicious talk, evil suspicions and constant friction between men of corrupt mind, who have been robbed of the truth and who think that godliness is a means to financial gain."* Instead of these men being flatly condemned and rejected by the Christian community as the false prophets they have proven themselves to be, the majority of preachers and churches have actually accepted and now teach this same false doctrine.

This "chicken little" message that the sky is falling is one of the primary hindrances to the acceptance of Christianity by non-believers today. Every decade since Lindsay's has seen a multitude of books written and prophecies proclaimed by well known "Christian" theologians about the end of the world. Every flare-up in the Middle East starts a new round of prophecies and books. And even though every such prophecy, including Lindsey's, has been proven false, the "Left Behind" doctrine attracts an ever increasing following. How many false prophets do we have to hear before we begin to question the validity of their message? By his own admission, Paul Crouch and his associates "misread the Scriptures." But the same failed misinterpretation keeps getting repeated over and over like a broken record. The world has heard the church cry "wolf" so many times they have begun to dismiss the entire Christian message as a hoax. Who can blame them?

Instead of proclaiming the good news of hope and redemption to a lost and dying world, these doomsday prophets are spreading a message of gloom and despair. According to them everything is terrible and going to get much worse until everything and everyone is finally destroyed by a revenge-seeking Jesus on a white horse. Why would anyone be concerned about the condition of the world when it is all going to be destroyed "in just a little while?" The church's urgent message to a lost world, the *good news*, is not, "The sky is falling!"

More importantly, this "end times" philosophy is simply false doctrine and compromises the fundamental teachings of Jesus and the apostles regarding salvation and the purpose of the church in the world. If this doctrine is true, and we follow what Scripture teaches about the "last days," the following must also be true:

1. The miraculous "gifts of the Holy Spirit," speaking in tongues, healing, raising the dead, being immune to poisonous snake bites, prophecy, and divine revelation, are still a vital part of the church and everyday Christian experience.
2. The church is still in its infancy, dependent upon these "childish" gifts, not having grown to the "maturity" Paul describes in his first letter to the Corinthians.
3. Scripture is not complete as the Holy Spirit continues to reveal God's word to divinely

inspired men and women.

4. Death still has mastery over us and we are still living under the Law of Moses, since the "*...sting of death is sin and the power of sin is the Law,*" and death will not be destroyed until Jesus returns (1 Corinthians 15).
5. The atonement sacrifice of Jesus on the Cross is still incomplete, and we stand outside the Holy of Holies guilty of sin, waiting to find out if God accepts his sacrifice for our forgiveness.
6. The temple in Jerusalem must still be standing. (Many proponents of the "future coming" doctrine do understand the key role the Jerusalem temple plays in Biblical eschatology, which is why they believe the Jews must be restored as a nation and the temple rebuilt before the Lord can come again...so he can destroy it, AGAIN!)

Acceptance of this doctrine also explains why so many, even in conservative Christian churches, have either embraced the "Pentecostal" view that miraculous gifts are still with us and God is still personally revealing his will to "Spirit-filled" men and women today, or they are at a complete loss to explain why not. If we are truly living in the "last days," one cannot honestly hold any other view and be consistent with Scripture. "Jesus is coming soon, morning or night or noon" may be an emotionally exciting message, but as one preacher often said of good sounding, but false, teachings, "it is a doctrine of the Devil, comes straight from the pits of Hell, and smells like smoke!"

In order to comprehend the meaning of the "last days" and the significance of what Jesus taught concerning the events that transpired during those days leading up to the destruction of the temple in Jerusalem, we must first understand what the Bible refers to as the "mystery of God" and a concept known as the "consummation (fulfillment) of the ages." The answers can only come from God's word.

The Apostle Paul discusses the mystery of God at great length in his letter to the church in Ephesus. In Ephesians 1:9-10 he says, *"And he (God) made known to us the mystery of his will according to his good pleasure, which he purposed in Christ, to be put into effect when the times will have reached their fulfillment—to bring all things in heaven and on earth together under one head, even Christ."* And in chapter 3:4-6, *"In reading this, then, you will be able to understand my insight into the mystery of Christ, which was not made known to men in other generations as it has now been revealed by the Spirit to God's holy apostles and prophets. This mystery is that through the gospel the Gentiles are heirs together with Israel, members together of one body, and sharers together in the promise in Christ Jesus."* He further identifies that body as the church in verses 10-11, *"His intent was that now, through the church, the manifold wisdom of God should be made known to the rulers and authorities in the heavenly realms, according to his eternal purpose which he accomplished in Christ Jesus our Lord."*

According to Paul the establishment of the church would be the means by which the mystery of God would be revealed and that would be when the times will have reached their fulfillment. He writes the same thing in Colossians 1:26-27 where he speaks again of *"...the mystery that has been kept hidden for ages and generations, but is now disclosed to the saints. To them God has chosen to make known among the Gentiles the glorious riches of this mystery, which is Christ in you, the hope of glory."*

In 1 Peter 1:12 Peter refers to the same revealing of this mystery when he is speaking of the message of the prophets of the Old Testament. *"It was revealed to them that they were not serving themselves but you, when they spoke of the things that have now been told you by those who have preached the gospel to you by the Holy Spirit sent from heaven. Even angels long to look into these things."*

This mystery was revealed at a time called the "consummation (fulfillment) of the ages." Paul, speaking of some of the things that happened to the Israelites during the time of Moses, said in 1 Corinthians 10:11, *"These things happened to them as examples and were written down as warnings for us, on whom the fulfillment (consummation) of the ages has come."* The King James Version renders this verse, *"Now all these things happened unto them for examples: and they are written for our admonition, upon whom the ends of the world are come."* And the Amplified Bible says, *"Now these things befell them by way of a figure [as an example and warning to us]; they were written to admonish and fit us for right action by good instruction, we in whose days the ages have reached their climax (their consummation and concluding period)."*

John, in Revelation 10:7, writing at the very end of this time period says, *"But in the days when the seventh angel is about to sound his trumpet, the mystery of God will be accomplished, just as he announced to his servants the prophets."* There is only one "mystery of God" discussed in the Bible. It was how he would redeem all of mankind from the curse of sin and bring them together into one body, one spiritual kingdom, known today as the church, and this terminology is found in numerous passages, especially in the writings of the Apostle Paul. All these verses speak of the same mystery and the same time period for its revelation. It was a time known as the consummation of the ages. The apostles clearly identified this time period as during their lifetime. This would be the same "last days" of Israel described earlier.

What exactly was going to transpire during this "consummation of the ages" and why was this time referred to as an "age-changing" period? Why did Jesus put so much importance on the destruction of Jerusalem and its temple? Is it important for us to understand these things today? If we are to properly understand the times in which we are living and what the future holds for Christians and the world, we must know what changed and when. We will see from our study there was a change from one age to another, from one world to another, from one kingdom to another, from one covenant to another, from one priesthood to another. Perhaps the best source of information regarding these age-changing events and their timing is the New Testament book of Hebrews. With the exception of the last chapter which contains some final encouragements and greetings, the entire book is dedicated to explaining the consummation of the ages.

In the first three verses the author lays out the basis of what he is going to be teaching. Hebrews 1:1-3, *"In the past God spoke to our forefathers through the prophets at many times and in various ways, but in these last days he has spoken to us by his Son, whom he appointed heir of all things, and through whom he made the universe. The Son is the radiance of God's glory and the exact representation of his being, sustaining all things by his powerful word. After he had provided purification for sins, he sat down at the right hand of the Majesty in heaven."* He immediately identifies the "ages past" when God spoke through the prophets, the time in which he is living as "these last days," and the subject of his letter; Christ, the Son of God. As we will see, he will spend the remainder of the book comparing the old covenant of Moses with new covenant in Christ, the one that was ending with the one that was just beginning, the physical kingdom with the spiritual kingdom, the inferior one to the superior one.

In chapter two the writer urges his readers to pay careful attention to the gospel message they had heard, for if people were punished for disobeying the Old Testament teachings, how can we escape punishment if we ignore the message of salvation *"...which was first announced by the Lord, was confirmed to us by those who heard him. God also testified to it by signs, wonders and various miracles, and gifts of the Holy Spirit distributed according to his will"* (2:3-4). In verse 5 he says *"...it is not to angels that he (God) has subjected the world to come, about which we are speaking,"* but it is subjected to Christ. Please notice two things in this verse. First, the passage says the spiritual kingdom of Christ is the "world to come," and second, this "world to come" is the subject of the text. He then speaks of the preeminence of Christ, how he shared our humanity so that *"...by his death he might destroy him who holds the power of death—that is, the devil—and free those who all their lives were held in slavery by their fear of death"* (2:14-15). Jesus did this by making atonement for sin.

In chapters 3 and 4 the author admonishes his Jewish readers to *"...fix their eyes on Jesus"* because he is far superior to Moses and has become the "Great High Priest." The subject of Jesus as the Great High Priest introduces us to the means by which the consummation of the ages will be possible. This is the main theme of this letter...atonement. Only the High Priest could make atonement for the sins of the people. But the Jewish priests were sinners and could only offer the blood of bulls and goats, which could not actually atone for sin. It would take a better sacrifice to do that. Jesus was that better sacrifice.

The writer explains in chapters 5 and 7 how Jesus' priesthood was not based on genealogy as required by the Law of Moses. Rather he was appointed by God Himself, "after the order" or similar to Melchizedek. This was one of the "age-changing" events, a change in the priesthood. *"For when there is a change of the priesthood, there must also be a change of the law"* (7:12). The Law of Moses gave specific and detailed instructions about the appointment of priests, and especially the High Priest. These men had to be of the tribe of Levi, direct descendants of Aaron who served as Israel's first High Priest.

Outside the book of Hebrews, Melchizedek is mentioned only two times in the Bible (Genesis 14:18, Psalm 110:4). He lived during the time of Abraham over four hundred years before the Law was given to Moses on Mt. Sinai. We are not given many details of his life, but Melchizedek was chosen by God to serve as a priest and when Abraham met him, he gave him a tenth of all his possessions. Melchizedek's priesthood was not based on his genealogy, but solely upon God's divine selection and appointment.

Jesus was a descendant of the tribe of Judah, not Levi. Based on his genealogy he had no claim to the priesthood. Under the Law of Moses he could not have served as High Priest. This is why the Hebrew writer says his priesthood is after the order of Melchizedek, not Aaron. In chapter 7:16 he says, Jesus *"...has become a priest not on the basis of a regulation as to his ancestry but on the basis of the power of an indestructible life."*

Also in verse 12 we see another "age-changing" event was a change in the law. As he said, if there was a change in the priesthood there had to be a change in the law since the law required the High Priest to be a direct descendant of Aaron. *"The former regulation is set aside because it was weak and useless (for the law made nothing perfect), and a better hope is introduced, by which we draw near to God"* (7:18-19). Unlike the former priests under the Old Law, Jesus would remain the High Priest forever, and he could actually save people from their sins because of his superior sacrifice.

In the first part of chapter 8 we see this Great High Priest serves at a different sanctuary. The Old Levitical high priest served at a copy of God's sanctuary here on earth, which was first located in a "traveling tabernacle" built by the Israelites in the wilderness. This tabernacle had one room designated the Holy of Holies, which symbolized the place where God lived. Only the High Priest could enter the presence of God in the Holy of Holies once each year to offer the annual atonement sacrifice for sin. Once the Israelites moved into their promised land and the kingdom was established under King David, Jerusalem was selected as the permanent site of the tabernacle. Solomon built the temple to replace the original tent that had been used since the wilderness wanderings. It was in this temple the High Priests continued to serve. Jesus was not appointed High Priest under the Law of Moses. He did not enter the Holy of Holies in the temple in Jerusalem. He offered his blood sacrifice in the heavenly Holy of Holies before the very throne of God.

As we continue we see another "age-changing" event, a new covenant. *"The time is coming, declares the Lord, when I will make a new covenant with the house of Israel and with the house of Judah. It will not be like the covenant I made with their forefathers when I took them by the hand to lead them out of Egypt...By calling this covenant 'new,' he has made the first one obsolete; and what is obsolete and aging will soon disappear"* (8:8-13).

The old covenant was passing away. The text clearly says *"...what is obsolete and aging will soon disappear."* It was not yet gone. Doesn't the Bible say the Old Law was "nailed to the cross"? Yes, in Colossians 2:14 Paul wrote, *"He forgave us all our sins, having canceled the written code, with its regulations, that was against us and that stood opposed to us; he took it away, nailing it to the cross."* Hebrews was written some thirty years after the crucifixion of Jesus. Why did it not say the old covenant had already disappeared? Because, as we shall soon see, the atonement work of Jesus was not finished. The cross was the fatal blow to the power of the Old Law. The perfect sacrifice of Jesus on the cross rendered it obsolete. But until the old Jewish system (world, heaven and earth) was destroyed, the law would remain.

Jesus said in Matthew 5:17-18, *"Do not think that I have come to abolish the Law or the Prophets; I have not come to abolish them but to fulfill them. I tell you the truth,* **until heaven and earth disappear**, *not the smallest letter, not the least stroke of a pen, will by any means disappear from the Law until everything is accomplished."*

In Isaiah 51 God told the Israelites he had led them out of Egypt across the Red Sea, given them his law, *"That I may plant the heavens, lay the foundations of the earth, and say to Zion, 'You are My people.' "* It was this "heaven and earth" (kingdom of Israel) to which Jesus referred when he said not the least part of the Law of Moses would disappear until "heaven and earth" had disappeared. The Law could not disappear until everything in it was fulfilled. Jesus said that is what he came to do.

Jesus' death on the cross was what made all of the "age-changing" events possible, but the actual changing of the ages did not occur on the day of his crucifixion. Nothing could change until the atonement sacrifice had been completed. Once that had happened there would indeed have been a change in the law and the priesthood. Then the old covenant, its temple and worship, would disappear. The atonement sacrifice was not complete with the slaying of the sacrificial lamb. The blood still had to be taken into the Holy of Holies and sprinkled on the Mercy Seat covering the Ark of the Covenant. Jesus' death was the beginning of this ritual, not the completion of it.

This may be the most critical point to understand concerning the "second coming" of Jesus. The old covenant was a prototype of the new one to be revealed during the "last days" of Israel. In the first covenant only the High Priest could enter the Holy of Holies, only to offer a blood sacrifice...first for his own sin, then for the sins of the people. This ritual is described in Leviticus 16 and required the High Priest to enter the Most Holy Place (and reappear) *twice*. There were actually two atonement sacrifices. The first time the High Priest entered with blood for himself. When he went behind the veil, he was entering (symbolically) into the presence of God, which was a place a sinful person could not enter and live. Since death was the consequence of sin, he was, in a very real sense, entering the "realm of death." If he or his sacrifice was not acceptable to God, he would die. His first appearance indicated to the people that he was acceptable to God as the High Priest to offer the sacrifice for the people.

He would then take a second amount of blood from their offering, return behind the veil, and make the sacrifice for the sins of the people. They anxiously waited for his second appearing, proving that God had accepted this blood for their sins. Only then were they assured of their atonement and could know they were justified before God for one more year.

Jesus is the High Priest of the new covenant. The ritual was exactly the same as under the old covenant...only the sacrifice was better. His perfect blood was the permanent remedy for sin. But he had to go through the same exercise as every previous High Priest. On the cross he shed his own blood that would be used for the atonement for sin. However, when Jesus died he did not enter the realm of death with a sin offering. As a matter of fact, technically his blood was not actually spilled until after he was dead. He entered death with NO sacrifice for Himself. This was the ultimate test of his complete lack of sin. This was equivalent to the High Priest walking into the Holy of Holies with NO blood offering.

The Bible teaches that Jesus had no sin. Anyone can make that claim. It was his resurrection from the grave that absolutely proved him to have been sinless. Had Jesus had even one sin, he would still be dead and would have never returned. The Apostle Paul said it was his resurrection that God used to declare that he was who he claimed to be, the Son of God. Paul says of Jesus, *"…who through the Spirit of holiness was declared with power to be the Son of God by his resurrection from the dead: Jesus Christ our Lord"* (Romans 1:3-5). And in Hebrews 7:16 it says, Jesus *"...has become a priest not on the basis of a regulation as to his ancestry but on the basis of the power of an indestructible life."*

The most important ritual God ever gave was the atonement, and Jesus had to complete all of it. Anybody could have claimed to be the Messiah, and even claimed to be sinless. His appearing from the grave was absolutely necessary to establish not only his High Priesthood, but that no additional sacrifices were needed. He had truly overcome death! His first appearing (bodily resurrection) proved that God had accepted him as the Great High Priest for the people. But Jesus still had to take his blood, go into the heavenly Holy of Holies, and fulfill the sacrifice for the sins of the people. By doing this he became *"...the lamb of God who takes away the sins of the world"* (John 1:29). To finish the second and final part of the atonement ritual, he had to go away again, after he had appeared the first time from the grave. This is why he explained to Mary at the tomb she could not "hold onto him" now because he had to return to the Father.

So after Jesus had been seen by a sufficient number of people to prove beyond any doubt that he was alive and accepted as God's High Priest, he left this earth to make the final sacrifice in the Most Holy Place. Hebrews 9:24 says, *"For Christ did not enter a man-made sanctuary that was only a copy of the true one; he entered heaven itself, now to appear for us in God's presence."* The eager anticipation of his "second coming" that we read about in the New Testament was because they understood the significance and the details of the atonement. His return would announce to the world that the sacrifice had been accepted by God and that the people were forgiven!

This same writer in Hebrews 9:28 said, *"Christ was sacrificed once to take away the sins of many people; and* ***he will appear a second time****, not to bear sin, but* ***to bring salvation to those who are waiting for him****."* It was in view of the completion of the atonement sacrifice for sin that Jesus taught that his coming would complete our redemption. In Luke 21:27-28, speaking of the destruction of Jerusalem and its temple, Jesus said, *"At that time they will see the Son of Man coming in a cloud with power and great glory. When these things begin to take place, stand up and lift up your* *heads,* ***because your redemption is drawing near.*** *"*

Paul taught the same thing in his letters. To the Romans in 13:11 he said, *"And do this, understanding the present time. The hour has come for you to wake up from your slumber, because* ***our salvation is nearer now than when we first believed.*** *"* In Galatians 5:5 he said, *"But by faith we eagerly await through the Spirit the righteousness for which we hope."* And in Titus 2:11-14, *"For the grace of God that brings salvation has appeared to all men. It teaches us to say 'No' to ungodliness and worldly passions, and to live self-controlled, upright and godly lives in this present age, while we wait for the blessed hope—the glorious appearing of our great God and Savior, Jesus Christ, who gave himself for us to redeem us from all wickedness and to purify for himself a people that are his very own, eager to do what is good."*

The Apostle Peter was also guided by the Holy Spirit to teach the same expectation of the Lord's coming to signify the completion of the atonement and finish the work of salvation. In 1 Peter 1:3-7 he wrote, *"Praise be to the God and Father of our Lord Jesus Christ! In his great mercy he has given us new birth into a living hope through the resurrection of Jesus Christ from the dead, and into an inheritance that can never perish, spoil or fade—kept in heaven for you, who through faith are shielded by God's power* ***until the coming of the salvation that is ready to be revealed in the last time.*** *In this you greatly rejoice, though now for a little while you may have had to suffer grief in all kinds of trials. These have come so that your faith—of greater worth than gold, which perishes even though refined by fire—may be proved genuine and may result in praise, glory and honor when Jesus Christ is revealed."* Jesus was ready to be revealed at the "last time," bringing to fruition the great mystery of God, completing the atonement ritual and God's plan of salvation.

This is why he left no doubt how everyone could tell he had returned. Jesus linked the destruction of Jerusalem, the temple, and the former Holy of Holies to that event. *"This is how you will know...when you see the abomination of desolation spoken of by the prophet Daniel, let the reader understand"* (Matt. 24). *"When you see Jerusalem surrounded by armies...this is the time of punishment in fulfillment of all that has been written...Stand up, lift up your heads,* ***because your redemption is drawing near****"* (Luke 21)! They both go on to say, *"This generation will certainly not pass away until all these things have happened."* Why the destruction of the temple as the final sign? It was the place of the atonement sacrifice. Once the real atonement was completed in heaven there was no need for the earthly temple. No more sacrifice for sin is required!

If the Lord did not "come again" as he promised and the Gospel writers predicted during that generation; if we are still awaiting his return, then the sacrifice of the High Priest was not accepted and our redemption is still not a reality. A careful study of Hebrews 9 makes this abundantly clear. In verse 8 the writer says that the sacrifice of the High Priest was the Spirit's way of *"...showing that the way into the Most Holy Place had not yet been disclosed* ***as long as the first tabernacle was still standing****."* When one saw the old temple destroyed, one would KNOW that the sacrifice had been accepted and the way into the Most Holy Place was open for all! Christ was sacrificed once to take away the sins of all people; and was to appear a second time, not to bear sin, but to bring salvation to those who were waiting for him. This is the same "appearing of our Great God and Savior Jesus Christ" of whom Paul, Peter, James and all the other New Testament writers speak. We are NOT still waiting for salvation!

In chapter 10 the writer continues to parallel the old covenant with the new covenant of Jesus Christ. He explains how we *"...have confidence to enter the Most Holy Place by the blood of Jesus"* (10:19). He encourages the Hebrew Christians to persevere through their trials and encourage each other more and more as they *"...see the Day approaching."* Isaiah, Joel and many other prophets had promised a "great and notable day of the Lord" would come to usher in the eternal kingdom and bring judgment on the nations. At the end of chapter 10 the encouragement is to hang on because *"…in just a little while (literally soon, very soon) he who is coming will come and not delay…"*

The writer here quotes from Habakkuk 2:3-4. The prophet's warnings were not only to the Jews of his day but also foreshadowed the coming events of Israel's "last days." We read in Acts 13:38-41, *"Therefore, my brothers, I want you to know that through Jesus the forgiveness of sins is proclaimed to you. Through him everyone who believes is justified from everything you could not be justified from by the Law of Moses. Take care that what the prophets have said does not happen to you: 'Look, you scoffers, wonder and perish, for I am going to do something in your days that you would never believe, even if someone told you.' "* Quoting from Habakkuk 1:5 Paul clearly confirmed that the prophecy saw its ultimate fulfillment in Jesus' death, resurrection and subsequent establishment of the church.

Hebrews quotes from Habakkuk 2:3, *"For the revelation awaits an appointed time; it speaks of the end and will not prove false. Though it linger, wait for it; it will certainly come and will not delay."* What was coming and would not delay was the appearing of Jesus Christ to bring salvation to those who were waiting. There is no discrepancy between Acts and Hebrews. They were both discussing events that would occur in that generation. Once again, the Bible interprets itself.

Hebrews chapter 12 concludes this concept with the explanation of God's "shaking the earth" to take away the physical kingdom so *"…what cannot be shaken may remain."* In verses 26-29 it says, *"At that time his voice shook the earth, but now he has promised, 'Once more I will shake not only the earth but also the heavens.' The words 'once more' indicate the removing of what can be shaken—that is, created things—so that what cannot be shaken may remain. Therefore, since we are receiving a kingdom that cannot be shaken, let us be thankful, and so worship God acceptably with reverence and awe, for our God is a consuming fire."*

To understand what the Hebrew writer is saying we must first understand the prophesies from which he is quoting. In Isaiah 2 the prophet describes a coming time during the "last days" of Judah and Jerusalem when the Lord would establish his new eternal kingdom. At that time, in verse 19, he says, *"Men will flee to caves in the rocks and to holes in the ground from dread of the Lord and the splendor of his majesty, when he rises to shake the earth."*

So as not to leave anything to speculation, God set up a graphic demonstration to show what he meant by "shaking the earth." In 586 B.C. God brought the Babylonians to bring his judgment against Israel because of their disobedience just as he had warned them in Habakkuk chapter one. Jerusalem was overrun, the temple was desecrated, and they were carried off into captivity. Their world was indeed shaken. Then in Isaiah 13 the prophet tells what was going to happen to the Babylonian kingdom.

> *"See, the day of the Lord is coming —a cruel day, with wrath and fierce anger— to make the land desolate and destroy the sinners within it. The stars of heaven and their constellations will not show their light. The rising sun will be darkened and the moon will not give its light. I will punish the world for its evil, the wicked for their sins. I will put an end to the arrogance of the haughty and will humble the pride of the ruthless. I will make man scarcer than pure gold, more rare than the gold of Ophir. Therefore I will make the heavens tremble; and the earth will shake from its place at the wrath of the Lord Almighty, in the day of his burning anger"* (Isaiah 13:9-13).

Notice in this description the prophetic language that was used to describe God's judgment against a nation. The heavens tremble;

the earth shakes. The stars and constellations do not shine; the sun and moon are darkened. This was the description of his coming judgment on Babylon. The Medes came and overthrew their empire, and it was never rebuilt.

Then in Haggai 2:6-9 the Bible says, *"This is what the Lord Almighty says: 'In a little while I will once more shake the heavens and the earth, the sea and the dry land. I will shake all nations, and the desired of all nations will come, and I will fill this house with glory,' says the Lord Almighty. 'The silver is mine and the gold is mine,' declares the Lord Almighty. 'The glory of this present house will be greater than the glory of the former house,' says the Lord Almighty. 'And in this place I will grant peace,' declares the Lord Almighty."*

Haggai lived after the Babylonian exile and was predicting the ultimate outcome of the kingdom of Israel. This "shaking of the earth" would result in a new house into which the desired of all nations would come. He also says the glory of the former house (temple in Jerusalem) would be replaced with a house far more glorious. To what else could the prophet be referring than the removal of the physical kingdom of Israel and the establishment of the eternal kingdom of God? That is also exactly what Isaiah had originally predicted.

Not surprisingly, Jesus quoted from some of the same verses and used the same imagery when telling his apostles about the coming destruction of Jerusalem in Matthew 24:29-30. *"Immediately after the distress of those days the sun will be darkened, and the moon will not give its light; the stars will fall from the sky, and the heavenly bodies will be shaken. At that time the sign of the Son of Man will appear in the sky, and all the nations of the earth will mourn. They will see the Son of Man coming on the clouds of the sky, with power and great glory."*

Luke leaves no doubt when he explains this same discussion to his Gentile readers. Luke 21:20-28, *"When you see Jerusalem being surrounded by armies, you will know that its desolation is near…*

There will be signs in the sun, moon and stars. On the earth, nations will be in anguish and perplexity at the roaring and tossing of the sea. Men will faint from terror, apprehensive of what is coming on the world, for the heavenly bodies will be shaken. At that time they will see the Son of Man coming in a cloud with power and great glory. When these things begin to take place, stand up and lift up your heads, because your redemption is drawing near." Given the prophetic history and background of this coming event, why would anyone be surprised to see the destruction of Jerusalem in the New Testament described in these very same terms? If it were not, how would we know it was the fulfillment of the prophetic Scriptures? One must have a lot of help to twist these Scriptures into a future coming of the Lord.

During the first century, between the first and second appearance of Jesus, they were receiving (present tense) a kingdom. It came! God indeed "shook the earth," removing what could be shaken (the earthly kingdom of Israel) and leaving only that which cannot be shaken...the eternal kingdom, the church. We are not still awaiting the kingdom. The writer of Hebrews, as well as the other New Testament writers, understood the consummation of the ages.

Below is a simple chart showing the things that were changing during the consummation (fulfillment) of the ages. These things were all to happen during the "last days" of Judah and Jerusalem. When asked by his apostles when these things would happen and what would be the sign of his coming and the end of the age, Jesus' response was the destruction of Jerusalem and the temple would be the final sign that all was accomplished (Matthew 24). In 1 Corinthians 10:11 the Apostle Paul said the "fulfillment of the ages" had come on his generation.

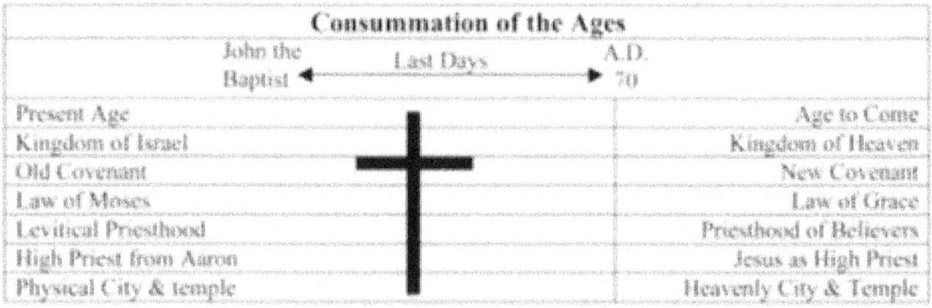

Consummation of the Ages		
John the Baptist ◄	Last Days	► A.D. 70
Present Age		Age to Come
Kingdom of Israel		Kingdom of Heaven
Old Covenant		New Covenant
Law of Moses		Law of Grace
Levitical Priesthood		Priesthood of Believers
High Priest from Aaron		Jesus as High Priest
Physical City & temple		Heavenly City & Temple

The consummation of the ages is a Biblical concept rooted in the completed atonement sacrifice of Jesus as seen most clearly in the Book of Hebrews. There are two additional major components of this consummation which are not discussed in detail in this one letter. One is the resurrection of the dead and the other the judgment. These are explained in other texts which will be discussed in detail later.

As for all the Christian Chicken Littles, Henny Pennys, Ducky Luckys, Goosey Looseys, Turkey Lurkeys, and especially Foxy Loxys…an acorn fell. It is called gravity. The sky is not falling! Accept it and move on.

CHAPTER 5

Miraculous Gifts of the Holy Spirit

She was sitting less than ten feet away in a crowd of about two thousand people who had come to worship God. I could not help but notice the large growth in her throat. Her eyes were hollow and her movements slow. She was in obvious pain as she tried with every effort she could muster to follow the pastor as he led the congregation in prayer after prayer. He proclaimed that the Lord had given him a prophetic message that Jesus would personally appear during that Sunday morning service and pour out his blessings on the people. Just as he had promised his disciples in John 14:13-14, *"I will do whatever you ask in my name, so that the Son may bring glory to the Father. You may ask me for anything in my name, and I will do it."* The crowd cheered and shouted as the pastor promised that in just a few minutes Jesus would appear in person and every disease would be healed, every hurting marriage would be mended, every curse of poverty would be loosed, every prayer of faith would be answered.

I could see the doubt and utter despair in her face but, living in one of the poorest countries in the world with no access to even the most basic health care, a miracle was her only glimmer of hope. So she went through the motions. She faithfully raised her hands on cue, repeated all the words as directed, and prayed earnestly for Jesus to come for her healing. Two hours later she, and two thousand other worshippers, left the service, taking with them the same diseases and broken lives with which they had come. Jesus, and the promised healing, never came.

The pastor? He received his blessing. The offering baskets were full. He and his wife can continue to wear designer clothes and live a lifestyle light years above most members of their church. Every week the people will return to hear a similar "message of hope." Why do they continue to come? When people live in such deplorable conditions, even false hope is better than no hope at all. And they have been taught the Bible promises "miraculous gifts of the Holy Spirit" to all believers. Not properly understanding the time frame for these gifts, Christians by the millions, especially the poor and underprivileged, are being misled. To comprehend what the Bible teaches about this vital subject one must consider not only the times in which the Scriptures were written, but also the times in which we are living today.

The very nature of God is, by all human understanding and standards, miraculous. Genesis 1:1 says, *"In the beginning God created the heavens and the earth."* That was a miracle! All efforts to explain creation in any other terms, whether it be evolution, the big bang theory, or any other imagination of man, is to deny the nature and very existence of an all-powerful God. We cannot understand God, but simply accept by faith that "I AM." Hebrews 3:3 says, *"By faith we understand that the universe was formed at God's command, so that what is seen was not made out of what was visible."*

One cannot believe in God and not believe in miracles. The world came into existence and is sustained by the miraculous hand of a loving God. This same God who created the universe has, on occasion, seen fit to interject Himself into the affairs of men in miraculous ways. Moses witnessed a miracle when he listened to God speak from a burning bush (Exodus 3). When the waters of the Red Sea and Jordan River parted so that the Israelites walked through on dry ground, that was a miracle (Exodus 14, Joshua 3). Jesus being born of a virgin was a miracle. While on earth, Jesus performed many miracles. God has not changed (Hebrews 13:8, James 1:17). He can and does still intervene in the affairs of men and women when and how he sees fit. Prayer is based on this fundamental Christian belief.

It is necessary for us to understand the definition of "miracle." While it may be argued that almost everything that happens is a miracle because it is only possible by the creative and sustaining power of God, the Bible teaches a much more limited view of the term "miracle" as it relates to human life and interaction and particularly the "gifts of the Holy Spirit." When God created Adam from dirt and Eve from one of Adam's ribs, those were miracles. When a healthy young couple give birth to a new baby, that is not a miracle in the same sense. Procreation is a "normal" part of God's already created universe. People do nothing "out of the ordinary" when they conceive and have a child. People who have no faith in God bear children. When a ninety-year-old woman and a one hundred-year-old man have a baby…that's a miracle (Genesis 17:17)! A miracle is something that someone does that is clearly outside the normal boundaries of nature God has set in place. Flying an airplane seems like a miracle to me, but it is a simple case of understanding and using the principles of the universe that God has already established. Using chemicals to kill the parasites that attack one's body and cause malaria, resulting in the patient regaining health, is not a miracle. Again, it is understanding and using God's creation in an effective and helpful manner.

There have also been occasions when God has given certain men and women the power or "gift" to perform miracles. This is what the New Testament refers to as "miraculous gifts of the Holy Spirit." God is able to perform miracles any time he chooses because he is omnipotent. Human beings are not omnipotent;

therefore, humans can only perform miracles when empowered by God to do so. There is a big difference between God answering the prayer of one of his servants and God giving that same servant his divine power, through the Holy Spirit, to perform miracles. In the New Testament where we read of Christians possessing these miraculous gifts of the Holy Spirit, we also find that God carefully explained when, where, and how these "gifts" were to be given and used, so there would be no deception regarding his will versus that of the Devil or false teachers. A careful and thorough study of Scripture will reveal exactly the time and purpose for the miraculous gifts of the Holy Spirit spoken about in the New Testament.

Whether or not Christian men and women today believe it is still possible to possess miraculous gifts of the Holy Spirit described in the New Testament for the early church is dependent upon one's understanding of the historical time frame of the "last days," discussed earlier in this book. According to Joel and Peter, the "miraculous gifts" of the Holy Spirit to confirm the word were promised for the "last days." If we are currently living in these "last days," we will also still have these miraculous gifts. The prophet Micah told of the miracles that would occur in the last days and how long they would last when in verse fifteen of chapter seven he said, *"As in the days when you came out of Egypt, I will show them my wonders."* Miraculous gifts were promised and given during the "last days" of Israel and were to last for a period of forty years, during which the Spirit would reveal and confirm the word (Heb. 2:1-4). At the end of these days "vision and prophecy" would be "sealed up" (Daniel 9:24). Failure to understand the Biblical time frame of the "last days" has led to much confusion over these "gifts." Kept in their context, everything makes perfect sense.

Describing the strange events happening on the Day of Pentecost when the Jewish audience was assembled in Jerusalem,

Acts 2:14-21 says,

> *"Then Peter stood up with the Eleven, raised his voice and addressed the crowd: 'Fellow Jews and all of you who live in Jerusalem, let me explain this to you; listen carefully to what I say. These men are not drunk, as you suppose. It's only nine in the morning! No, this is what was spoken by the prophet Joel: 'In the last days, God says, I will pour out my Spirit on all people. Your sons and daughters will prophesy, your young men will see visions, your old men will dream dreams. Even on my servants, both men and women, I will pour out my Spirit in those days, and they will prophesy. I will show wonders in the heaven above and signs on the earth below, blood and fire and billows of smoke. The sun will be turned to darkness and the moon to blood before the coming of the great and glorious day of the Lord. And everyone who calls on the name of the Lord will be saved.' "*

To properly understand that to which Peter was referring, we need to look at the book of Joel, from which he quoted. We learn from beginning to end that Joel's prophetic book is about the ultimate future of Israel that would include a "great day of the Lord" and culminate in the realization of God's promise to Abraham of an eternal kingdom.

Joel 1:15 says, *"Alas for that day! For the day of the Lord is near; it will come like destruction from the Almighty."* In chapter 2:1-2, *"Blow the trumpet in Zion; sound the alarm on my holy hill. Let all who live in the land tremble, for the day of the Lord is coming. It is close at hand - a day of darkness and gloom, a day of clouds and blackness. Like dawn spreading across the mountains a large and mighty army comes, such as never was of old nor ever will be in ages to come."* His battle language continues and in 2:9-11, speaking of the coming chariots, *"They rush upon the city; they run along the wall. They climb into the houses; like thieves they enter through the windows. Before them the earth shakes, the sky trembles, the sun and moon are darkened, and the stars no longer shine. The Lord thunders at the head of his army; his forces are beyond number, and mighty are those who obey his command. The day of the Lord is great; it is dreadful. Who can endure it?"*

Then we come to the part quoted by Peter in chapter 2:28-32, *"I will pour out my Spirit on all people. Your sons and daughters will prophesy, your old men will dream dreams, your young men will see visions. Even on my servants, both men and women, I will pour out my Spirit in those days. I will show wonders in the heavens and on the earth, blood and fire and billows of smoke. The sun will be turned to darkness and the moon to blood before the coming of the great and dreadful day of the Lord. And everyone who calls on the name of the Lord will be saved."*

Joel continues where Peter left off, *"...for on Mount Zion and in Jerusalem there will be deliverance, as the Lord has said, among the survivors whom the Lord calls."* Chapter three continues with the explanation of what would ensue, *"In those days and at that time, when I restore the fortunes of Judah and Jerusalem, I will gather all nations and bring them down to the Valley of Jehoshaphat. There I will enter into judgment against them concerning my inheritance, my people Israel, for they scattered my people among the nations and divided up my land. And God pronounced judgment against the enemies of Israel..."* (Joel 3:1-2). That Joel was speaking of the establishment of the church during the first century when Peter lived cannot be questioned, since Peter said "this is that." Therefore, restoring the fortunes of Judah and Jerusalem must have been the ultimate fulfillment of God's promise to Abraham that *"...through you and your seed all nations will be blessed."* That was Israel's ultimate fulfillment, even if they did not understand it at the time.

To erase any doubt, look at the way Joel concludes his prophecy. In Joel 3:14-21 he says, *"Multitudes, multitudes in the valley of decision! For the day of the Lord is near in the valley of decision. The sun and moon will be darkened, and the stars no longer shine. The Lord will roar from Zion and thunder from Jerusalem; the earth and the sky will tremble. But the Lord will be a refuge for his people, a stronghold for the people of Israel… Then you will know that I, the Lord your God, dwell in Zion, my holy hill. Jerusalem will be holy; never again will foreigners invade her. In that day the mountains will drip new wine, and the hills will flow with milk; all the ravines of Judah will run with water. A fountain will flow out of the Lord's house and will water the valley of acacias. But Egypt will be desolate, Edom a desert waste, because of violence done to the people of Judah, in whose land they shed innocent blood. Judah will be inhabited forever and Jerusalem through all generations.* ***Their bloodguilt, which I have not pardoned, I will pardon.*** *The Lord dwells in Zion!"*

Pardon from the guilt of sin was only accomplished after Jesus died on the cross. Joel could have been prophesying about nothing other than the establishment of the "eternal kingdom" where forgiveness would finally be available in Jesus. Even though the physical nation was headed for some terrible times and ultimately would be destroyed in what was called "that great day of the Lord," the new kingdom would be established as an eternal one where all the faithful would receive a full pardon. This can only be the new Jerusalem, the heavenly Jerusalem, the city of the Living God, the church, which we read about in Hebrews 12 and Revelation 21.

Isaiah also prophesied of the same eternal kingdom when in Isaiah 2:1-3 he said, *"This is what Isaiah son of Amoz saw concerning Judah and Jerusalem: In the last days the mountain of the Lord's temple will be established as chief among the mountains; it will be raised above the hills, and all nations will stream to it. Many peoples will come and say, 'Come, let us go up to the mountain of the Lord, to the house of the God of Jacob. He will teach us his ways, so that we may walk in his paths.' The law will go out from Zion, the word of the Lord from Jerusalem."* We know the establishment of the eternal kingdom, the church, was begun on that day of Pentecost where over 3,000 people were baptized following Peter's sermon. The word of the Lord did go out from Jerusalem, just as the prophets had foretold. And in keeping with the prophets, the Holy Spirit of God was poured out enabling Peter and the others to speak in other tongues (languages) and perform many other miracles to confirm the word they were receiving was from God. This was promised for and came to pass in the "last days" of Judah and Jerusalem. Peter understood it.

Jesus also promised miraculous gifts would follow his apostles and early disciples. In Mark 16:15-18 he said, *"Go into all the world and preach the good news to all creation. Whoever believes and is baptized will be saved, but whoever does not believe will be condemned. And these signs will accompany those who believe: In my name they will drive out demons; they will speak in new tongues; they will pick up snakes with their hands; and when they drink deadly poison, it will not hurt them at all; they will place their hands on sick people, and they will get well."*

We read of many instances where the apostles, and others, healed the sick, spoke in foreign languages, raised the dead, and were unharmed when bitten by deadly snakes. One occurrence is recorded in Acts 28:1-6. *"Once safely on shore, we found out that the island was called Malta. The islanders showed us unusual kindness. They built a fire and welcomed us all because it was raining and cold. Paul gathered a pile of brushwood and, as he put it on the fire, a viper, driven out by the heat, fastened itself on his hand. When the islanders saw the snake hanging from his hand, they said to each other, 'This man must be a murderer; for though he escaped from the sea, Justice has not allowed him to live.' But Paul shook the snake off into the fire and suffered no ill effects. The people expected him to swell up or suddenly fall dead, but after waiting a long time and seeing nothing unusual happen to him, they changed their minds and said he was a god."*

We know that, beginning on the day of Pentecost, miraculous gifts of the Holy Spirit were part of the early church experience. The Bible also tells us the purpose of these gifts. In Hebrews 2:1-4 the writer says, *"We must pay more careful attention, therefore, to what we have heard, so that we do not drift away. For if the message spoken by angels was binding, and every violation and disobedience received its just punishment, how shall we escape if we ignore such a great salvation? This salvation, which was first announced by the Lord, was confirmed to us by those who heard him. God also testified to it by signs, wonders and various miracles, and gifts of the Holy Spirit distributed according to his will."*

The Apostle Paul says essentially the same thing in Rom 15:18-20. *"I will not venture to speak of anything except what Christ has accomplished through me in leading the Gentiles to obey God by what I have said and done - by the power of signs and miracles, through the power of the Spirit."*

In the early days of the church there were no New Testaments. The Scripture was being revealed by the Holy Spirit to these men and women as they went about teaching and preaching. God gave these people "gifts" that enabled them to perform miracles to confirm that what they received was from him in much the same way as he enabled Moses to perform miracles to prove he had sent him to Egypt to deliver the Israelites (Exodus 4).

How long were these "gifts" to last? According to the prophet in Micah 7:15, *"As in the days when you came out of Egypt, I will show them my wonders."* There is a very interesting parallel between the establishment of the physical kingdom of Israel and the establishment of the spiritual kingdom, the church. The physical kingdom was a prototype of the spiritual one that would follow.

Every aspect of that first kingdom has its counterpart in the second. If we fail to understand the first, we will not understand the second. This is the reason it is so important for Christians to study and understand the Old Testament. It was God's physical demonstration of everything he was going to do in the spiritual kingdom.

That physical kingdom began with deliverance from the bondage of slavery in Egypt, a prototype of man's bondage to sin. The crossing of the Red Sea and the physical destruction of the Egyptians (their captors) is a prototype of our baptism, whereby we symbolically accept God's deliverance from sin, our old "man of sin" is buried in the water, and we come out on the other side free from bondage. The High Priest and his offering of blood for the sins of the people is a prototype of Jesus and his perfect sacrifice on the cross. The Old Testament is a wealth of information that helps us better understand the spiritual kingdom into which we are "born again."

From the time of the crossing of the Red Sea to entering the "promised land" was a period of forty years. These "first days" of the kingdom of Israel were accompanied by signs, wonders, and the outpouring of the Holy Spirit. Moses and a few others were given "miraculous gifts" that included graphic demonstrations to confirm his will, which was revealed during this period. This physical kingdom had "first days" and it also had "last days." The "last days" of physical Israel were also the "first days" of the spiritual kingdom, the church. This was also a period of forty years.

These "last days" of the old and "first days" of the new were from the baptism of Jesus by John the Baptist, an example of how we would be delivered from bondage and enter the new kingdom, to the literal destruction of Israel and its temple in A.D. 70 (40 years). Jesus clearly said the revealing of the kingdom of heaven (church) and the ending of the former kingdom began with John.

In Matthew 11:12 he said, *"From the days of John the Baptist until now, the kingdom of heaven has been forcefully advancing, and forceful men lay hold of it. For all the Prophets and the Law prophesied until John."* Just like the beginning of the physical kingdom, the spiritual kingdom began with signs, wonders, and miraculous gifts of the Holy Spirit. During that forty year period the New Testament was revealed, God confirming it with these miracles. This was the fulfillment of Micah's prophecy. Once again, the Bible interprets itself. The physical kingdom of Israel had a beginning and an end, first days and last days. The spiritual kingdom of heaven is eternal; it can have no "last days" because it will never end. "The end," of which the Bible speaks, is the end of the physical kingdom of Israel, not the end of the physical universe. (See chart below.)

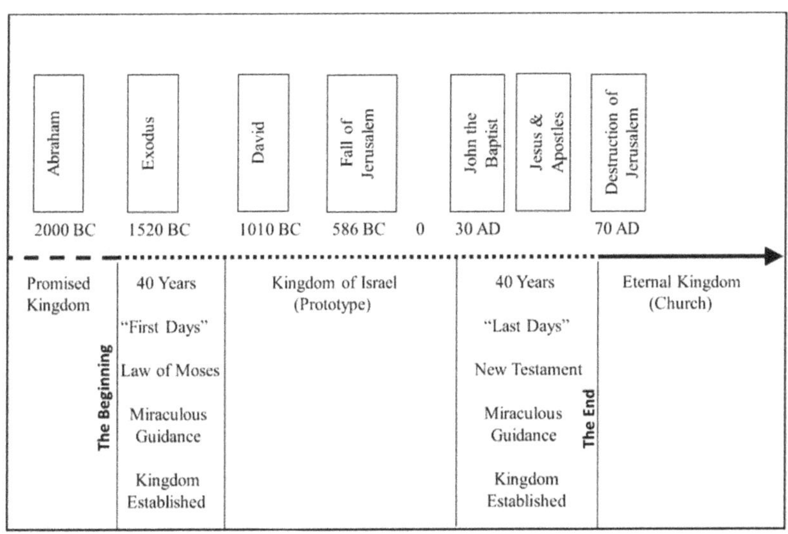

Were these miraculous gifts of the Holy Spirit to continue past the "last days" of Israel and "first days" of the church? Let us *"...examine the Scriptures to see if this is true."*

The Apostle Paul in 1 Corinthians 12:1-3 said to the early

Christians in Corinth, *"Now about spiritual gifts, brothers, I do not want you to be ignorant. You know that when you were pagans, somehow or other you were influenced and led astray to mute idols. Therefore I tell you that no one who is speaking by the Spirit of God says, "Jesus be cursed," and no one can say, 'Jesus is Lord,' except by the Holy Spirit."* The New Testament was not yet written, it was being revealed to the apostles and other divinely inspired teachers and writers. As Paul pointed out, nobody could even say "Jesus is Lord" except by this divine revelation. How else would they know?

He goes on to explain how people received those gifts. 1 Corinthians 12:7-11 continues, *"Now to each one the manifestation of the Spirit is given for the common good. To one there is given through the Spirit the message of wisdom, to another the message of knowledge by means of the same Spirit, to another faith by the same Spirit, to another gifts of healing by that one Spirit, to another miraculous powers, to another prophecy, to another distinguishing between spirits, to another speaking in different kinds of tongues, and to still another the interpretation of tongues. All these are the work of one and the same Spirit, and he gives them to each one, just as he determines."* Paul said God was the one who gave these gifts to whomever he chose. Not everyone had them and there is no Biblical teaching anywhere that indicates one could "learn how to get them."

What was the purpose of these gifts? The only purpose the Bible ever gives for people having miraculous gifts was to confirm God's word. Moses was given the power to perform miracles to convince Pharaoh, as well as the Israelites, that his message was from God. Old Testament prophets were inspired by the Holy Spirit and performed miracles to prove their messages were from God. The same is true in the New Testament. Hebrews 2:3-4 says, *"This salvation, which was first announced by the Lord, was confirmed to us by those who heard him. God also testified to it by signs, wonders and various miracles, and gifts of the Holy Spirit distributed according to his will."* The miraculous gifts of the Holy Spirit were specifically given to confirm that the revelation given to the early Christians was from God.

Problems arose in the Corinthian church because some who had received these special gifts thought they were better than those who did not. Paul spent three chapters explaining how these gifts were never intended for anything other than the mutual edification of all. In 1 Corinthians 12:7 he says, *"Now to each one the manifestation of the Spirit is given for the common good."* He recognized God had given different ones different gifts, but severely condemned the divisiveness that resulted from their abuse.

In 1 Corinthians 12:27-31 he continues, *"Now you are the body of Christ, and each one of you is a part of it. And in the church God has appointed first of all apostles, second prophets, third teachers, then workers of miracles, also those having gifts of healing, those able to help others, those with gifts of administration, and those speaking in different kinds of tongues. Are all apostles? Are all prophets? Are all teachers? Do all work miracles? Do all have gifts of healing? Do all speak in tongues? Do all interpret? But eagerly desire the greater gifts."* And in 1 Corinthians 14:26 he says, *"What then shall we say, brothers? When you come together, everyone has a hymn, or a word of instruction, a revelation, a tongue or an interpretation. All of these must be done for the strengthening of the church."*

The apostle wrote the same message to the church in Ephesus. In Ephesians 4:11-16 we read, *"It was he (Christ) who gave some to be apostles, some to be prophets, some to be evangelists, and some to be pastors and teachers, to prepare God's people for works of service, so that the body of Christ may be built up until we all reach unity in the faith and in the knowledge of the Son of God and become mature, attaining to the whole measure of the fullness of Christ. Then we will no longer be infants, tossed back and forth by the waves, and blown here and there by every wind of teaching and by the cunning and craftiness of men in their deceitful scheming. Instead, speaking the truth in love, we will in all things grow up into him who is the Head, that is, Christ. From him the whole body, joined and held together by every supporting ligament, grows and builds itself up in love, as each part does its work."* We clearly see from these passages that the purpose of the "gifts of the Holy Spirit," whether speaking in tongues, healing, prophecy, whatever, was to build up the church by teaching and confirming the word of God that was being revealed.

Were these gifts to last forever, or were they to come to an end? Going back to Paul's letter to the Corinthian church, in 1 Corinthians 13:8-13 he writes, *"Love never fails. But where there are prophecies, they will cease; where there are tongues, they will be stilled; where there is knowledge, it will pass away. For we know in part and we prophesy in part, but when perfection comes, the imperfect disappears. When I was a child, I talked like a child, I thought like a child, I reasoned like a child. When I became a man, I put childish ways behind me. Now we see but a poor reflection as in a mirror; then we shall see face to face. Now I know in part; then I shall know fully, even as I am fully known. And now these three remain: faith, hope and love. But the greatest of these is love."*

Applying the second fundamental principle and keeping Paul's discussion in context, we know he is still discussing the miraculous gifts of the Holy Spirit (1 Corinthians 12:1). He calls these gifts "childish things" which will cease. When will they cease? When "perfection comes." The Greek word here is "teleios" which means, "having reached its end" (telos), "finished, complete, perfect." It is used of persons, primarily of physical development, then, with ethical import, "fully grown, mature," (Vines Expository Dictionary of New Testament Words). Vines gives the literal translation as, *"...but when that which is complete arrives, that which is partial will be done away with."*

For Paul's analogy to make sense, something in his discussion was in its infancy and, like a child learning to walk, needed special assistance until it could mature to a point when it could walk on its own. The entire letter is about the church. The church was in its infancy. With no written New Testament, Christians needed special assistance to know what God's will was. Miraculous gifts of the Holy Spirit were the "special helps" necessary to guide them through this "childish" period. That which was "imperfect" or incomplete was the Bible. The New Testament was in the process of being revealed. According to Paul, once the entire Bible was complete, these special helps, the miraculous gifts of the Holy Spirit, would no longer be needed, so they would cease.

Let's look again at the passage in Ephesians 4:11-16 and compare it to what Paul taught the Corinthian church. (The emphasis is mine.) *"It was* ***he*** *(Christ)* ***who gave some*** *to be apostles, some to be prophets, some to be evangelists, and some to be pastors and teachers…"* (These were the same "childish things," the miraculous gifts.) *"…* ***to prepare God's people*** *for works of service,* ***so that the body of Christ may be built up****…"* (Here we see the exact same purpose.) *"…* ***until*** (something better is coming) *we all* ***reach unity in the faith and in the knowledge of the Son of God and become mature, attaining to the whole measure of the fullness of Christ."*** (This is the same as "when perfection comes.")

*"****Then*** (when the word of God is complete) *we will* ***no longer be infants,*** (same childish analogy) *tossed back and forth by the waves, and blown here and there by every wind of teaching and by the cunning and craftiness of men in their deceitful scheming.* ***Instead,*** (the better, mature way of love) *speaking the truth in love, we will in all things* ***grow up*** (become mature) *into him who is the Head, that is, Christ. From him the whole body, joined and held together by every supporting ligament, grows and builds itself up in love, as each part does its work."*

What could possibly be the purpose of miraculous gifts of the Holy Spirit in the church today? Is the word of God not complete? If the Bible is the complete, fully revealed word of God, there is no need for further revelation or for God to confirm such. Divine revelation and miraculous gifts of the Holy Spirit to confirm it were promised "during the last days" (Joel 2-3). In view of all Biblical prophecy and evidence, the last inspired message from God had to be received prior to the destruction of Jerusalem in A.D. 70. Beyond that event there can be no divine inspiration. Also, there is no Scriptural basis for miraculous gifts of the Holy Spirit beyond that point. Using the Apostle Paul's analogy, a Christian (or church) today who still desires "miraculous gifts of the Holy Spirit" is like a grown man still wanting a baby walker.

Aside from basic theological inconsistencies, current practices within most charismatic churches today are not in keeping with the Scriptures and result in the same problems that afflicted the early Corinthian church. A close examination of 1 Corinthians 14 will illustrate this point. Paul begins by addressing those Christians who were "speaking in tongues" without an interpreter. He says that if someone does this the only one who can understand is God, which is absolutely no benefit the others present. In verse 5 he says, *"I would like every one of you to speak in tongues, but I would rather have you prophesy. He who prophesies is greater than one who speaks in tongues, unless he interprets, so that the church may be edified."*

It is important to understand the modern concept of "unknown tongues" is not only **un**-biblical, it is **anti**-biblical. The gift of "tongues" was the gift to speak in a foreign language. The only purpose for that gift was to enable one to speak the will of God to people of other nations and languages. In verse 10 Paul says, *"Undoubtedly there are all sorts of languages in the world, yet* ***none of them is without meaning.****"* He goes on to say if nobody understands the language of the speaker, it is useless. The practice of speaking gibberish that nobody understands in the public gathering of the church is flatly condemned. The apostle said in verses 18-19, *"I thank God that I speak in tongues (languages) more than all of you. But in the church I would rather speak five intelligible words to instruct others than ten thousand words in a tongue."* And in verse 28 he said, *"If there is no interpreter, the speaker should keep quiet in the church."* Yet today, speaking in "unknown tongues" is the most widely seen and demonstrated "miraculous gift of the Holy Spirit."

In 1 Corinthians 14:22-25 the apostle wrote, *"Tongues, then, are a sign, not for believers but for unbelievers; prophecy, however, is for believers, not for unbelievers. So if the whole church comes together and everyone speaks in tongues, and some who do not understand or some unbelievers come in, will they not say that you are out of your mind? But if an unbeliever or someone who does not understand comes in while everybody is prophesying, he will be convinced by all that he is a sinner and will be judged by all, and the secrets of his heart will be laid bare. So he will fall down and worship God, exclaiming, 'God is really among you!' "*

Paul first says in these verses that, used properly with an interpreter, tongues are a sign for unbelievers, NOT believers. Most Christians today who believe in the miraculous gifts of the Holy Spirit also believe that being able to "speak in tongues" is a sign that one has been "baptized in the Holy Spirit." This makes tongues a sign for the believer and is the exact opposite of what the Bible says. The only proper use of tongue speaking is to impart the will of God to unbelievers or to edify the church. This demands that the language be understood by the hearers.

Perhaps the biggest problem with the misuse of these spiritual gifts, especially speaking in tongues, is the adverse effect it has on non-believers. As Paul said, if someone visits a church and hears people speaking in "unknown tongues," he or she will think these people have lost their minds. It is difficult to even imagine how many lost people have been turned away from Christianity because of the abuse of what are called "gifts of the Holy Spirit."

Paul's contrast in these verses is between the gift of tongues and the gift of prophesy. Both of these were miraculous gifts requiring divine inspiration because they both required knowledge and/or ability beyond the physical capabilities of the person doing the speaking. While tongues gave an individual the ability to speak the gospel to someone of a different language, prophesy was the revelation of God's will to Christians and was always presented in the language of the hearer. Prophesy was for believers, not unbelievers.

The Greek word translated "prophesying" is "*propheteia.*" Vines Expository Dictionary of New Testament Words defines this as, "the speaking forth of the mind and counsel of God…It is the declaration of that which cannot be known by natural means, the forth-telling of the will of God, whether with reference to the past, the present, or the future." According to Paul, prophesy was the best gift because it was the one that enabled the body of Christ to be built up in the knowledge of God's word. These gifts were necessary during the first century until the Scriptures were fully revealed, but they did come to an end.

Greek scholars agree there was a distinction between "prophesying" and "teaching" in the New Testament. "With the completion of the canon of Scripture prophecy apparently passed away. (1 Corinthians 13:8-9) In his measure the teacher has taken the place of the prophet, the significant change in 2 Peter 2:1. The difference is that, whereas the message of the prophet was a direct revelation of the mind of God for the occasion, the message of the teacher is gathered from the completed revelation contained in the Scriptures." (Notes on Thessalonians by Hogg and Vine, pp. 196,197.)

Does this mean we do not have the Holy Spirit with us today? Absolutely not! When one becomes a Christian the Spirit of God comes to live within us. We are "led by the Spirit," "walk by the Spirit," and are "guided by the Spirit." There is a distinct difference in Scripture between the indwelling of God's Holy Spirit, which is available to every child of his, and having the "miraculous gifts" of the Holy Spirit to perform miracles, speak in tongues, heal the sick, raise the dead, etc. The confusion of these differences is a direct result of our failure to understand the times in which we live.

Does this mean that there is no such thing as a miracle today? Absolutely not! God is still God and can and will do whatever he chooses. And he chooses to continually listen to his people and answer our prayers. It is very Biblical to ask God to do things that are "out of the ordinary." Should we pray for God to heal someone who is sick? Yes! Can he do it? Yes! But has he given his miraculous power to men and women of faith today to perform miracles on his behalf? There is no evidence in the Bible to support such a claim. And though many evangelists today say they have such healing powers, they cannot produce one single verifiable example of having done so.

A word of caution is appropriate as we consider what may appear to be "divine miraculous powers" claimed by humans. The Scriptures warn us not to be fooled by those who falsely claim to be following Christ and claim to have powers from God. Jesus said in Matthew 7:22-23, *"Many will say to me on that day, 'Lord, Lord, did we not prophesy in your name, and in your name drive out demons and perform many miracles?' Then I will tell them plainly, 'I never knew you. Away from me, you evildoers!' "* In Matthew 24:24 he said, *"For false Christs and false prophets will appear and perform great signs and miracles to deceive even the elect—if that were possible."* And Paul said in 2 Thessalonians 2:9, *"The coming of the lawless one will be in accordance with the work of Satan displayed in all kinds of counterfeit miracles, signs and wonders..."* Not everything that appears to be from God actually is.

A close examination of the miracles of Jesus and his disciples reveals sharp contrasts between them and the so-called miracles of men and women today who claim to have the same powers of the Holy Spirit. In the New Testament we see people being healed of hemorrhaging (Matthew 9:20-22), blindness (Matthew 20:30-34), fever (Luke 4:38-39), leprosy (Luke 5:12-13), paralysis (Luke 5:17-25), deformity (Luke 13:11-13), infirmity (John 5:5-9), even death (Luke 8:49-55). Jesus walked on water, calmed the stormy seas, and took a sack lunch and fed thousands. Paul was bitten by a deadly snake and suffered no harm (Acts 28:1-6). The miracles of the New Testament had the following characteristics:

1. The conditions were clearly visible and verifiable.
2. The result was instantaneous and complete.
3. They were very diverse.
4. They were never staged.
5. They required no fanfare or emotional frenzy, only a simple prayer, statement or command.

The miracles of "faith healers" today are dubious at best. The healers only perform a select few types of miracles. The vast majority of their healings cannot be perceived by the senses. Preliminary inquiries weed out the hard cases. You will never see them drink deadly poison or be unharmed by the bite of a venomous snake. They will not raise the dead. Success for the few conditions they do claim to heal requires a highly emotional, almost hysterical atmosphere; something never seen in Scripture. Services are staged. Today's healers will not submit their work to verification or testing. They become indignant when questioned. They avoid investigation and they commonly teach false doctrine. The Apostle John warned the early Christians, *"Do not believe every spirit, but test the spirits to see whether they are from God, because many false prophets have gone out into the world"* (1 John 4:1).

The miraculous gifts of the Holy Spirit were "childish things" to help the church through its infancy period. They were promised only for the period known in Scripture as the "last days" of Judah and Jerusalem. They were vitally important for the revelation of God's final will for mankind. The Bible clearly says they would last for that period after which they would cease. Unless we are still living in the last days of Judah and Jerusalem, they ceased.

But what about the passages which say we will receive whatever we ask in the name of Jesus? Matthew and Mark both record an incident where Jesus cursed a tree that had no fruit. Responding to the amazement of his disciples, Jesus replied in Mark 11:23-24, *"I tell you the truth, if anyone says to this mountain, 'Go, throw yourself into the sea,' and does not doubt in his heart but believes that what he says will happen, it will be done for him. Therefore I tell you,* ***whatever you ask for in prayer, believe that you have received it, and it will be yours.****"* John 14:12-14, *"I tell you the truth, anyone who has faith in me will do what I have been doing. He will do even greater things than these, because I am going to the Father. And I will do whatever you ask in my name, so that the Son may bring glory to the Father.* ***You may ask me for anything in my name, and I will do it.****"* 1 John 5:14-15, *"This is the confidence we have in approaching God: that if we ask anything according to his will, he hears us.* ***And if we know that he hears us—whatever we ask—we know that we have what we asked of him.****"*

Unfortunately, these passages have been taken completely out of context and used by many to promote a new social gospel of earthly health and prosperity which is not supported by any serious study of the Bible. As with virtually all of Jesus' teachings, he used physical, earthly examples to teach spiritual lessons. Whatever he meant by the above statements must align with the entirety of Scripture. Jesus spoke these words to his apostles. The next day he told them they would be falsely accused, arrested, beaten, face unfair trials, and eventually put to death…all because of their faith. Can anyone honestly believe these men faced these severe trials and never once asked God to spare them? Did Jesus forget what he had just promised the day before? Did the apostles not live a life of health and prosperity because they lacked faith to believe their own prayers? When Jesus faced his own crucifixion he repeatedly prayed, *"Father, let this cup be taken from me!"* He was crucified anyway. Did Jesus not have enough faith for God to answer his prayer?

While contemporary preachers are promising physical healings and financial prosperity based on these statements of Jesus, 2 Timothy 3:12-13 says, *"In fact, everyone who wants to live a godly life in Christ Jesus will be persecuted, while evil men and impostors will go from bad to worse, deceiving and being deceived."* This does not sound like the faithful get whatever they ask for while the ungodly do not. Is it possible we have totally missed Jesus' message?

John's gospel account definitely connects Jesus' promise of receiving whatever one asks to spiritual, heavenly blessings. The contrast between the earthly and the spiritual cannot be missed in John's later writings. In 1 John 2:15-17 he says, *"Do not love the world or anything in the world. If anyone loves the world, the love of the Father is not in him. For* ***everything in the world*** *– the cravings of sinful man, the lust of his eyes and his pride in possessions –* ***comes not from the Father but from the world.*** *The world and its desires pass away, but the man who does the will of God lives forever."* Continuing in verses 24-25, *"See that what you have heard from the beginning remains in you. If it does, you also will remain in the Son and in the Father.* ***And this is what he promised us – even eternal life.****"*

John continues describing the spiritual blessings we have in Christ because of our faith in him. In the context of eternal, spiritual blessings he says in 1 John 5:11-15, *"God has given us eternal life, and this life is in his Son. He who has the Son has life; he who does not have the Son of God does not have life. I write these things to you who believe in the name of the Son of God so that you may know that you have eternal life. We have this assurance in approaching God, that if we ask anything according to his will, he hears us. And if we know that he hears us - whatever we ask – we know that we have what we ask of him."* Jesus never promised that we can have any *earthly* thing we want. In fact, John clearly says in this context that everything in the world; especially our desires for and pride in material possessions, are NOT from the Father, but from the world. But we can have any spiritual blessing for which we ask! The Apostle Paul wrote in Ephesians 4:3, *"Praise be to the God and Father of our Lord Jesus Christ, who has blessed us* ***in the heavenly realms*** *with every* ***spiritual blessing*** *in Christ."*

There is another contrast between the physical and spiritual that can be made from Scripture. Physical things, virtually anything that can be imagined, can be done by man. We are created in the image of God. The ability of the human mind is incredibly great. When the people were building the Tower of Babel God said in Genesis 11:6, *"If as one people speaking the same language they have begun to do this, then* ***nothing they plan to do will be impossible for them.****"* The great pyramids of Egypt are there because people believed they could be built. Air travel is possible today because people believed we could fly. A space station exists because people believed it could be done. Jesus said if one wanted a mountain to be removed and thrown into the sea, and believe it could be done, it would happen. Napoleon Hill, the founder and creator of the popular "Success" magazine said, "Whatever the mind of man can conceive and believe, it can achieve." It is likely Jesus was contrasting the physical capabilities of the mind of man, when coupled with absolute belief in the success of the desired result, to the unlimited power of his Father to grant any desired spiritual blessing. Unlike the physical, spiritual life and blessings are only possible with God. When it comes to eternal life and spiritual blessings, Jesus said, *"You may ask me for anything in my name, and I will do it."* He was not promising a new Mercedes or divine healing of a physical condition.

The purpose of miracles has never been to bless men and women with their every desire. The social prosperity gospel being proclaimed today, based on the miraculous gifts of the Holy Spirit, is a false gospel. It may be what people want to hear; but it is not what the Bible teaches. Miraculous gifts given to men and women by the pouring out of the Holy Spirit were for a specific time and purpose. They were promised for the last days of Israel and Judah. God is still God. He can do whatever he chooses. But the miraculous gifts of the Holy Spirit given to Christians are no longer necessary, and therefore ceased exactly when the Bible says they would.

We are always tempted to believe something we want to hear. Too many people today are looking for a church that teaches what they want to hear, rather than one that will challenge them to *"examine the Scriptures to see if these things are true."* As Paul said in 2 Timothy 4:3, *"For the time will come when men will not put up with sound doctrine. Instead, to suit their own desires, they will gather around them a great number of teachers to say what their itching ears want to hear."* Doctrine matters!

What one believes about the last days, the kingdom of heaven, the consummation of the ages, and the miraculous gifts of the Holy Spirit must be consistent with what is taught throughout the Old and New Testaments. As we move forward, we will examine in greater detail what Jesus, his apostles, and other Bible authors had to say about these vital subjects.

Section Two

Explaining the Times

CHAPTER 6

The Teaching of Jesus

When one considers how much time Jesus spent teaching about the coming destruction of Jerusalem and its temple, and the significance of this event related to the coming spiritual kingdom, it seems rather amazing that most Christians today have never studied the subject and consider it virtually irrelevant to their lives. This has given rise to a seemingly endless number of unchallenged prophecies based on his words. While the theories may seem plausible and the Bible references they use may seem to fit their story, are they really what Jesus was teaching? What did Jesus actually say?

We will spend this chapter looking specifically at what Jesus taught would happen and when he said all these things would occur. Three of the Gospel writers included Jesus' teachings on the subject in their narratives. Matthew and Mark are written from the Jewish perspective. Luke's account is written to a Gentile in language more easily understood by someone not steeped in Jewish tradition. All three accounts tell of the same events and the same time of fulfillment. Since they are all inspired by the Holy Spirit, they are in total agreement on the truth. Most of us share Luke's Gentile heritage; therefore, his account is particularly helpful to us in understanding some of the Old Testament prophecies being fulfilled by these events.

We will continue to employ the three basic principles of Biblical understanding and interpretation and begin by comparing the three parallel accounts. The charts in this section list some of the major points Jesus made and how the same message is conveyed to different readers so all can understand. Each chart contains questions or statements that are parallel; that is, they are expressing the exact same part of Jesus' message in their own individual linguistic style as divinely guided by the Holy Spirit. In addition to comparing the three accounts of the actual text we will also examine a few other Scriptural passages which refer to this same conversation.

Matthew 24	**Mark 13**	**Luke 21**
[1] Jesus left the temple and was walking away when his disciples came up to him to call his attention to its buildings.	*[1] As he was leaving the temple, one of his disciples said to him, "Look, Teacher! What massive stones! What magnificent buildings!"*	*[5] Some of his disciples were remarking about how the temple was adorned with beautiful stones and with gifts dedicated to God.*

The Bible begins the narrative by unmistakably identifying the subject of the conversation. Jesus and his disciples were leaving the temple area and the disciples were commenting on the marvelous structures. In the above passage we see how each writer introduced the subject, calling attention to the temple buildings and their construction.

Matthew 24	**Mark 13**	**Luke 21**
[2] "I tell you the truth, not one stone here will be left on another; every one will be thrown down."	*[2] "Not one stone here will be left on another; every one will be thrown down."*	*[6] "As for what you see here, the time will come when not one stone will be left on another; every one of them will be thrown down."*

Jesus immediately said something that shocked them. These beautiful buildings with their massive stones would be utterly destroyed! *"Not one stone will be left on another."* The temple, and all its surrounding buildings, would be completely gone.

Matthew 24	Mark 13	Luke 21
[3]*As Jesus was sitting on the Mount of Olives, the disciples came to him privately. "Tell us," they said, "when will this happen, and what will be the sign of your coming and of the end of the age?"*	[3]*As Jesus was sitting on the Mount of Olives opposite the temple, Peter, James, John and Andrew asked him privately,* [4]*"Tell us, when will these things happen? And what will be the sign that they are all about to be fulfilled?"*	[7]*"Teacher," they asked, "when will these things happen? And what will be the sign that they are about to take place?"*

This led to two obvious questions from the disciples. WHEN WILL THIS HAPPEN? HOW WILL WE KNOW? Here is where we must begin to apply the principles of proper Biblical study. Some teachers, in an effort to support their own world view, take the account in Matthew, ignoring Mark and Luke, and say there were actually multiple questions about different events, then proceed to divide Matthew 24 into sections with Jesus answering these very different questions and discussing entirely different historical periods of time. How many questions did the disciples ask and how many did Jesus answer? Were the questions about one event, or multiple events? The answer is clear when we compare the three accounts.

Luke says, *"When will these things* (destruction of temple buildings) *happen? And what will be the sign that they* (same things) *are all* (not some) *about to be fulfilled?"* Mark says about the same in his account; *"When will these things happen? And what will be the sign that they are about to take place?"* There is only one subject being discussed, the destruction of the temple buildings, and only one subject of the disciples' questions. They wanted to know when this would happen and what would be the signs that it was about to take place. Matthew was not wrong in his recording of the questions when he referred to the Lord's coming and the end of the age. Writing from his Jewish perspective and understanding Old Testament prophecies, he knew the destruction of Jerusalem and its temple would be at the "coming of the Son of Man" to establish the eternal kingdom (Daniel 7:13-14) and be at the "end of the age (world-KJV)" (Daniel 7). The writer of Hebrews confirms the time in which they were living as this "age-ending" time. Hebrews 9:26 says, *"But now he (Christ) has appeared once for all* ***at the end of the ages*** *to do away with sin by the sacrifice of himself."* Matthew did not record different questions, nor did he record questions about different subjects or time periods. The three gospel accounts are in perfect agreement. They do, however, shed light on the subject from differing perspectives. The subject is still the temple buildings and the questions are about when they will be destroyed and the signs that will precede this great age-changing event.

Matthew 24	Mark 13	Luke 21
4Jesus answered: "Watch out that no one deceives you. 5For many will come in my name, claiming, 'I am the Christ,' and will deceive many.	*5Jesus said to them: "Watch out that no one deceives you. 6Many will come in my name, claiming, 'I am he,' and will deceive many*	*8He replied: "Watch out that you are not deceived. For many will come in my name, claiming, 'I am he,' and, 'The time is near.' Do not follow them*

Jesus then began to answer their questions, and he first cautioned them to watch out for false teachers (false or "anti" christs) who would try to deceive people about what was going to take place. It was critical in the teaching of Jesus for people to properly understand these events. It is just as critical today if we are to comprehend the age-changing nature of his sacrifice on the cross which made it possible for the old temple, with its animal sacrifices, to finally be destroyed. This is fundamental to understanding our atonement and the eternal kingdom (church) which he was about to bring to fruition.

It is interesting to note how many modern religious prophets are still predicting the coming of the "antichrist" to usher in the return of Jesus and the establishment of his sovereign reign. The Apostle John was the only Bible author who used the word "antichrist" (antichristos). The term appears four times in his writings and he makes it very clear that he understood their coming as one of the signs Jesus said to watch for, and further identified that time in which he was living as "the last hour." In 1 John 2:18-22 he said, *"Dear children, this is the last hour; and as you have heard that the antichrist is coming, even now many antichrists have come. This is how we know it is the last hour."* Again in 1 John 4:3, *"But every spirit that does not acknowledge Jesus is not from God. This is the spirit of the antichrist, which you have heard is coming and* ***even now is already in the world."*** John said the spirit of the antichrist, which they had been told was coming, was already in the world, which is how he knew it was the last hour. The only other conversation recorded in the Bible about false or "anti-christs" was that of Jesus in his description of signs that would precede the destruction of Jerusalem and its temple buildings. There is not one Scripture that mentions any other coming of some "antichrist." If we are to believe the Bible, the antichrist came, just as Jesus and John said, prior to the destruction of the temple. There is no mysterious "antichrist" in our future.

Matthew 24	**Mark 13**	**Luke 21**
6You will hear of wars and rumors of wars, but see to it that you are not alarmed. Such things must happen, but the end is still to come. 7Nation will rise against nation, and kingdom against kingdom. There will be famines and earthquakes in various places. 8All these are the beginning of birth pains.	*7When you hear of wars and rumors of wars, do not be alarmed. Such things must happen, but the end is still to come. 8Nation will rise against nation, and kingdom against kingdom. There will be earthquakes in various places, and famines. These are the beginning of birth pains.*	*9When you hear of wars and revolutions, do not be frightened. These things must happen first, but the end will not come right away." 10"Nation will rise against nation, and kingdom against kingdom. 11There will be great earthquakes, famines and pestilences in various places, and fearful events and great signs from heaven.*

Jesus then told the disciples there would be "wars and rumors of wars," but they should not be too alarmed because the end will not come right away. Why the warning about wars? Practically every decade of human history has had its share of wars and rumors of war. The first century was no exception, but Jesus was talking about a particular war. There would be only one war in all of human history that would utterly destroy the temple and its buildings, as well as the entire Jewish world, to complete extinction. That they would be destroyed in a seemingly "human" war was God's plan, but not just any war and not just any time. It would happen in God's time and in a "God-directed" war. That's why he gave them many other signs and told them the end would not come right away. Keeping within the context of the subject, Jesus was talking about the end of the temple and the Jewish world...not the end of the physical universe. The end of the temple, its complete and total annihilation, came at the hands of the Romans in A.D. 70. Just as Jesus had predicted, John was the only apostle who "remained alive" until these things happened.

Matthew 24	**Mark 13**	**Luke 21**
9"Then you will be handed over to be persecuted and put to death, and you will be hated by all nations because of me.	*9"You must be on your guard. You will be handed over to the local councils and flogged in the synagogues. On account of me you will stand before governors and kings as witnesses to them.*	*12"But before all this, they will lay hands on you and persecute you. They will deliver you to synagogues and prisons, and you will be brought before kings and governors, and all on account of my name.*

The apostles would be persecuted and tortured before this time would come. Jesus was telling them of things that would signify his coming. If this time is still to come, the first century persecution of the apostles would have had little or no meaning. He has not changed the subject.

Matthew 24	**Mark 13**	**Luke 21**
14And this gospel of the kingdom will be preached in the whole world as a testimony to all nations, and then the end will come.	*10And the gospel must first be preached to all nations.*	*13This will result in your being witnesses to them.*

Prior to the destruction of the Jewish temple, the Gospel would be preached among all nations of that day. The apostles were commissioned by Jesus Himself to *"...go into all the world and preach the gospel to every nation."* That great commission was, and is, the mission of the church in every generation, but it had "age-changing" implications in the first century and specifically applied to the Jewish world. Before God would take away the temple and its worship under the Law of Moses, he would first announce the new covenant to his chosen people. As we learn from Daniel's prophecy, he would confirm a covenant with his people for one "seven." Once they had been informed of the "new and better covenant" in Jesus Christ, the old temple had no further use. As Matthew's account says, *"Then the end will come."* He was still speaking of the end of the temple and surrounding buildings. This "sign" of the end of the age was fulfilled in that generation. Representatives of every nation heard the very first gospel sermon. Acts 2:5 describes the crowd gathered. *"Now there were staying in Jerusalem God-fearing Jews from every nation under heaven."* In Romans 1:8 Paul said the faith of the Roman Christians was being reported *"all over the world."* And this same apostle said in Colossians 1:23, *"This is the gospel that you heard and that has been proclaimed to every creature under heaven, and of which I, Paul, have become a servant."* If only every generation of Christians could make the same claim.

Matthew 24	Mark 13	Luke 21
15So when you see standing in the holy place 'the abomination that causes desolation, spoken of' through the prophet Daniel—let the reader understand—16then let those who are in Judea flee to the mountains.	*14When you see 'the abomination that causes desolation' standing where it does not belong—let the reader understand—then let those who are in Judea flee to the mountains.*	*20When you see Jerusalem being surrounded by armies, you will know that its desolation is near. 21Then let those who are in Judea flee to the mountains, let those in the city get out, and let those in the country not enter the city.*

Jesus then explained how this event would fulfill the prophecy of Daniel. Matthew and Mark, being Jewish and understanding the significance of that prophetic event, give us the prophecy-fulfilling account. So we Gentiles would understand, Luke put it in "plain Greek" and simply said, when you see Jerusalem being surrounded by armies…RUN! All three described the same event, the coming destruction of Jerusalem and its temple. Thanks to Luke we know for sure what time frame Daniel was talking about in his prophecy.

One might wonder, if the city was surrounded by Roman armies, how anyone could escape? The answer to that dilemma comes from the historical records of the Roman Empire. In A.D. 66 there was a fairly successful revolt against the Roman armies in Jerusalem. In A.D. 67 the Emperor Nero sent his general Vespasian to squash the uprising and restore Rome's credibility and dominance as the world power. He completely surrounded the city of Jerusalem and was preparing for a final assault. Before he could implement his plan, news of Nero's death came. Vespasian withdrew his troops and went back to Rome where, after some months of upheaval in the empire, in December A.D. 69 he became the Emperor. In A.D. 70 Vespasian sent his son Titus to finish the job he had started in Judea. Anyone who listened to Jesus and was watching for the signs would have had ample opportunity to flee the city between sieges. God works in mysterious ways!

Matthew 24	Mark 13	Luke 21
	22*For this is the time of punishment in fulfillment of all that has been written.*	22*For this is the time of punishment in fulfillment of all that has been written.*

Matthew continually related his writing to the fulfillment of prophecy knowing his Jewish readers would readily recognize and understand what he was talking about. The Holy Spirit, not leaving anything to speculation, inspired both Mark and Luke to include Jesus' statement that this would be in fulfillment of all that had been written. That is a very important point, especially to non-Jewish folks who may not have the grasp of Old Testament prophecies Matthew's audience had. It also leads one to ask, if that event was the fulfillment of "all that has been written," where is the basis for future "age-ending" prophecies? The Bible here clearly says the events that transpired up to and including the destruction of the temple were all that had been prophesied about the "coming of the Lord" and the "end of the ages."

Matthew 24	**Mark 13**	**Luke 21**
19How dreadful it will be in those days for pregnant women and nursing mothers! 20Pray that your flight will not take place in winter or on the Sabbath. 21For then there will be great distress, unequaled from the beginning of the world until now—and never to be equaled again. 22If those days had not been cut short, no one would survive, but for the sake of the elect those days will be shortened.	*17How dreadful it will be in those days for pregnant women and nursing mothers! 18Pray that this will not take place in winter, 19because those will be days of distress unequaled from the beginning, when God created the world, until now—and never to be equaled again. 20If the Lord had not cut short those days, no one would survive. But for the sake of the elect, whom he has chosen, he has shortened them.*	*23How dreadful it will be in those days for pregnant women and nursing mothers! There will be great distress in the land and wrath against this people. 24They will fall by the sword and will be taken as prisoners to all the nations. Jerusalem will be trampled on by the Gentiles until the times of the Gentiles are fulfilled.*

Next Jesus talked about the intense persecution that would accompany those times. He said it would be a time of distress *"…unequaled from the beginning, when God created the world, until now…and never to be equaled again."* This was exactly what Daniel prophesied would happen in Daniel 12:1, *"At that time Michael, the great prince who protects your people, will arise. There will be a time of distress such as has not happened from the beginning of nations until then. But at that time your people—everyone whose name is found written in the book—will be delivered."* If what happened leading up to and during the destruction of Jerusalem and its temple buildings was a time of distress "never to be equaled again," how can anyone today predict a more terrible time still coming in our future?

Matthew 24	Mark 13	Luke 21
29*Immediately after the distress of those days the sun will be darkened, and the moon will not give its light; the stars will fall from the sky, and the heavenly bodies will be shaken.'*	24*But in those days, following that distress, the sun will be darkened, and the moon will not give its light;* 25*the stars will fall from the sky, and the heavenly bodies will be shaken.*	25*There will be signs in the sun, moon and stars. On the earth, nations will be in anguish and perplexity at the roaring and tossing of the sea.* 26*Men will faint from terror, apprehensive of what is coming on the world, for the heavenly bodies will be shaken.*

All three writers recorded Jesus as saying *"the heavenly bodies will be shaken."* What is the significance of this phrase? As we have already noted, this is but one more example of New Testament events fulfilling Old Testament prophecy. In Isaiah 2, speaking of all the events that would unfold when God established his eternal kingdom, the church, verse 19 says, *"Men will flee to caves in the rocks and to holes in the ground from dread of the Lord and the splendor of his majesty, when he rises to shake the earth."* Again in Haggai 2:6-9, speaking of the future fulfillment of Israel's promises and how that future spiritual temple will far surpass the former physical one, *"This is what the Lord Almighty says: 'In a little while I will once more shake the heavens and the earth, the sea and the dry land. I will shake all nations, and the desired of all nations will come, and I will fill this house with glory,' says the Lord Almighty. 'The silver is mine and the gold is mine,' declares the Lord Almighty. 'The glory of this present house will be greater than the glory of the former house,' says the Lord Almighty. 'And in this place I will grant peace,' declares the Lord Almighty."* We see clearly the fulfillment of these prophecies in Hebrews where in chapter twelve he so vividly compared the receiving of the old covenant of Moses with receiving the new covenant in Christ and in verses 26-29 said, *"At that time his voice shook the earth, but now he has promised, 'Once more I will shake not only the earth but also the heavens.' The words 'once more' indicate the removing of what can be shaken—that is, created things—so that what cannot be shaken may remain. Therefore, since we are receiving a kingdom that cannot be shaken, let us be thankful, and so worship God acceptably with reverence and awe, for our "God is a consuming fire."*

The "shaking of the earth" was a term applied to the removal of the old physical kingdom of Israel and its earthly temple to be replaced with the new spiritual kingdom, the church, and the heavenly temple in which all the redeemed have access to the Holy of Holies. A large portion of the book of Hebrews deals with the significance of this "age-changing" event when the physical temple was being replaced with the spiritual one. In chapter 9:9 the writer put particular emphasis on the destruction of the physical one when he said, *"The Holy Spirit was showing by this that the way into the Most Holy Place had not yet been disclosed as long as the first tabernacle was still standing."* You may be thinking, "I thought the Holy of Holies was opened when Jesus died on the cross and the veil was symbolically torn." Jesus' death on that cross was the sacrifice that opened the way, but not until he took his blood into the very presence of God and offered it for our sins were we actually granted forgiveness. This is an exact parallel with the annual sacrifice of the High Priest under the old covenant which was covered in detail in our discussion of the Hebrew letter.

In case anyone still wonders when and where all this was to happen, Luke said *"Jerusalem will be trampled on..."* Neither the context nor the subject has changed. Jesus was still answering the same two questions; when will these buildings be destroyed and what will be the signs this event is about to happen.

If we believe Daniel, we must also believe that the archangel Michael was present and guiding the events as they unfolded and every righteous person who had ever lived was finally cleansed by the blood of Jesus and delivered from death. And it gets even more exciting...read on!

Matthew 24	Mark 13	Luke 21
30 They will see the Son of Man coming on the clouds of the sky, with power and great glory. 31 And he will send his angels with a loud trumpet call, and they will gather his elect from the four winds, from one end of the heavens to the other.	*26 At that time men will see the Son of Man coming in clouds with great power and glory. 27 And he will send his angels and gather his elect from the four winds, from the ends of the earth to the ends of the heavens.*	*27 At that time they will see the Son of Man coming in a cloud with power and great glory. 28 When these things begin to take place, stand up and lift up your heads, because your redemption is drawing near."*

Jesus would come in the clouds of the sky with power and great glory! How was this possible? Did he physically return to earth when the temple was destroyed? Let us examine the Scriptures. When Moses received the old covenant on Mt. Sinai the presence of God was in the form of a cloud. Exodus 24:15-16, *"When Moses went up on the mountain, the cloud covered it, and the glory of the Lord settled on Mount Sinai. For six days the cloud covered the mountain, and on the seventh day the Lord called to Moses from within the cloud."* Moses did not physically see God…he, and the Israelites, saw the cloud.

When the tabernacle was built and God descended to fill the Tent of Meeting, the Bible says in Exodus 40:34-35, *"Then the cloud covered the Tent of Meeting, and the glory of the Lord filled the tabernacle. Moses could not enter the Tent of Meeting because the cloud had settled upon it, and the glory of the Lord filled the tabernacle."* The children of Israel did not physically see God…they saw him in a cloud.

In Acts 1:9-11 the apostles watched as Jesus was taken up and hidden from their sight…in a cloud. *"After he said this, he was taken up before their very eyes, and a cloud hid him from their sight. They were looking intently up into the sky as he was going, when suddenly two men dressed in white stood beside them. 'Men of Galilee,' they said, 'why do you stand here looking into the sky? This same Jesus, who has been taken from you into heaven, will come back in the same way you have seen him go into heaven.' "* How had they seen him go? In a cloud. What was the purpose of the cloud? To hide him from their sight. How did he say he would return? In a cloud. Does that imply he could be physically seen? Just the opposite. Jesus said, *"My kingdom does not come visibly"* (Luke 17:20).

Those who teach a future coming of Jesus base much of their logic on this passage in Acts. They reason that since he was physically seen ascending and the angels said he would come back in the same manner, his return must also be physical. This point is usually made in connection with what John said in Revelation 1:7, *"Look, he is coming with the clouds, and every eye will see him, even those who pierced him; and all the peoples of the earth will mourn because of him. So shall it be! Amen."*

One must first question the inconsistency of connecting these two passages to prove a physical return of Jesus. Applied in this way the two reasons are mutually exclusive. Jesus' literal ascension was witnessed by only a handful of people…not every person in the world. If he is going to return in exactly the same manner as he left, only a handful will see his return. In addition, if he is going to literally return to Jerusalem with the same body in which he left, only a few people could see him, not "every eye." How could someone in the Americas possibly see a physical person in Jerusalem? At some point everyone who espouses a view of the second coming must admit it will be vastly different from his ascension. Scripture says at the time of Jesus' ascension the clouds **concealed him from view.** This is exactly why the angels said he will come again "in like manner," and Jesus personally said he would come "in the clouds," concealed from view.

The "coming of the Lord" was not a foreign concept to the disciples to whom Jesus was speaking. The phrase was used repeatedly in Old Testament Scripture referring to God's coming in judgment on nations and in prophecies about this very time Jesus was describing and is often described as his "coming in the clouds." In Isaiah 19:1, *"An oracle concerning Egypt: See, the Lord rides on a swift cloud and is coming to Egypt. The idols of Egypt tremble before him, and the hearts of the Egyptians melt within them."* How was the Lord going to "come on a cloud" to Egypt? He came in exactly the same way he came to destroy the temple, in the form of an invading army.

Again In Isaiah 26:21, *"See, the Lord is coming out of his dwelling to punish the people of the earth for their sins."* And in Isaiah 66:6, *"Hear that uproar from the city, hear that noise from the temple! It is the sound of the Lord repaying his enemies all they deserve."* In verse 15 of the same chapter he says, *"See, the Lord is coming with fire, and his chariots are like a whirlwind; he will bring down his anger with fury, and his rebuke with flames of fire."* And in Micah 1:3, *"Look! The Lord is coming from his dwelling place; he comes down and treads the high places of the earth."*

The prophecy of the Lord's coming to destroy Jerusalem was described in Daniel 7:13, *"In my vision at night I looked, and there before me was one like a son of man, coming with the clouds of heaven. He approached the Ancient of Days and was led into his presence."*

That Jesus would use the same language to describe the age-changing events that were about to take place did not surprise his disciples, nor should it confuse any student of the Bible today. Not one example of the Lord coming in the clouds involved a physical sighting of the Almighty. When Jesus lived on earth, he had a physical body people could see and touch. Following his death, burial, resurrection, and ascension he resumed his role as God. He is Spirit, and human eyes cannot see spiritual beings. Just as God appeared in a cloud to confirm the first covenant, Jesus said he would appear in a cloud to remove the first and confirm the second. Why would anyone believe this would be a physical return of Jesus in a physical body?

The passage in Revelation 1 is connected to the one in Acts 1, but not as the futurist doctrine would explain it. John began his Revelation of Jesus Christ by referring to what the angels told the disciples in Acts 1. *"Look, he is coming in the clouds..."* John then added the phrase, *"...and every eye shall see him."* As opposed to the ascension which only a few saw, everyone will "see" his return. John was not saying every person who ever lived would literally see Jesus. He was saying the event of the Lord's return would be such that every person would know it had happened.

The Greek word "ophthalmos," translated "eye" comes from a "root signifying 'penetration, sharpness' " (Vines Expository Dictionary of New Testament Words). It can be used to refer to the physical organ, but usually refers to sight in the sense of knowing something, such as in Ephesians 1:18 *"...the eyes of your heart having been enlightened..."*

This is consistent with how the Lord has revealed Himself throughout history. In Exodus 7:4-5, *"Then I will lay my hand on Egypt and with mighty acts of judgment I will bring out my divisions, my people the Israelites. And the Egyptians will know that I am the Lord when I stretch out my hand against Egypt and bring the Israelites out of it."* This passage could be translated "...every eye will see that I am the Lord" and nobody would misunderstand the meaning.

John connected the promise of the angels at the ascension to the prophecy in Zachariah 12:10, *"And I will pour out on the house of David and the inhabitants of Jerusalem a spirit of grace and supplication. They will look on me, the one they have pierced, and they will mourn for him as one mourns for an only child, and grieve bitterly for him as one grieves for a firstborn son."* Zachariah was describing the Lord's coming Judgment on Jerusalem and in 13:1 said, *"On that day a fountain will be opened to the house of David and the inhabitants of Jerusalem, to cleanse them from sin and impurity."* Jerusalem's "cleansing from sin" was fulfilled with Jesus' atonement sacrifice. No other event could do so.

The same concept was used in reference to the establishment of the new covenant under which "all people" would "know" the Lord. Quoting Jeremiah 31, Hebrews 8:10-12 says, *"This is the covenant I will make with the house of Israel after that time, declares the Lord. I will put my laws in their minds and write them on their hearts. I will be their God, and they will be my people. No longer will a man teach his neighbor, or a man his brother, saying, 'Know the Lord,' because they will all know me, from the least of them to the greatest. For I will forgive their wickedness and will remember their sins no more."*

Obviously not every person in the world knows the Lord, but the new covenant is for all, not just the Jews, and with the complete revelation of his word, everyone can know him. The concept in both Revelation and in Jesus predictions of the destruction of Jerusalem and its temple in Matthew 24 is that his coming would be so clear that "every eye will see" it has occurred.

In Matthew 24:27 Jesus said, *"For as lightning that comes from the east is visible even in the west, so will be the coming of the Son of Man."* The destruction of Jerusalem and its temple was an event unlike any other in human history. Just as Daniel and the other Old Testament prophets had predicted, God used the armies of the Roman Empire (Daniel's fourth kingdom or beast) to bring his divine judgment on the nations and ultimately on Jerusalem. The destruction of the temple was known all over the world and has been known by every generation since. Nobody missed this event. It was indeed a "shot heard around the world." Even today one can visit the temple site and will find exactly what Jesus said, *"Not one stone left on top of another."* As lightning from the East can be seen in the West, the absence of the temple is proof of the validity of Scripture and is an everlasting testimony of the completed atonement sacrifice of Jesus. It will never be rebuilt.

So how would anyone know when it happened? Jesus said to watch for the signs.

Matthew 24	Mark 13	Luke 21
32Now learn this lesson from the fig tree: As soon as its twigs get tender and its leaves come out, you know that summer is near. 33Even so, when you see all these things, you know that it is near, right at the door.	*28Now learn this lesson from the fig tree: As soon as its twigs get tender and its leaves come out, you know that summer is near. 29Even so, when you see these things happening, you know that it is near, right at the door.*	*29He told them this parable: "Look at the fig tree and all the trees. 30When they sprout leaves, you can see for yourselves and know that summer is near. 31Even so, when you see these things happening, you know that the kingdom of God is near.*

When they saw all these things happening around them, they would know. Of course, the final sign of his return, signifying the acceptance by God of his sacrifice confirming the new covenant was now in full force and the Holy of Holies was now open to all, was the destruction of the temple. They all saw that!

Jesus said when they saw these signs, they would know that this event was *near*, not two thousand or two million years in the future, *right at the door*. To make sure nobody misunderstood the timing of these events, Jesus concluded his teachings about the signs with the following statement:

Matthew 24	Mark 13	Luke 21
34I tell you the truth, this generation will certainly not pass away until all these things have happened. 35Heaven and earth will pass away, but my words will never pass away.	*30I tell you the truth, this generation will certainly not pass away until all these things have happened. 31Heaven and earth will pass away, but my words will never pass away.*	*32I tell you the truth, this generation will certainly not pass away until all these things have happened. 33Heaven and earth will pass away, but my words will never pass away.*

The generation in which Jesus and his apostles were living was not going to end until *all* these things happened. Many have tried to rationalize this statement of Jesus to mean something entirely different by "stretching" the meaning of "this generation" to some undetermined amount of time that could be centuries long. Is this a correct interpretation? The Greek word translated here is "genea" from "ginomai" which means begotten. The literal meaning is, "The whole multitude of men living at the same time," (Matt. 24:34, Mark 13:30, Luke 1:48, 21:32, Phil 2:15) especially those of the Jewish race living at the same period. (Matt. 11:16) Transferred from people to the time in which they lived, the word came to mean an age, i.e. a period ordinarily occupied by each successive generation, say, of thirty or forty years (Acts. 14:16, 15:21, Eph. 3:5, Col. 1:26, Gen. 15:16). The word "genea" is to be distinguished from "aion", as not denoting a period of unlimited duration." (Vines Expository Dictionary of New Testament Words)

Here is a sample of the different translations of this verse:

> King James Version: *"Verily I say unto you, this generation shall not pass till all these things be fulfilled."*
>
> Williams Translation: *"I solemnly say to you, the present age will not pass away before all this takes place."*
>
> New Century Bible: *"I tell you the truth, all these things will happen while the people of this time are still living."*
>
> Revised Standard Version: *"Truly I say to you, this generation will not pass away till all things take place."*
>
> Amplified Bible: *"Truly, I tell you, this generation…that is, the whole multitude of people living at the same time, in a definite given period…will not pass away till all these things taken together take place."*

If Jesus had meant a period of unlimited duration, he would

have used "aion." He did not. He said exactly what he meant here, which is the same thing he said in Mark 9:1, *"I tell you the truth, some who are standing here will not taste death before they see the kingdom of God come with power."* A look at other passages of Scripture that speak of this generation might be helpful.

> Genesis 7:1, *"The Lord then said to Noah, 'Go into the ark, you and your whole family, because I have found you righteous in this generation.' "*
>
> Matthew 11:16-17, *"To what can I compare this generation? They are like children sitting in the marketplaces and calling out to others: 'We played the flute for you, and you did not dance; we sang a dirge and you did not mourn.' "*
>
> Mark 8:12, *"He sighed deeply and said, 'Why does this generation ask for a miraculous sign? I tell you the truth, no sign will be given to it.' "*
>
> Luke 11:30, *"For as Jonah was a sign to the Ninevites, so also will the Son of Man be to this generation."*
>
> Luke 17:25, *"But first he* (Jesus) *must suffer many things and be rejected by this generation."*

In none of the other passages where "this generation" is used do we have any difficulty with its meaning. Why do we feel the necessity to change its meaning only in the one place where it refers to the coming of the Lord? Jesus said exactly what he meant. That generation would not pass until all these things happened.

Matthew's account of these events is the most lengthy of the three and actually encompasses all of chapters 24 and 25 of his

Gospel. To keep the reader on subject and context, he weaved into his narrative language to connect everything he said to Jesus' discussion of the questions at hand. In 24:10-11 he said, *"**At that time** many will turn away from the faith and will betray and hate each other, and many false prophets will appear and deceive many people."* What time? The time when all these buildings would be destroyed. In verse 23, *"**At that time** if anyone says to you, 'Look, here is the Christ!' or, 'There he is!' do not believe it."* What time? Again in verse 30, *"**At that time** the sign of the Son of Man will appear in the sky..."*

In verse 36 he said, *"No one knows about **that day or hour**, not even the angels in heaven, nor the Son, but only the Father."* To what day or hour was he referring? He was still speaking of the time of the destruction of the temple. They would not know the exact day and hour, but they would know it was approaching by watching for the signs.

Some have tried to suggest Jesus' language here does denote a change from his discussion of the destruction of Jerusalem to the end of time, because they would be able to tell when the armies were advancing on Jerusalem, but nobody will know when the final end will come. This interpretation actually denies the very thing Jesus was trying to teach. Neither subject nor context has changed. Jesus' point was they would know by the signs as the end approached, but he was not giving them an exact day and hour.

Much like a woman who announces she is expecting a baby cannot tell you the exact day and hour of the approaching birth. She can tell you it will come within the next nine months. As the time approaches, there will be signs that will narrow the time frame, but they still will not identify the exact hour. When labor begins, she will recognize the signs and know it is time...soon.

This is exactly what Jesus was saying and what we see fulfilled in Scripture. John, who heard his teaching and was watching the signs, wrote in his first letter, *"It is the last hour."* The Revelation given him was about those things that were soon to happen. The time had come. In Revelation 9 we read the four angels *"...who had been kept ready for this very hour and day and month and year were released..."* Finally the exact day and hour had come.

Matthew 25 begins, *"**At that time** the kingdom of heaven will be like ten virgins who took their lamps and went out to meet the bridegroom."* At what time? Jesus is still speaking of the same time. He concludes this parable with, *"Therefore keep watch, because you do not know **the day or the hour.**"*

The parable of the talents begins in verse 14 with these words, *"**Again, it will be like** a man going on a journey, who called his servants and entrusted his property to them."* What did he mean **again** and what was **"it"**? One more example of what that time would be like.

The parable of the sheep and goats starts in verse 30 with, *"**When the Son of Man comes in his glory,** and all the angels with him, he will sit on his throne in heavenly glory."* This is an obvious reference back to what he had just said in chapter 24 about the coming of the Son of Man. Nowhere in these two chapters does Matthew change the subject. He begins and ends with Jesus' answer to the disciples two questions; "When will these temple buildings be destroyed?" And "...what will be the sign that it is about to happen?" Matthew 26 begins, *"When Jesus had finished all these sayings..."* Not until here does he change the subject.

Rule number two: **Keep Scripture in its context.**

That is what Jesus said. Everything he said happened just as he said it would at the exact time he said it would happen...or he is not the Son of God and Christianity is a false religion.

CHAPTER 7

The Teaching of Peter

Before Jesus left his apostles and ascended back into heaven he promised the Holy Spirit would come to guide them. In John 16:12-14 he told them, *"I have much more to say to you, more than you can now bear. But when he, the Spirit of truth, comes, he will guide you into all truth. He will not speak on his own; he will speak only what he hears, and he will tell you what is yet to come. He will bring glory to me by taking from what is mine and making it known to you."* The Holy Spirit's role in the lives of these early disciples was to help them remember what Jesus had taught and continue to reveal God's will to them, **including things that were yet to happen**, so they could write it down for our benefit.

Peter was keenly aware of the importance of the Holy Spirit's guidance in God's revelation. In 1 Peter 1:20 he said, *"Above all, you must understand that no prophecy of Scripture came about by the prophet's own interpretation. For prophecy never had its origin in the will of man, but men spoke from God as they were carried along by the Holy Spirit."* Peter was one of those men from God who would speak and write as he was guided by the Holy Spirit.

In his first letter, following his usual salutation, he began to explain some things about salvation that may seem a bit strange. He said in verse 3-4, *"Praise be to the God and Father of our Lord Jesus Christ! In his great mercy he has given us new birth into a living hope through the resurrection of Jesus Christ from the dead, and into an inheritance that can never perish, spoil or fade—kept in heaven for you, who through faith are shielded by God's power until the coming of the salvation that is ready to be revealed in the last time."* Here the apostle was writing many years after the death, burial, and resurrection of Jesus speaking of the **coming of the salvation** that **is** (not was) **ready to be revealed in the last time.** What was there about salvation that was still to be revealed? To what time period was he referring when he said "the last time"? Remember this was the same apostle who preached the first gospel sermon on the day of Pentecost. In that sermon he was the one who identified these times as the ones spoken of by the prophet Joel when he said, *"In the last days God will pour out his Spirit..."*

Throughout the New Testament letters there is expressed time after time the concept of salvation being present, yet still coming. We saw this in our study of Hebrews in regard to the kingdom where the writer said, *"...we are receiving a kingdom."* Jesus' death on the cross was the sacrifice for our sin. His blood was shed for our atonement, which made possible our salvation. The sacrificial lamb had been slain. But there was more to come.

Continuing in verse 10 of the same chapter, *"Concerning this salvation, the prophets, who spoke of the grace that was to come to you, searched intently and with the greatest care, trying to find out the time and circumstances to which the Spirit of Christ in them was pointing when he predicted the sufferings of Christ and the glories that would follow."* Not only did the prophets predict the sufferings of Christ, but also the **"...glories that would follow."** There must have been more to these "last days" than the crucifixion of Jesus. Peter also understood the consummation of the ages. He knew Jesus had been sacrificed for the sins of the world. He was at the trial. He also knew, by divine guidance of the Holy Spirit, that there was more to be accomplished. Peter knew the ritual the High Priest went through in sacrificing blood for sin. He had taken many animals to the priest and waited anxiously for his emergence from the Holy of Holies to know his sacrifice was accepted by God.

In 1 Peter 4:7 he said, *"The end of all things is near. Therefore be clear minded and self-controlled so that you can pray."* Is it even remotely logical that he was speaking of the end of the physical universe? If so, Peter and the other New Testament writers were sadly misguided by the Holy Spirit in regard to the timing. Are we still waiting for salvation to be revealed? In keeping with what Jesus and Scripture says on the subject, salvation was to be completely revealed in the last days of Israel. Once all the things the prophets had foretold and Jesus said would have to happen were fulfilled, the atonement would be complete and our Great High Priest would appear signifying not only God's acceptance of his blood for our sins, but the end of the old covenant. Then the physical temple would be forever removed from the earth. This was the "end of all things" necessary to complete God's wonderful mystery of salvation. A few of these things were still to be revealed at the time of Peter's writing. If they have not yet happened, our salvation is not yet complete.

In his second letter, Peter continued with a much more detailed account of these final things that remained to be revealed concerning this salvation. In 2 Peter 3:1-2 he said, *"Dear friends, this is now my second letter to you. I have written both of them as reminders to stimulate you to wholesome thinking. I want you to recall the words spoken in the past by the holy prophets and the command given by our Lord and Savior through your apostles."* He said he had written both of his letters to remind his readers of what the prophets said and what Jesus taught.

Peter began this chapter telling them what he was saying was nothing new. It could be found in the Old Testament prophecies and in the teachings of Jesus. Remember study principle number one...**Let the Bible interpret itself.** In verse 3-4 he said, *"First of all, you must understand that in the last days scoffers will come, scoffing and following their own evil desires. They will say, 'Where is this 'coming' he promised? Ever since our fathers died, everything goes* *on as it has since the beginning of creation.' "*

Who had predicted scoffers and false teachers? Jesus. These people were now taunting the first century Christians with Jesus' own words. *"Where is this 'coming' he promised?"* Everyone understood exactly what Jesus had said, that this generation would not pass away until all these things happened. They were some thirty years beyond the death of Jesus and it had not happened. Jesus must have been a fake.

Peter began to answer their argument with a comparison to the days of Noah. Verses 5-6, *"But they deliberately forget that long ago by God's word the heavens existed and the earth was formed out of water and by water. By these waters also the world of that time was deluged and destroyed."* Imagine the scoffers in Noah's day. You are building a *what?* The entire earth is going to be flooded? Yeah, right! After about a hundred years of listening to Noah, I can believe a lot of people were saying, "Where is this flood he promised?" But they were wrong. God did exactly what he said he would do. Notice Peter said the *"...world of that time was destroyed."* He was now telling them the "world of this time" is about to be destroyed.

Peter repeated precisely what Jesus had taught in verse 7, *"By the same word the present heavens and earth* (world) *are reserved for fire, being kept for the day of judgment and destruction of ungodly men."* In Matthew 25:31-33 Jesus had said, *"When the Son of Man comes in his glory, and all the angels with him, he will sit on his throne in heavenly glory. All the nations will be gathered before him, and he will separate the people one from another as a shepherd separates the sheep from the goats. He will put the sheep on his right and the goats on his left."* Jesus continued, *"Then he will say to those on his left, 'Depart from me, you who are cursed, into the eternal fire prepared for the devil and his angels"* (vs. 41).

In one of the most misunderstood and misapplied verses in the Bible, Peter explained to them why they should not listen to the scoffers. In verse 8 he said, *"But do not forget this one thing, dear friends: With the Lord a day is like a thousand years, and a thousand years are like a day. The Lord is not slow in keeping his promise, as some understand slowness. He is patient with you, not wanting anyone to perish, but everyone to come to repentance."*

Many Christians today have been taught that one cannot take God literally when he makes a statement about time because God doesn't keep time like we do. A day is like a thousand years to God, so when God says he will do something in forty years, he may mean forty thousand years. And, in this case, when Jesus said all these things will happen in this generation, he may have meant a thousand generations. This is utter nonsense and is the complete opposite of what Peter was saying.

When God makes an explicit time statement, he means it and he keeps it. When he told the Israelites they would have to wander in the desert for forty years, he meant exactly forty years. And forty years **to the day** they crossed over the Jordan into the promised land. When God said forty years, he meant forty years.

Daniel started praying to God to deliver Israel from Babylonian captivity and return them to their own land in the seventieth year of that captivity. Why? Because in Jeremiah 25:11-12 God had said, " *'This whole country will become a desolate wasteland, and these nations will serve the king of Babylon seventy years. But when the seventy years are fulfilled, I will punish the king of Babylon and his nation, the land of the Babylonians, for their guilt,' declares the Lord, 'and will make it desolate forever.'* " It is no accident that in Daniel 9:2 we read, *"In the first year of his (Darius') reign, I, Daniel, understood from the Scriptures, according to the word of the Lord given to Jeremiah the prophet, that the desolation of Jerusalem would last seventy years."* Daniel knew that if God were true to his word, the captivity was almost over because it was the seventieth year. God is not slow keeping his promise! He never has been, he never will be, and he wasn't in the days of Peter.

Peter's message to the first century Christians was clear. God can remember a thousand years as easily as he can remember one day. God does not forget over time, nor does he forget what he says about time. He had not forgotten Jesus' promise. He said he would come in their generation…HE DID!

Then Peter proceeded to explain how the end would come and again chose the same terminology used by Jesus. 2 Peter 3:10-13, *"But the day of the Lord will come like a thief. The heavens will disappear with a roar; the elements will be destroyed by fire, and the earth and everything in it will be laid bare. Since everything will be destroyed in this way, what kind of people ought you to be? You ought to live holy and godly lives as you look forward to the day of God and speed its coming. That day will bring about the destruction of the heavens by fire, and the elements will melt in the heat. But in keeping with his promise we are looking forward to a new heaven and a new earth, the home of righteousness."*

Peter used the Greek word "ouranos" which is translated "heavens" to denote that which would be destroyed. This is the same term Jesus used in Matthew 24:33 when he said, *"Heaven and earth will pass away…"* Had either of them meant the physical universe, they would have used the word "kosmos." It is the same terminology from the prophecy of Isaiah 67:17, speaking of the time when the physical nation of Israel would find her ultimate fulfillment in the eternal kingdom. The prophet said, *"Behold, I will create new heavens and a new earth. The former things will not be remembered, nor will they come to mind."* The Scriptures contain numerous similar passages referring to the old kingdom of Israel as a world that would pass away, replaced by a "new heaven and earth." Remember that Peter said he would bring to mind the things spoken by the prophets and what Jesus had taught. This is one more example of just that.

He also said the *"…elements will melt in the heat."* The word "elements" is the Greek word "stoicheion" and appears seven times in the New Testament. Twice in Galatians (4:3 & 9) and twice in Colossians (2:8 & 20) it refers to the basic principles of this world to which we die when we become Christians. Once in Hebrews 5:12 it refers to the elementary truths of God's word. The other two times the word is used is here in 2 Peter 3:10 & 12. The word means the principles upon which a society is built. It refers here to the basic principles or "elements" of that world which was passing away, the world of physical Israel, the Jewish world. Never does this word refer to trees and dirt. There is nothing in these verses that teach the physical universe would be destroyed. Actually the opposite is true. The universe was going to undergo a "consummation" or changing of the ages. Something imperfect (physical Israel) was going to be destroyed and the perfect spiritual kingdom would replace it, which is exactly what happened. What a blessing that was to the kosmos!

No wonder Peter's next comment in 2 Peter 3:14 was, *"So then, dear friends, since you are looking forward to this, make every effort to be found spotless, blameless and at peace with him."* It is difficult to see how a cataclysmic destruction of the universe would be something to look forward to, but the revealing of God's salvation and the establishment of his eternal spiritual kingdom…now that is something to get excited about!

Before leaving this subject Peter had some interesting words to say about the Apostle Paul's writings and those who would distort the teachings about these matters. In verses 15-16 he said, *"Bear in mind that our Lord's patience means salvation, just as our dear brother Paul also wrote you with the wisdom that God gave him. He writes the same way in all his letters, speaking in them of these matters. His letters contain some things that are hard to understand, which ignorant and unstable people distort, as they do the other Scriptures, to their own destruction."*

CHAPTER 8

The Teaching of Paul

According to the inspired Apostle Peter, some of the things Paul wrote concerning these matters are difficult to understand. Peter did not say they could not be understood. He did not say they were secret things or disputable matters. These are things that require careful, thorough study. Since we have access to the complete revealed word of God, unless we are content to live on milk, we should be able to discern Paul's meaning.

The Apostle Paul was a highly educated Jewish scholar who was well versed in the Old Testament Scriptures. He had been taught all his life, prior to his conversion to Christianity, about the coming Messiah, the "last days" of Judah and Jerusalem, and the coming of a "great day of the Lord" to bring salvation to the righteous and judgment on the nations. As a result, these themes are woven throughout his writings, and he often assumes his readers know the background and history behind things he describes.

To the Church in Rome

Beginning with his letter to the Romans, much of which was directed to his fellow Jewish believers, he began the first four verses by saying, *"Paul, a servant of Christ Jesus, called to be an apostle and set apart for the gospel of God—the gospel he promised beforehand through his prophets in the Scriptures regarding his Son, who as to his human nature was a descendant of David, and who through the Spirit of holiness was declared with power to be the Son of God by his resurrection from the dead: Jesus Christ our Lord."* There is no doubt in Paul's mind that Jesus was the fulfillment of the Old Testament prophecies and the promised Messiah.

In chapter 2:5 he mentioned *"...the day of God's wrath, when his righteous judgment will be revealed."* Much of Paul's text is given to a comparison between the burden of the Law of Moses and the riches we have under a new covenant of grace. In chapter 5:20-21 he said, *"The law was added so that the trespass might increase. But where sin increased, grace increased all the more, so that, just as sin reigned in death, so also grace might reign through righteousness to bring eternal life through Jesus Christ our Lord."* Sin reigned in death, but in the following chapter he explained how through our baptism we share in Jesus' death, burial, and resurrection and become free of sin by the perfect sacrifice of Christ's blood. He concluded that chapter by saying, *"For the wages of sin is death, but the gift of God is eternal life in Christ Jesus our Lord."*

Chapter seven begins with a statement that Paul is writing to people who know the Law and how, while the Law was perfect and good, it resulted in condemnation because nobody could keep it. He asked an important question in verse 24. *"Who will rescue me from this body of death?"* His answer; *"Thanks be to God—through Jesus Christ our Lord!"* In chapter 10:4 he said, "**Christ is the end of the law** *so that there may be righteousness for everyone who believes."*

In chapter 13:11-12 he wrote, *"And do this, understanding the present time. The hour has come for you to wake up from your slumber, because our salvation is nearer now than when we first believed. The night is nearly over; the day is almost here."* Paul pointed out the importance of understanding the time in which they were living, that "the day" was almost here and salvation was

"...nearer than when we first believed." Does he mean believers in his day were not yet saved? Not at all, but he and his Jewish readers did understand the ritual of atonement. He knew the blood sacrifice for sin had been offered and taken into the Holy of Holies. But he also understood the final confirmation of God's acceptance of that sacrifice was yet to come, and that it would come soon, confirming their salvation.

In Romans 16:20 he said, *"The God of peace will soon crush Satan under your feet."* And he concluded his letter with these words; *"Now to him who is able to establish you by my gospel and the proclamation of Jesus Christ, according to the revelation of the mystery hidden for long ages past, but now revealed and made known through the prophetic writings by the command of the eternal God, so that all nations might believe and obey him—to the only wise God be glory forever through Jesus Christ! Amen."*

Just as in the letter to the Hebrews, Paul was looking forward to "the great day of the Lord' when the final step in the atonement ritual of the High Priest would be proclaimed "finished." The entire plan of salvation would be complete. That day would bring about the end of the Law, which had already been rendered obsolete by the cross. The dispensation of law would end with the total destruction of the temple, just as the Scriptures and Jesus had prophesied. Since the wages of sin was death and the power of sin was the Law, that event would also crush Satan's dominion over death forever.

Remember, Paul was writing to those who knew the Old Testament and understood the prophecies concerning these things. Let's now examine what he said in some of his other writings.

To the Church in Corinth

In his first letter to the church in Corinth Paul mentioned the same coming events when in verses 7-8 of the first chapter he said, *"Therefore you do not lack any spiritual gift as you eagerly wait for our Lord Jesus Christ to be revealed. He will keep you strong to the end, so that you will be blameless on the day of our Lord Jesus Christ."* There is an important link between the miraculous gifts of the Holy Spirit and the coming of Jesus, as Paul indicated in this passage. We will study this in detail as we go forward, but it is noteworthy to point out here that these spiritual gifts were to last until Jesus' return.

We read in chapter 4:5, *"Therefore judge nothing before the appointed time; wait till the Lord comes. He will bring to light what is hidden in darkness and will expose the motives of men's hearts. At that time each will receive his praise from God."* The Apostle Paul knew the judgment of God was to happen when the Lord returned.

Again encouraging the first century Christians to understand the times in which they were living, he said in chapter 7:29-31, *"What I mean, brothers, is that the time is short...For this world in its present form is passing away."* The Greek word translated "world" in this passage is the word "schema, which means "...a figure, fashion of the world, signifying that which comprises the manner of life, actions, etc. the outwardly perceptible mode and shape of things." Had Paul been referring to the physical universe he would have used the word "kosmos." This text is referring to the same world Jesus and the other New Testament writers were describing with similar language, the former manner of life under the Old Law. That world, the Jewish world, would soon pass away.

Paul also recognized this time as the consummation of the ages. After reminding his readers of examples from the Old Testament, he said in chapter 10:11, *"These things happened to them as examples and were written down as warnings for us,* ***on whom the fulfillment of the ages has come.****"*

The apostle also linked their observation of the Lord's Supper with the coming of Jesus in 1 Corinthians 11:26. In this verse he said, *"For whenever you eat this bread and drink this cup, you proclaim the Lord's death until he comes."* Most Christians understand this to be a "proof text" that the Lord has not yet come. Since Paul said we take communion to remember his death "until he comes," they reason that if he has already come, we would no longer take it.

We should understand from 1 Corinthians that Paul's instructions to that first century church were very much related to the times in which they were living. His instructions not to marry, about women wearing head coverings, how to properly handle the miraculous gifts of the Holy Spirit, and many other issues were clearly related to the specific time frame of that day. They were living in the Biblical time known as the "last days" of Judah and Jerusalem, just prior to the coming destruction of Jerusalem. In Scripture that was to be the final event to fulfill all prophecy concerning the establishment of the eternal kingdom of Jesus Christ (Matthew 24-25, Mark 13, Luke 21). These passages emphatically state that this would be the time when *"...you will see the Son of Man coming in the clouds with great glory..."* This was the "out with the old – in with the new" event that had been prophesied for centuries and would finally be coming to fruition.

Consider what Jesus said when he instituted the Communion Supper in Matthew 26:29, *"I tell you, I will not drink of this fruit of the vine from now on until that day when I drink it anew with you in my Father's kingdom."* This same conversation is also recorded in Mark 14:25, *"I tell you the truth, I will not drink again of the fruit of the vine until that day when I drink it anew in the kingdom of God."*

When was "that day" when Jesus would "drink it anew" in the kingdom? In Luke 21:31-32, at the conclusion of Jesus' teaching about the coming destruction of the temple and its buildings, he said, *"Even so, when you see these things happening, you know that the* ***kingdom of God is near****. I tell you the truth, this generation will certainly not pass away until all these things have happened."* He said the kingdom of God will have come when "these things" (destruction of Jerusalem and its temple) have happened.

In Hebrews 12:28 it is clear that, although years after the crucifixion of Jesus and the day of Pentecost, the kingdom was still coming. The writer said, *"Therefore, since we* ***are receiving a kingdom*** *that cannot be shaken, let us be thankful, and so worship God acceptably with reverence and awe."* The coming kingdom which was proclaimed by John, began adding members on the day of Pentecost, but was not fully complete until all the prophecies concerning it had been fulfilled.

Since the kingdom of Israel was a prototype of the church, we should not be surprised to learn it began in much the same way. The Lord delivered the Israelites from Egyptian bondage and brought them through their baptism in the Red Sea (1 Corinthians 10:2). From the time they left Egypt until they crossed the Jordan into the Promised Land they were a nation, the chosen people of God…yet their kingdom had not yet been fully established. During this forty year period God miraculously cared for them, revealed their law, and continued to instruct them in the ways of their "coming kingdom."

We see many parallels with the establishment of the spiritual kingdom. Jesus was crucified on the cross, providing the sacrifice for the bondage of sin. Those who were baptized into Christ received forgiveness and were called into the fellowship of a "coming kingdom." They were a new Holy Nation, God's chosen people, yet the kingdom had not yet been fully established. During the following forty year period God miraculously cared for them (miraculous gifts of the Holy Spirit), revealed his New Testament or covenant law, and continued to instruct them in the ways of this "coming kingdom." With this in mind, let us go back to Jesus' statement of "drinking it anew in the kingdom" and what Paul said about the Lord's Supper showing his death "until he comes."

A very important consideration of what Jesus and Paul said comes from an understanding of exactly what the Lord's Supper commemorates, which is the sacrifice of the Passover Lamb for our deliverance from death. The observance of the Passover comes from the Old Testament. The final plague in Egypt, which resulted in the Israelites being freed from hundreds of years of bondage, was the death of the firstborn. The only escape from this plague was to kill a sacrificial lamb and place its blood over the door of their home. When the death angel came through the land, if he saw the blood of the Passover Lamb on the doorpost he would "pass over" that house. They were to cook and eat the meat with bitter herbs, unleavened bread, and wine (fruit of the vine). Anyone who failed to participate in this Passover would not be covered by the blood of the Lamb. He would suffer the consequences of the death angel.

This became a lasting ordinance for the Jews to celebrate and served as a reminder not only of their cruel bondage, but the price of their deliverance, the death of the firstborn. They were given specific instructions about this commemorative meal which also became known as the Feast of Unleavened Bread. In Exodus 12 we read about the very first Passover meal. On the 14th day of the first month of each year they were to take a lamb, cook and eat it with unleavened bread and wine. Why was this day so important? Verse 17 says, *"Celebrate the Feast of Unleavened Bread, because it was on this very day that I brought your divisions out of Egypt. Celebrate this day as a lasting ordinance for the generations to come."*

They were to celebrate the Passover on the very day they were freed from bondage. The importance of this celebration is seen in the instructions God gave Moses in Numbers 9:13. *"But if a man who is ceremonially clean and not on a journey fails to* *celebrate the Passover, that person must be cut off from his people because he did not present the Lord's offering at the appointed time. That man will bear the consequences of his sin."* Failure to keep this ordinance would result in one's expulsion from the kingdom.

The place of this observance was also decreed by God in Deuteronomy 16:5-8. *"You must not sacrifice the Passover in any town the Lord your God gives you except in the place he will choose as a dwelling for his Name."* That place was Jerusalem where the temple was built. However, the instructions were given and the feast began to be commemorated many years before the kingdom of Israel was fully established and the temple built in Jerusalem. From the time God gave them the instructions, they knew that one day there would be a special place for this feast. It would be in the city that bore his name, in the kingdom to which he was leading them.

We see in Ezra 6:19-21, when the Israelites were finally returned to their homeland from Babylonian captivity, they celebrated the Passover in Jerusalem. *"On the fourteenth day of the first month, the exiles celebrated the Passover. The priests and Levites had purified themselves and were all ceremonially clean. The Levites slaughtered the Passover lamb for all the exiles, for their brothers the priests and for themselves. So the Israelites who had returned from the exile ate it, together with all who had separated themselves from the unclean practices of their Gentile neighbors in order to seek the Lord, the God of Israel."* They could not celebrate the Passover while they were held in captivity because God had instructed them to do it in the City that bore his name.

Jesus' parents understood this teaching, and we see in Luke 2:41, *"Every year his (Jesus') parents went to Jerusalem to celebrate the Passover."* Jesus continued this practice in his adult life and ministry and it was at this feast he instituted what we now call the Lord's Supper. At that supper he took the unleavened bread and said, *"This is my body,"* and told them all to eat it. Then he took the cup and said, *"This is my blood of the covenant...drink it."* This memorial "Feast of Unleavened Bread" is to be done "in remembrance of Jesus" as our Passover Lamb sacrificed to free us from the bondage of sin.

Is it important? Consider the words of Jesus in John 6:53-56, *"Jesus said to them, 'I tell you the truth, unless you eat the flesh of the Son of Man and drink his blood, you have no life in you...Whoever eats my flesh and drinks my blood remains in me, and I in him.' "* Remember, any Israelite who willingly failed to participate in the original Passover celebration suffered the consequences of the death angel. Those in subsequent years who did not participate were cut off from Israel. To remain in the kingdom they had to celebrate this feast. Jesus said, *"If you eat my flesh and drink my blood you will remain in me and I in you."*

The Apostle Paul underscored the importance of this observance in 1 Corinthians 11:27-30 when he said, *"Therefore, whoever eats the bread or drinks the cup of the Lord in an unworthy manner will be guilty of sinning against the body and blood of the Lord. A man ought to examine himself before he eats of the bread and drinks of the cup. For anyone who eats and drinks without recognizing the body of the Lord eats and drinks judgment on himself. That is why many among you are weak and sick, and a number of you have fallen asleep."*

Is there a specific day on which to observe the Lord's Supper? The Jews were to celebrate the Passover on the very day they were delivered from bondage. We are delivered from the much greater bondage of sin by the sacrifice of Jesus on the cross. On what day were we delivered? Scripture says in 1 Peter 1:3, *"Praise be to the God and Father of our Lord Jesus Christ! In his great mercy he has given us new birth into a living hope* ***through the resurrection of Jesus Christ from the dead."*** Jesus' death on the cross was the Passover sacrifice, but it was the power of his resurrection that overcame death and made possible our deliverance from sin.

(Remember, avoiding death was what the first Passover was about.) Jesus arose from the grave on the first day of the week. It is no accident the only recorded examples in Scripture we have of the early Christians' observance of the Lord's Supper are on this day. It was **that very day** we were delivered from death.

Where is this Passover Feast to be observed? In the city that bears his name. In the Old Testament kingdom of Israel that was the city of Jerusalem. In the New Testament it is the spiritual Jerusalem, still called the City of God. Hebrews 12:22-24 says, *"But you have come to Mount Zion, to the heavenly Jerusalem, the city of the living God. You have come to thousands upon thousands of angels in joyful assembly, to the church of the firstborn, whose names are written in heaven. You have come to God, the judge of all men, to the spirits of righteous men made perfect, to Jesus the mediator of a new covenant, and to the sprinkled blood that speaks a better word than the blood of Abel."*

This is the same new Jerusalem John saw in Revelation 21:2-3, *"I saw the Holy City, the new Jerusalem, coming down out of heaven from God, prepared as a bride beautifully dressed for her husband. And I heard a loud voice from the throne saying, 'Now the dwelling of God is with men, and he will live with them. They will be his people, and God himself will be with them and be their God.' "* John further pointed out in verse 22, *"I did not see a temple in the city, because the Lord God Almighty and the Lamb are its temple."*

Paul and the other New Testament writers were all in agreement about the nature and timing of this "coming kingdom." We learn from Daniel this heavenly kingdom would not be complete until the events of "the time of the end" had been completed. Jesus confirmed the same in Luke 21:31 when he said, *"Even so, when you see these things happening, you know that the kingdom of God is near."* This is why the writer of Hebrews said, *"We are receiving* (not have received) *a kingdom"*. The destruction of the Jewish temple was the final sign of the completion of the new kingdom, which would not need a physical temple.

When the Jews celebrated the first Passover, and subsequently celebrated it in their forty years of wilderness wanderings, they were doing it not only to remember their deliverance, but also in anticipation of when they could celebrate it "anew" in their physical kingdom in the physical city of Jerusalem. This is Paul's analogy when he said they were partaking to show his death "until he comes." Paul clearly understood the "coming of the Lord" was to usher in the new eternal kingdom and take the old Jewish kingdom and its temple away forever.

Paul did not err when he said the first century Christians who were partaking of the Lord's Supper prior to the destruction of the temple were doing so "to proclaim his death until he comes". We, on the other hand, live beyond those "last days". He has come! The temple is no longer standing, indicating the completion of the kingdom of heaven, the new Jerusalem. We celebrate the Passover Feast, not in anticipation of the fulfillment of a coming kingdom, but indeed "drink anew with him in the kingdom!"

The Bible says in Hebrews 10:1, *"The law is only a shadow of the good things that are coming—not the realities themselves."* Later in that same chapter it says, *"Anyone who rejected the law of Moses died without mercy on the testimony of two or three witnesses. How much more severely do you think a man deserves to be punished who has trampled the Son of God under foot, who has treated as an unholy thing the blood of the covenant that sanctified him, and who has insulted the Spirit of grace?"* How important is the observance of the Lord's Supper on the first day of the week? You decide.

When we get to chapter 15 of Paul's letter to the Corinthians, we find him refuting the idea of some that there is no resurrection. He basically says if there is no resurrection, Christianity is a hoax. Christians today all accept the resurrection as a fact, but there is still much confusion surrounding the subject. Since resurrection life and the eternal kingdom are both spiritual, and we cannot literally see into the spirit world, it is likely we will not fully understand all these things until we leave this earth to be with him in Glory.

The Apostle Paul had a distinct advantage in that, not only were things divinely revealed to him through the Holy Spirit, but *"...he was caught up to paradise. He heard inexpressible things, things that man is not permitted to tell"* (2 Corinthians 12:1-6). Some things that relate to eternity are secret. God has not permitted them to be revealed yet. We should concern ourselves with what has been written in the Bible for our learning.

1 Corinthians 15:20-37 says, *"But Christ has indeed been raised from the dead, the firstfruits of those who have fallen asleep. For since death came through a man, the resurrection of the dead comes also through a man. For as in Adam all die, so in Christ all will be made alive. But each in his own turn: Christ, the firstfruits; then, when he comes, those who belong to him. Then the end will come, when he hands over the kingdom to God the Father after he has destroyed all dominion, authority and power. For he must reign until he has put all his enemies under his feet. The last enemy to be destroyed is death. For he 'has put everything under his feet.' Now when it says that 'everything' has been put under him, it is clear that this does not include God himself, who put everything under Christ. When he has done this, then the Son himself will be made subject to him who put everything under him, so that God may be all in all."*

One thing on which we can all agree is that without the atonement of Jesus Christ there would be no resurrection for us. Speaking to Martha on the occasion of her brother's death, Jesus said to her, *"I am the resurrection and the life. He who believes in me will live, even though he dies; and whoever lives and believes in me will never die. Do you believe this"* (John 14:25-26)? Here is the irony of the story of Lazarus. He died physically, and even though Jesus brought him back from the grave, he was still dead. Jesus brought life back to his physical body but had not yet shed his blood to atone for his sins. Lazarus, though alive again physically, still had not experienced "resurrection life." Jesus used the resurrection of Lazarus to demonstrate that he had power over death. It was a physical demonstration of what would soon become a spiritual reality. In the context of salvation and eternity, death and resurrection are always spiritual concepts, never physical. Most people, like Mary and Martha, get the two confused. In order to understand the resurrection of which Jesus and Paul spoke we must first understand this difference between physical and spiritual.

In the beginning God warned Adam and Eve not to eat of the tree of knowledge of good and evil. He said, *"The day you eat thereof, you shall surely die."* They ate…but did they die **that day?** Some would argue they "began to die" that day or they "became subject to death" that day. That is not what God said. If we do not understand the meaning of death, we will certainly not understand the resurrection from death.

Death literally means "a separation." When Adam and Eve sinned, they died spiritually. They were banished from the garden and separated from the presence of God **that day.** Physical death may have been a subsequent consequence of their spiritual death, but Jesus proved that physical death cannot separate one from God. If it did, he could not have come back from the grave. Had Adam and Eve not sinned, even if they died a physical death, what would have happened to them? They would have continued to live with God throughout all eternity! When Paul says in Romans 6:23, *"The wages of sin is death,"* he is not talking of physical death. The consequence of sin is spiritual death, eternal separation from the presence of God. Jesus did not die on the cross to overcome physical death, but spiritual death, the death that resulted from sin. The same verse says, "The gift of God is eternal life in Christ Jesus our Lord." Just as the wages of sin is eternal spiritual death, the gift of God is eternal, spiritual life.

In the context of redemption, death always refers to spiritual death and the resurrection always refers to spiritual life. Jesus could not have given Lazarus spiritual life when he raised his physical body because he had not yet made atonement for his sin. The wages of sin is death…spiritual death. Physical death is just a "side effect" of spiritual death.

When a person sins, he dies. In Romans 7:9 Paul says, *"Once I was alive apart from law; but when the commandment came, sin sprang to life and **I died.**"* That is the whole problem with being justified by law. Since nobody can keep God's law, everyone sins and everyone dies…spiritually. When does one die? When he or she sins.

In the same way, when one receives forgiveness from sin, he or she is "resurrected" to life. Jesus said in John 5:24, *"I tell you the truth, whoever hears my word and believes him who sent me has eternal life and will not be condemned; **he has crossed over from death to life.**"* Describing how we die to sin and are raised in Christ when we are baptized Paul said, *"We were buried therefore with him through baptism unto death: that like as Christ was raised from the dead through the glory of the Father, so we also might walk in newness of life"* (Romans 6:4). Once we receive forgiveness of our sins through the death, burial, and resurrection of Christ, we are "resurrected" or raised to walk in new life…resurrection life. Most Christians believe they are waiting on the resurrection because they don't understand they already have it!

What about Lazarus and all the other righteous people who died before the atonement of Jesus? Daniel was shown a vision of the "last days" in which atonement would be made and God would put an "end to sin" (Daniel 9:24) and in chapter 12:1-4 & 13 said, *"At that time Michael, the great prince who protects your people, will arise. There will be a time of distress such as has not happened from the beginning of nations until then. But at that time your people—everyone whose name is found written in the book—will be delivered. Multitudes who sleep in the dust of the earth will awake: some to everlasting life, others to shame and everlasting contempt. Those who are wise will shine like the brightness of the heavens, and those who lead many to righteousness, like the stars forever and ever. But you, Daniel, close up and seal the words of the scroll until the time of the end. Many will go here and there to increase knowledge...As for you, go your way till the end. You will rest, and then at the end of the days you will rise to receive your allotted inheritance."*

When was the resurrection from death going to be a reality? At the "time of the end" following the "time of distress such as has not happened from beginning of nations until then." We know from Jesus' quotation of this very same prophecy this time would be when the temple would be destroyed (Matthew 24:15-25, Mark 13:14-23). What was allowing the power of death to keep its hold over these people? **SIN!** Once the atonement of Jesus was complete, there was no way death could continue to hold them. Did they come to life? YES! If they did not, it means death still has dominion and, since death is the result of sin, forgiveness must not yet be available. This view ultimately nullifies the death and resurrection of Jesus.

Once all these things were fulfilled, the atonement was complete and the curse of sin was forever destroyed. Death no longer has its control over mankind. The eternal kingdom, which Jesus came to establish, is complete and has been handed over to the Father...**mission accomplished!**

We should not be surprised to read the statement of Jesus in John 5:25-27, *"I tell you the truth, a time is coming and has now come when the dead will hear the voice of the Son of God and those who hear will live. For as the Father has life in himself, so he has granted the Son to have life in himself. And he has given him authority to judge because he is the Son of Man. Do not be amazed at this, for a time is coming when all who are in their graves will hear his voice and come out—those who have done good will rise to live, and those who have done evil will rise to be condemned."* The redemption of the righteous and the condemnation of the wicked (the resurrection and judgment) was drawing near.

This is perhaps one of the concepts to which Peter was referring when he said Paul wrote some things that were difficult to understand. It is difficult for us to truly grasp eternal, resurrection life. Do we still die physically? Yes, but as Jesus said, we don't really die. We have already experienced the resurrection from death in Christ because we have received forgiveness for our sin. Remember, the wages of sin is death. With no sin there is no death.

But what about the body? Paul continued in 1 Corinthians 15:35-50, *"But someone may ask, 'How are the dead raised? With what kind of body will they come?' How foolish! What you sow does not come to life unless it dies. When you sow, you do not plant the body that will be, but just a seed, perhaps of wheat or of something else. So will it be with the resurrection of the dead. The body that is sown is perishable, it is raised imperishable; it is sown in dishonor, it is raised in glory; it is sown in weakness, it is raised in power; it is sown a natural body, it is raised a spiritual body. I declare to you, brothers, that flesh and blood cannot inherit the kingdom of God, nor does the perishable inherit the imperishable."* Are we going to have a flesh and blood body? Paul said we will not. We may speculate all we want about what our eternal spiritual existence may look like, but let's not miss the true meaning of the resurrection. Spiritual resurrection life is granted to everyone the moment he receives the atonement sacrifice for sin.

Paul continued explaining the mystery of resurrection in verses 51-57. *"Listen, I tell you a mystery: We will not all sleep, but we will all be changed—in a flash, in the twinkling of an eye, at the last trumpet. For the trumpet will sound, the dead will be raised imperishable, and we will be changed. For the perishable must clothe itself with the imperishable, and the mortal with immortality. When the perishable has been clothed with the imperishable, and the mortal with immortality, then the saying that is written will come true: "Death has been swallowed up in victory." "Where, O grave, is your victory? Where, O death, is your sting?" The sting of death is sin, and the power of sin is the law. But thanks be to God! He gives us the victory through our Lord Jesus Christ."*

He began these final comments of the chapter about the resurrection by stating that what he was about to say was a mystery. (Remember what Peter said!) Paul said a day was coming when a trumpet would sound and the dead would be raised. Those who had not died would be changed. That change would be from perishable to imperishable, from mortal to immortality. When would this happen? When "death has been swallowed up in victory." That happened, according to Scripture, when the atonement ritual was complete in heaven, at which time the Jewish temple on earth was destroyed.

Philippians 3:20-21, *"But our citizenship is in heaven. And we eagerly await a Savior from there, the Lord Jesus Christ, who, by the power that enables him to bring everything under his control, will transform our lowly bodies so that they will be like his glorious body."* How a person is transformed from being spiritually dead to spiritually alive is a mystery. This is, however, something that happens to all those who accept Jesus as Savior and receive a full pardon for their sins. Paul said we are dead in sin but alive in Christ. He was not speaking of life after death in heaven but the spiritual life we are granted when we receive his grace. At the appearing of Jesus, the atonement was confirmed and all who belonged to God were eternally changed. Although we long to see with our physical eyes, the truth is we cannot see into the spiritual realm as long as we are in this body. As difficult as it may be, the apostle said, *"So we fix our eyes not on what is seen, but on what is unseen. For what is seen is temporary, but what is unseen is eternal"*

(2 Corinthians 4:18).

Paul was teaching exactly the same thing as did Jesus in Matthew 24:31-34, *"And he will send his angels with a loud trumpet call, and they will gather his elect from the four winds, from one end of the heavens to the other...this generation will not pass away until all these things have happened."* It was the consummation of the ages, the culmination and revelation of the great mystery of God. As John recorded in Revelation 10:7, *"But in the days when the seventh angel is about to sound his trumpet, the mystery of God will be accomplished, just as he announced to his servants the prophets."*

Please consider seriously the consequences of any other explanation. Paul said the mystery would be complete when death would be swallowed up in victory. One may wonder how this can be since we still die. He was not speaking of physical death. The subject was spiritual death and spiritual life. He further said, *"The sting of death is sin, and the power of sin is the law."* The power of sin was the law. If death has not yet been swallowed up in victory, we are still living under the Law, the sacrifice of Jesus on the cross is nullified, and we are still in our sin. But death has been destroyed. In 2 Timothy 1:9-10 this same apostle told the young preacher, *"This grace was given us in Christ Jesus before the beginning of time, but it has now been revealed through the appearing of our Savior, Christ Jesus,* **who has destroyed death** *and has brought life and immortality to light through the gospel."*

Jesus' sacrifice and resurrection from the grave destroyed death. It had no mastery over him because he was sinless. Now that the atonement for us is complete, it no longer has any power over us because we too, cleansed by his blood, are sinless. We can say with Paul, *"But thanks be to God! He gives us the victory through our Lord Jesus Christ."*

To the Church in Thessalonica

The Apostle Paul wrote two short letters to the church in Thessalonica. He began the first by complementing them on their faith that was well known in the region. He said the churches in Macedonia and Achaia had given glowing reports of their understanding of Scripture. In 1 Thessalonians 1:8-10 he said, *"Therefore we do not need to say anything about it, for they themselves report what kind of reception you gave us. They tell how you turned to God from idols to serve the living and true God, and to wait for his Son from heaven, whom he raised from the dead—Jesus, who rescues us from the coming wrath."* As we already know from his other writings and will soon discover in this letter as well, Paul was speaking of the same coming Jesus predicted and the same time of wrath that was to have greater consequences than anything that had ever happened before or would ever happen again.

We learn in chapter 4:13-18 of their concern about those faithful disciples who had died before the coming of the Lord. What would happen to them? Paul said, *"Brothers, we do not want you to be ignorant about those who fall asleep, or to grieve like the rest of men, who have no hope. We believe that Jesus died and rose again and so we believe that God will bring with Jesus those who have fallen asleep in him. According to the Lord's own word, we tell you that we who are still alive, who are left till the coming of the Lord, will certainly not precede those who have fallen asleep."* Jesus had said earlier to the disciples, *"I tell you the truth, some who are standing here will not taste death before they see the kingdom of God come with power"* (Mark 9:1, Luke 9:27). Paul knew some Christians to whom he was writing would be *"...left till the coming of the Lord"* and live to see these events unfold.

Verse 16 continues, *"For the Lord himself will come down from heaven, with a loud command, with the voice of the archangel and with the trumpet call of God, and the dead in Christ will rise first."*

It's beginning to sound like a broken record, but this is the same coming, the same trumpet sound, that Jesus said would come before that generation passed, it would signal the consummation of the ages and that the mystery of God has been accomplished (Revelation 10:7).

Then Paul explained what would happen to those who live beyond those last days. *"After that, we who are still alive and are left will be caught up together with them in the clouds to meet the Lord in the air. And so we will be with the Lord forever. Therefore encourage each other with these words"* (vs. 17-18). Paul did not say all those who remain would be immediately caught up to heaven in a worldwide "rapture." The question he was answering was what will happen to the dead. His answer was simple. Those who died prior to the coming of the Lord, all the way back to Adam, would be raised and be with him at that time. Those who die "after that," those who live beyond that event, will actually never die. When they experience physical death, they will simply be caught up to be with the Lord and all those who have gone on before. That is exactly what Jesus said in John 11:26, *"...and whoever lives and believes in me* ***will never die.*** *Do you believe this?"*

Remember, in the context of redemption, Scripture is always speaking of spiritual death and spiritual life. Death has been destroyed. We will still leave our physical body one day. But we have eternal life, resurrection life, NOW. We will never again be separated from God. We will never die.

It is interesting to notice the difference between what one hears in a typical Sunday sermon and what the same preacher may say at a funeral. There is one theology for Sundays and a completely different one for funerals. On Sunday, the Lord is yet to come, the resurrection is in the future, and "someday," when the Lord returns, the dead will rise to be with him. At a funeral it is usually said that the deceased has gone on to be with the Lord and is now in a much better place in heaven with Jesus. Our funeral theology is correct. May God help us understand that on Sundays.

Having answered the question about what happens to dead people, Paul turned his attention to the coming day of the Lord. Paul used the same analogy Jesus did about this day coming like a thief in the night. Jesus specifically said they would not know the exact day and hour. However, both Jesus and Paul said it should not surprise believers because there was a whole litany of signs for which they should be watching. Paul said in chapter 5:4-11, *"But you, brothers, are not in darkness so that this day should surprise you like a thief. You are all sons of the light and sons of the day…for God did not appoint us to suffer wrath but to receive salvation through our Lord Jesus Christ. Therefore encourage one another and build each other up, just as in fact you are doing."* We have already discussed how the Roman armies surrounded Jerusalem, withdrew, then came back to finish their task. This allowed those who were watching the signs time to escape. Those who were watching were not surprised.

In his second letter to this church in Thessalonica Paul continued to encourage them to remain faithful and watchful for the Lord's coming. We read in 2 Thessalonians 1:6-10, *"This will happen when the Lord Jesus is revealed from heaven in blazing fire with his powerful angels. He will punish those who do not know God and do not obey the gospel of our Lord Jesus. They will be punished with everlasting destruction and shut out from the presence of the Lord and from the majesty of his power on the day he comes to be glorified in his holy people and to be marveled at among all those who have believed. This includes you, because you believed our testimony to you."* Paul did not change the subject to some other coming. Earlier he told them not to worry about Christians who had died, or who would live beyond this time. Here he described the fate of those who had refused to believe and obey the gospel and accept the atonement sacrifice of the Lamb of God who could have taken away their sin. Just as the blessings of eternal life with Jesus await the saved, all who will ever live and refuse to obey the gospel have but one destiny. They will be punished with everlasting destruction and shut out from the presence of the Lord. Once again he was speaking of spiritual death the same as Adam and Eve experienced, being separated from God, banished from his presence.

As in every generation since, there were those in the first century who misunderstood the teaching of Jesus concerning his second coming and the day of the Lord. There were scoffers who had decided that, because it had been almost three decades since Jesus was crucified and he had not yet returned and destroyed the temple and its worship as he said he would, he must have been a false prophet. The Apostle Peter explained to the early Christians that God neither forgets nor fails to keep a promise, but would indeed come in that generation. (2 Peter 3) There were others who, perhaps in an effort to defend what they had believed and taught, were saying the day of the Lord had come and the resurrection of the dead had already taken place. Paul addressed this false doctrine in 2 Thessalonians 2:1-12:

> *"Concerning the coming of our Lord Jesus Christ and our being gathered to him, we ask you, brothers, not to become easily unsettled or alarmed by some prophecy, report or letter supposed to have come from us, saying that the day of the Lord has already come. Don't let anyone deceive you in any way, for that day will not come until the rebellion occurs and the man of lawlessness is revealed, the man doomed to destruction. He will oppose and will exalt himself over everything that is called God or is worshiped, so that he sets himself up in God's temple, proclaiming himself to be God.*
>
> *Don't you remember that when I was with you I used to tell you these things? And now you know what*

> *is holding him back, so that he may be revealed at the proper time. For the secret power of lawlessness is already at work; but the one who now holds it back will continue to do so till he is taken out of the way. And then the lawless one will be revealed, whom the Lord Jesus will overthrow with the breath of his mouth and destroy by the splendor of his coming. The coming of the lawless one will be in accordance with the work of Satan displayed in all kinds of counterfeit miracles, signs and wonders, and in every sort of evil that deceives those who are perishing. They perish because they refused to love the truth and so be saved. For this reason God sends them a powerful delusion so that they will believe the lie and so that all will be condemned who have not believed the truth but have delighted in wickedness."*

Paul identified two of these false teachers in 2 Timothy 2:17-18, *"Among them are Hymenaeus and Philetus, who have wandered away from the truth. They say that the resurrection has already taken place, and they destroy the faith of some."*

A third, and equally false, doctrine about the second coming and the day of the Lord is prevalent in the church today. Failing to properly understand the importance of the destruction of Jerusalem and its temple and the significance that event had in the atonement for sin and the establishment of the kingdom of heaven, many today believe and teach the day of the Lord and the resurrection have still not occurred. If Jesus and the apostles actually taught the coming of the Lord and the resurrection was to be the end of the entire universe, how could anyone in the first century have been deceived into believing it had already happened? The fact that Paul addressed this as a serious concern obviously meant neither he nor any first century Christians held this view of the second coming and the resurrection of the dead. They all understood exactly what Jesus had said about these things happening during their generation. And, just as Jesus had said would happen, there were false teachers, some claiming to be the "returned Christ" and others attempting to capitalize on their own imaginary version of his coming. Sound familiar?

Paul explained to the Christians in Thessalonica the Lord would not come until after the *"...man of lawlessness is revealed"* who will *"...set himself up in God's temple, proclaiming himself to be God."* Compare this to Daniel's prophecy of these same last days when he says in Daniel 9:26-27, *"The people of the ruler who will come will destroy the city and the sanctuary...And on a wing of the temple he will set up an abomination that causes desolation, until the end that is decreed is poured out on him."* We know for absolute certain from the teaching of Jesus in Matthew, Mark, and Luke that the *"...abomination of desolation spoken of by the prophet Daniel"* would immediately precede the destruction of the temple. The Apostle Paul could be speaking of no other event in history.

Paul did not identify by name the "man of lawlessness," but said the day of the Lord would not come until "the rebellion" occurred at which time this man would be revealed. In his historical account of the destruction of Jerusalem, Wars of the Jews, Josephus described the Jewish rebellion against Rome just prior to the city's destruction. According to this personal eyewitness of the events that unfolded, there was a man named John of Gischala who, with the help of the Idumaeans whose assistance he had requested, became the leader of the Jewish Zealots who were opposing the Roman occupation of Jerusalem. Ananus, the High Priest at the time, favored making peace with the Romans to spare the temple. Titus, the Roman General, intended to preserve the temple in Jerusalem as a monument to Roman conquest. Josephus personally pleaded with John of Gischala to surrender to the Romans.

Instead of listening to Ananus or Josephus, John of Gischala ordered the murder of the High Priest and set up his military defense in the temple. He deceived the Jews into believing they could defeat the Romans and brutally murdered anyone who attempted to escape. He melted down the temple utensils and defiled everything that was sacred to the Jews. He literally exalted himself *"...over everything that is called God or is worshiped"* and set himself up in God's temple in the place of God. It was his resistance that forced the Romans to destroy the temple. He was captured and condemned to life in prison by the Roman government. Paul had said Jesus would overthrow the man of lawlessness and destroy him *"...by the power of his coming."* That is exactly what happened.

At the time of Paul's writing, the fulfillment of these last days had not yet come. The man of lawlessness was yet to be revealed. The abomination of desolation set up in the temple was still a few years in their future. But it did come. It came before that generation passed away, just as Jesus said it would. Every writer of the New Testament is in total agreement on this subject. Some of it may be difficult to understand, especially for us Gentiles. But the second coming of Jesus Christ to affirm the completion of the atonement sacrifice, to fully accomplish the mystery of God, to bring an end to the Law, and to completely destroy the temple is a consistent, fully understandable teaching of God's word. All we have to do is study.

CHAPTER 9

The Teaching of James

James wrote a short letter to the Jewish Christians who had been dispersed because of persecution. In his opening salutation he said, *"James, a servant of God and of the Lord Jesus Christ, to the twelve tribes scattered among the nations: Greetings."*

The majority of his teaching had to do with daily Christian living. He encouraged them to be humble, not to show favoritism, to live their faith in actions, to watch their tongue, to seek the wisdom that is from above, to resist the Devil and the ways of the world, to not trust in earthly wealth, and to pray. The underlying theme of his message, which is seen in his opening and closing remarks, is patience in the face of suffering. While the principle of growth and maturity through adversity is true in any age, James had a special reason to write these words at that particular time.

Being Jews, his readers would have been very familiar with the prophecies in the Old Testament concerning "terrible times in the last days" of their nation. That they were also Christians meant they would also have been keenly aware of Jesus' teachings about those times coming during their generation. With that background James said in chapter 1:2-7, *"Consider it pure joy, my brothers, whenever you face trials of many kinds, because you know that the testing of your faith develops perseverance."* He went on to explain how that would ultimately lead to their becoming more mature in Christ, then in verse 12 he said, *"Blessed is the man who perseveres under trial, because when he has stood the test, he will receive the crown of life that God has promised to those who love him."*

James returned to this same subject in his final chapter. *"Be patient, then, brothers, until the Lord's coming. See how the farmer waits for the land to yield its valuable crop and how patient he is for the autumn and spring rains. You too, be patient and stand firm, because the Lord's coming is near. Don't grumble against each other, brothers, or you will be judged. The Judge is standing at the door"* (James 5:7-9)!

He then gave examples of patience in suffering. *"Brothers, as an example of patience in the face of suffering, take the prophets who spoke in the name of the Lord. As you know, we consider blessed those who have persevered. You have heard of Job's perseverance and have seen what the Lord finally brought about. The Lord is full of compassion and mercy"* (James 5:10-11).

James said:

1. Be patient until the Lord's coming.
2. The Lord's coming is near.
3. The judge is standing at the door.

Such language was very familiar to those Jewish Christians concerning the coming judgment of God on a nation. Remember, as previously noted concerning the consummation of the ages, what Isaiah said about the approaching judgment of God against Babylon. *"See, the day of the Lord is coming—a cruel day, with wrath and fierce anger—to make the land desolate and destroy the sinners within it. The stars of heaven and their constellations will not show their light. The rising sun will be darkened and the moon will not give its light. I will punish the world for its evil, the wicked for their sins. I will put an end to the arrogance of the haughty and will humble the pride of the ruthless"* (Isaiah 13:9-11). They had read dozens of similar passages of Scripture their entire lives.

James' point was for those first century Christians to be patient because *"the Lord's coming was near."* The message was not to be patient because we have no idea when the Lord will come, rather just the opposite, to be patient because the Lord's coming was SOON…at hand. That is exactly what the text says. Compare the words James used to those of Jesus in Matthew 24:33-34, *"Even so, when you see all these things, you know that it is* ***near, right at the door.*** *I tell you the truth, this generation will certainly not pass away until all these things have happened."*

The context, as seen in James 5, was the persecution the saints were facing in "the last days." They were living in "the last days." The Lord was not going to let them remain in their pain and suffering. He was going to return just as he had promised and fulfill all prophecies and bring the kingdom to fruition. The point of the farmer analogy was to look at the signs. They knew to wait patiently for the fall and spring rains and the harvest would come in just as sure as the sun rises and sets. In the same way, the first century disciples were told to "watch for the signs" of the Lord's coming. Yes, they were facing many trials and temptations at that time, but the Lord was faithful. He had not abandoned his promises. Just as surely as the farmer knows the rains will produce a crop, they could depend upon Jesus to come as he had promised to put an end to their suffering. And just a few short years later the very last words Jesus said to anyone on earth were, *"Yes, I am coming soon"* (Revelation 22:20).

There has been considerable effort by many religious teachers to ascribe various meanings to some words in the Scriptural texts to support a future, universe-ending interpretation. For instance, some versions of the Bible translate Revelation 22:20 to say, *"Yes, I am coming quickly."* They explain that "quickly" means his coming will be swift, but does not necessarily have an associated historical date. Once again, let's examine the Scriptures to see if these things are true.

There are three different Greek terms often associated with the Lord's coming. These same words are also used in many other passages of Scripture. It is sometimes helpful to look at the words and the ways in which they are used in context to get a better understanding of the intended meaning.

1. *Engus* – translated "near" or "at hand"
2. *Tachu* – translated "quickly" or "soon"
3. *Aiphnidios* (adjective) or *exaiphnes* (adverb) – translated "suddenly"

Below is a sampling of Bible passages that use the word "engus."

Matthew 3:2, *"Repent, for the kingdom of heaven is* ***near.****"*

John 6:4, *"The Jewish Passover Feast was* ***near.****"*

Matthew 26:18, *"Go into the city to a certain man and tell him, 'The Teacher says: My appointed time is* ***near****. I am going to celebrate the Passover with my disciples at your house.' "*

Matthew 24:32, *"Now learn this lesson from the fig tree: As soon as its twigs get tender and its leaves come out, you know that summer is* ***near****."*

Matthew 24:33-34, *"Even so, when you see all these things, you know that it is* ***near, right at the door****. I tell you the truth, this generation will certainly not pass away until all these things have happened."*

Luke 21:20, *"When you see Jerusalem being surrounded by armies, you will know that its desolation is* ***near****."*

1 Peter 4:7, *"The end of all things is **near**."*

James 5:8, *"The Lord's coming is **near**."*

Revelation 1:3, *"Blessed is the one who reads the words of this prophecy, and blessed are those who hear it and take to heart what is written in it, because the time is **near**."*

Revelation 22:10, *"Do not seal up the words of the prophecy of this book, because the time is **near**."*

The word "near" carries the same meaning in each of these verses. The event under discussion was close at hand, not in the distant future. Revelation 22:10 is particularly apparent when compared with Daniel 8:26 where the prophet was told, *"The vision of the evenings and mornings that has been given you is true, but seal up the vision, for it concerns the distant future."* Daniel's prophecy would not be fulfilled for 490 years. That was not near. John was specifically told not to seal his vision because the time was **near**. It makes absolutely no sense that God would tell Daniel something almost 500 years away was the distant future and tell John something thousands of years off was near. Whatever God was revealing to John had to be coming soon…in that generation.

The second term "*tachu*" is found in the following verses.

Matthew 5:25, *"Make friends **quickly** with your accuser, while you are going with him to court, lest your accuser hand you over to the judge, and the judge to the guard, and you be put in prison."*

John 11:31, *"When the Jews who were with her in the house, consoling her, saw Mary rise **quickly** and go out, they followed her, supposing that she was going to the tomb to weep there."*

> Matthew 28:7, *"Then go* ***quickly*** *and tell his disciples: 'He has risen from the dead and is going ahead of you into Galilee. There you will see him.' Now I have told you."*

> Revelation 22:20, *"Yes, I am coming* ***quickly.****"*

While this term indicates something to be done rapidly, it does not mean it will be done in the distant future. It carries with it a sense of urgency. One can hardly say the "coming" to which John refers in Revelation might be thousands of years in the future and be true to the original meaning.

The Greek adverb "aphno" or "*exaiphnes*" or the adjective form "aiphnidios, occurs in the following passages.

> Luke 2:13, *"And* ***suddenly*** *(exaiphnes) there was with the angel a multitude of the heavenly host praising God and saying…"*

> Acts 2:2, *"And* ***suddenly*** *(aiphnidios) a sound came from heaven like the rush of a mighty wind, and it filled all the house where they were sitting."*

> Acts 9:3, *"Now as he journeyed he approached Damascus, and* ***suddenly*** *(exaiphnes) a light from heaven flashed about him."*

> Luke 21:34, *"But pay attention to yourselves that your hearts never become weighed down with overeating and heavy drinking and anxieties of life, and* ***suddenly*** *(aiphnidios) that day be instantly upon you."*

> 1 Thessalonians 5:3, *"While people are saying, 'Peace and safety,' destruction will come on them*

> ***suddenly*** *(aiphnidios), as labor pains on a pregnant woman, and they will not escape."*

This term does refer to something that happens unexpectedly. It does not mean there are no signs that it is coming. The analogy of labor pains is the given example. A woman who is pregnant certainly knows the pains are coming, and she knows approximately when by counting the months. She does not know the exact day and hour they will begin. That is precisely what Jesus said about his coming and the destruction of the temple. He gave them the signs for which to watch. He told them it would be in that generation. But he also said they would not know the day or hour it would actually happen.

It is interesting to note all of these terms are used in connection with the "last days" coming of the Lord and the consummation of the ages. That day would come suddenly, so the disciples and early Christians were told to watch and wait. It would also come quickly, rapidly. But it was also near at the time of their writings. No possible Biblical definition of these terms allows any interpretation of the coming of the great day of the Lord beyond the generation in which the apostles lived.

Not only James, but all the New Testament writers believed the Lord's coming was going to happen "soon." Jesus Christ said, *"This generation will not end until all these things have happened."* One of "these things" was the Son of Man coming in the clouds. The language cannot be mistaken. Since they were divinely inspired by the Holy Spirit, the belief in an imminent coming must have also been "Holy Spirit inspired." Yet, according to many modern theologians, Jesus has still not come. Were the early Christians mistaken in their belief? Did the Holy Spirit misguide the writers of Scripture?

Atheists are quick to point out the inconsistency in our theology and denounce Christianity as a false religion and Jesus as a fake. Even many Christian writers publically say the apostles misunderstood Jesus and were mistaken in their belief about the timing of his coming. In his essay, *The World's Last Night*, the renowned Christian writer C. S. Lewis wrote the following in 1960:

> "Say what you like, the apocalyptic beliefs of the first Christians have been proven to be false. It is clear from the New Testament that they all expected the Second Coming in their own lifetime. And, worse still, they had a reason, and one you will find very embarrassing. Their Master had told them so. He shared, and indeed created, their delusion. He said in so many words, *'this generation shall not pass till all these things be done.'* And he was wrong. He clearly knew no more about the end of the world than anyone else. It is certainly the most embarrassing verse in the Bible."

Lewis is correct in his assessment of what Jesus said and what his disciples believed. Eschatology is no insignificant subject in the Scriptures. The imminent return of Jesus is a consistent, recurring theme throughout the entire New Testament. The doctrine of a "delayed coming" that is so prevalent today has done more damage to the believability of the Christian message than perhaps any other false doctrine. Those who espouse this view of Jesus' future return are completely helpless to explain the inconsistencies between their teaching and what the Scriptures actually say. Many Christians, in utter confusion, have completely abandoned any study of these end time events.

The confusion does not lie with the Scriptures. The Lord's coming, about which James and the others wrote, is not difficult to understand if we will simply believe what the Bible says. James was not mistaken about the timing of the Lord's coming. Jesus did know what he was talking about. The embarrassment is for the scoffers and false teachers of the first century, for C. S. Lewis, and all the others who proclaim something other than what the Bible so clearly teaches.

CHAPTER 10

The Teaching of John

Four times in Scripture John is referred to as the apostle whom Jesus loved. While Jesus certainly loved all the disciples, John had a very close, personal bond with the Master. Perhaps because of his special relationship, the writings of this apostle stress the personal relationship God (Father, Son, and Holy Spirit) wants to have with his people. John is the author of five New Testament books, the Gospel of John, 1 John, 2 John, 3 John, and The Revelation of Jesus Christ.

In his gospel John did not give a detailed account of Jesus' conversation predicting the destruction of Jerusalem and its temple, but his writings are obviously consistent with the other gospel writers since he was inspired by the same Holy Spirit. While John certainly understood the importance of the events of the "last days" in which he and the other apostles were living, he puts these events, the consummation of the ages, the fulfillment of the atonement sacrifice, and the establishment of the eternal kingdom in the context of their resulting effect for everyone who believes to have eternal life with God.

It was John who wrote, *"For God so loved the world that he gave his one and only Son, that whoever believes in him shall not perish but have eternal life. For God did not send his Son into the world to condemn the world, but to save the world through him"* (John 3:16-17). The message of the Bible from beginning to end is about life and death. Eternal death is the unavoidable result of sin, but eternal life is possible in Jesus Christ. In John's writings we see the final events that brought eternal life to fruition in the kingdom of heaven.

John 3:35-36 says, *"The Father loves the Son and has placed everything in his hands. Whoever believes in the Son has eternal life, but whoever rejects the Son* (remains in sin) *will not see life, for God's wrath* (death) *remains on him."* We are constantly reminded throughout Scripture that the problem facing mankind is spiritual death, eternal separation from the presence of God, because of sin. And as this same writer in 1 John 1:8 stated, *"If we claim to be without sin, we deceive ourselves and the truth is not in us."* The great mystery of God that was being revealed by John, and every writer of the Bible before him, was how God would redeem man from the penalty of sin and bring everyone together in one eternal kingdom.

For centuries the prophets foretold of this pre-planned, yet future event. The physical nation of Israel was a prototype of the spiritual kingdom that was to come. When the time was right and everything was in place, Jesus was born into the world for the final stage in God's grand mysterious plan. God entrusted his only Son, living in the world as a human being, to complete his plan of redemption. It was his ONLY plan! John says the Father *"...placed everything in his* (Jesus) *hands."* What an awesome responsibility he had.

Once Jesus fulfilled his mission, the plan would be complete, the mystery revealed, the atonement finished, and he could deliver to his Father the kingdom that had been planned from the beginning. In 1 Corinthians 15:20-28 the Apostle Paul wrote, *"But Christ has indeed been raised from the dead, the firstfruits of those who have fallen asleep. For since death came through a man, the resurrection of the dead comes also through a man. For as in Adam all die, so in Christ all will be made alive. But each in his own turn: Christ, the firstfruits; then, when he comes, those who belong to him.*

Then the end will come, when he hands over the kingdom to God the Father after he has destroyed all dominion, authority and power. For he must reign until he has put all his enemies under his feet. The last enemy to be destroyed is death. For he 'has put everything under his feet.' Now when it says that 'everything' has been put under him, it is clear that this does not include God himself, who put everything under Christ. When he has done this, then the Son himself will be made subject to him who put everything under him, so that God may be all in all."

The destruction of sin and death, its dominion, authority, and power was in the hands of Jesus. The establishment of God's eternal kingdom depended on Jesus' completion of his redemptive task. When it was complete, Jesus handed it back to the Father…It is finished! This is not some prediction of the end of the universe, it is the fulfillment of God's eternal plan of salvation.

We must never forget that in the context of redemption, spiritual death, separation from the presence of God, was the issue. In John 5:24 the beloved apostle records the words of Jesus, *"I tell you the truth, whoever hears my word and believes him who sent me has eternal life and will not be condemned; he has crossed over from death to life. I tell you the truth, a time is coming and has now come when the dead will hear the voice of the Son of God and those who hear will live. For as the Father has life in himself, so he has granted the Son to have life in himself. And he has given him authority to judge because he is the Son of Man. Do not be amazed at this, for a time is coming when all who are in their graves will hear his voice and come out—those who have done good will rise to live, and those who have done evil will rise to be condemned. By myself I can do nothing; I judge only as I hear, and my judgment is just, for I seek not to please myself but him who sent me."*

When would all those who were in the grave hear the voice of the Son of God and come out to receive their reward (or condemnation)? The clear answer comes from the prophet Daniel and Jesus' explanation of his prophecy. Daniel 12:1-2, *"There will be a time of distress such as has not happened from the beginning of nations until then. But at that time your people—everyone whose name is found written in the book—will be delivered. Multitudes who sleep in the dust of the earth will awake: some to everlasting life, others to shame and everlasting contempt."*

Jesus came into the world to fulfill the promises God had already made through the Old Testament Scriptures, not to make new promises. In Luke 24:44 he said, *"Everything must be fulfilled that is written about me in the Law of Moses, the Prophets and the Psalms."* At least forty-seven times the New Testament specifically says he came to fulfill the Scriptures. That was his mission. And when did Jesus say he would fulfill the promise God made to Daniel?

Matthew 24:15-21, *"So when you see standing in the holy place 'the abomination that causes desolation,' spoken of through the prophet Daniel—let the reader understand...For then there will be great distress, unequaled from the beginning of the world until now—and never to be equaled again."* Jesus said this *"...time of distress such as has not happened from the beginning of nations until then"* which Daniel predicted, and at which time *"...multitudes who sleep in the dust of the earth will awake: some to everlasting life, others to shame and everlasting contempt"* would happen at the same time Jerusalem and its temple would be destroyed. In case there is any lingering doubt as to Jesus' meaning, consider Luke's explanation to us Gentiles in Luke 21:20, *"When you see Jerusalem being surrounded by armies, you will know that its desolation is near."*

John 6:39-40 says, *"And this is the will of him who sent me, that I shall lose none of all that he has given me, but raise them up at the last day. For my Father's will is that everyone who looks to the Son and believes in him shall have eternal life, and I will raise him up at the last day."*

Jesus was not introducing here a different day when people

would be raised from death. This was the same day he had spoken of in chapter 5 when *"...all who are in their graves will hear his voice and come out."* Because of sin, death held absolute control over every person who ever lived. There was no escape. Once the atonement sacrifice was complete, death no longer had any hold over people. On that day Jesus, through his blood sacrifice for sin, destroyed the power and hold of death. There was a "last day" of the power of sin and death. On "that day" the grave could hold people no longer. Once death was destroyed, there was nothing to hold people, so they were assigned their eternal destiny by God. Those who had been righteous were cleansed of their sin by Jesus' blood and arose to everlasting life. Those who rejected God arose to everlasting contempt, banished forever from his presence.

All Christians accept as truth the sacrifice of Jesus on the cross as our Passover Lamb and our atonement offering for sin. It is easy to concentrate on the death of Jesus and overlook the other aspects of these rituals. There was more to both the Passover and the Atonement than killing the sacrificial animal. Once the animal had been killed, there were specific instructions given about the blood.

In the case of the Passover, the blood from the slain animal had to be taken and brushed over the doorposts. When the death angel came through Egypt, he was not looking for a carcass, nor was he looking for the place where the lamb was slain. He was looking at the doorposts of the houses. If the blood was not on the door, someone in that house died. It would have done no good to sacrifice a lamb if the blood was not subsequently used specifically as prescribed by God.

Similarly, the atonement sacrifice included much more than just the killing of an animal. The blood of the atonement sacrifice had to be collected by the High Priest and taken into the Holy of Holies inside the temple. There it was sprinkled over the Mercy Seat on top of the Ark of the Covenant which contained the tablets of the Law. Not until the blood was sprinkled on the Mercy Seat was there forgiveness of sin. The same is true concerning Jesus' crucifixion. His death on the cross was certainly the sacrifice for our sin. But the atonement ritual had not changed. After he was slain, his blood had to be taken into the Holy of Holies (in this case the eternal one in heaven) and sprinkled on the Great Mercy Seat before the Throne of Almighty God. Until the blood was sprinkled, there was no forgiveness.

That did not happen the day he died. We learned from Hebrews, before making atonement for the people, the High Priest first had to make an offering for himself, and his first appearing from behind the veil confirmed that God had accepted him as High Priest. Once he was accepted, then he could offer the blood sacrifice for the people. Following his death on the cross, Jesus first had to come back from the grave before he could serve as our High Priest. Since there was no sin offering for him, his resurrection (first appearing) proved he was the sinless Son of God. He was made our Great High Priest following his resurrection. Paul said in Romans 1:4 Jesus *"…was declared with power to be the Son of God by his resurrection from the dead."* The Hebrew writer said Jesus became our High Priest *"…not on the basis of a regulation as to his ancestry but on the basis of the power of an indestructible life"* (Hebrews 7:16).

Once Jesus was raised from the dead, declared with power to be the Son of God and our Great High Priest, there was still the blood requirement for the atonement of the people. When Jesus ascended to heaven, he went into the Holy of Holies as our newly appointed High Priest to sprinkle his own blood on the Mercy Seat of God's throne. Forgiveness was made possible by Jesus' death on the cross, but was not complete until the atonement ritual was finished in heaven. Once everything required by the law was finished, the atonement was complete and death was destroyed. The sign of his "second appearing" to confirm God's acceptance of the blood sacrifice for our sin was the removal of the earthly temple in Jerusalem. This makes perfect sense in the context of the atonement. Neither animal sacrifices nor the physical temple in which their blood was sprinkled were any longer necessary. Atonement had been made in heaven, no more need for an earthly temple. The destruction of the one confirmed the completion of the other. Since death no longer had control, those who had died were raised. In addition, since death no longer exists for the redeemed, when we die we go to be with the Lord forever.

This is precisely what the Apostle Paul explained to the Christians in Thessalonica who were concerned about those who had died before the Lord's coming. On that day they would be raised to be with Jesus. He went on to explain that those of us who live beyond that day, when we die physically, will go immediately to be with the Lord forever. As Jesus said in John 5:24, *"I tell you the truth, whoever hears my word and believes him who sent me has eternal life and will not be condemned; he has crossed over from death to life."* NO MORE DEATH!

So we are not surprised by what Jesus said in John 6:48-51, *"I am the bread of life. Your forefathers ate the manna in the desert, yet they died. But here is the bread that comes down from heaven, which a man may eat and not die. I am the living bread that came down from heaven. If anyone eats of this bread, he will live forever. This bread is my flesh, which I will give for the life of the world."* He speaks in chapter 12:30-33 of how his death would result in judgment, the destruction of Satan's power and salvation. " *'Now is the time for judgment on this world; now the prince of this world will be driven out. But I, when I am lifted up from the earth, will draw all men to myself.' He said this to show the kind of death he was going to die."*

In the twentieth chapter of his gospel John recorded the events of the morning of Jesus' resurrection from the grave. Several disciples had gone to see the empty tomb and eventually left to go back to their homes. Mary remained behind; and was crying. She explained to a man whom she assumed to be the gardener about the missing body and asked where they had taken it.

Picking up the conversation in verse 16, *"Jesus said to her, 'Mary.' She turned toward him and cried out in Aramaic, 'Rabboni!' (which means Teacher). Jesus said, 'Do not hold on to me, for I have not yet returned to the Father. Go instead to my brothers and tell them, I am returning to my Father and your Father, to my God and your God.' "* Jesus was explaining to her that he had not returned from the grave to stay with them physically on the earth. He had to return to the Father to complete the atonement sacrifice as High Priest, according to the pattern given to Moses.

During the course of the next fifty days he appeared to hundreds of disciples to prove that he had indeed come back from the grave. As we have already pointed out, the atonement sacrifice was carried out in two steps. Jesus' appearance following his resurrection not only proved he had overcome death, but that he was acceptable as High Priest to offer the blood sacrifice for our sins. This blood offering inside the Holy of Holies in heaven, the very presence of God, was what Jesus still had to do to fulfill the atonement ritual. He would not stay on the earth in his physical body, but would *"...appear a second time to bring salvation to those who are waiting for him"* (Hebrews 9:28). Had Jesus remained on the earth in his physical body following his personal resurrection from the grave the atonement sacrifice would have been left half completed. If he has still not "appeared" the second time, we are left waiting on confirmation of our salvation.

In the final chapter of his gospel John recorded a conversation he and Peter had with Jesus. After they had shared a meal, the Lord asked Peter three times if he loved him and three times told him to *"...feed my sheep."* Jesus then proceeded to tell Peter how he was going to die as a martyr. Joining the conversation in verse

20, *"Peter turned and saw that the disciple whom Jesus loved was following them. (This was the one who had leaned back against Jesus at the supper and had said, 'Lord, who is going to betray you?') When Peter saw him, he asked, 'Lord, what about him?' Jesus answered, 'If I want him to remain alive until I return, what is that to you? You must follow me.' Because of this, the rumor spread among the brothers that this disciple would not die. But Jesus did not say that he would not die; he only said, 'If I want him to remain alive until I return, what is that to you?' "*

Jesus had plans for each of his apostles. Peter was the one selected to preach the very first gospel sermon and introduce the kingdom of heaven to the world (Acts 2). He went on to become a great teacher in the early church and write two books of the New Testament. He also died a martyr's death, just as Jesus had predicted. However, Jesus had other plans for John. He was not making a casual, impossible remark about John remaining alive until he returned. That was the divine plan. John was the apostle selected to write the final chapter in God's revelation and live to witness the "great and notable day of the Lord," the "consummation of the ages," the "last day" of the "last days." His would be the last words of inspired Scripture ever given to man, the final summary of what had been prophesied throughout the ages and how it was about to be fulfilled.

Before he was given the final revelation, John wrote three very short letters to Christians living at that time. In 1 John 2:18 he said, *"Dear children, this is the last hour; and as you have heard that the antichrist is coming, even now many antichrists have come. This is how we know it is the last hour."* Being well acquainted with what Jesus had said about the events of the "last days" and the coming persecution and destruction of the temple, he wanted to make sure everyone understood "this was that" which Jesus had predicted. He recognized his time as "the last hour" of the old Jewish world and its temple worship. In verse 28 he says, *"And now, dear children, continue in him, so that when he appears we may be confident and unashamed before him at his coming."*

In chapter 4 he gave the same warning that Jesus gave years earlier to the apostles. *"Dear friends, do not believe every spirit, but test the spirits to see whether they are from God, because many false prophets have gone out into the world...This is the spirit of the antichrist, which you have heard is coming and even now is already in the world."* Where is the Scriptural justification for a future coming of some "antichrist?" Jesus said this would happen during that generation. John said the antichrist was already in the world when he wrote this letter. It would appear televangelists continue to misread the Scriptures. The sad truth is millions of Christians continue to be deceived by false prophets, defrauded out of millions of dollars and the assurance of a totally faithful Father God.

Section Three

Understanding the Revelation

CHAPTER 11

What Is It All About?

The last book in the Bible has been the subject of much debate and wild speculation for generations. It is a prophetic book, containing imagery that is difficult to fully understand. As a result this great book is the most misquoted and misapplied of all of God's word. Much of it is used to support any number of speculative theories about the "second coming" of Christ, the end of the world, and a host of other events. The following appeared in an article published on the internet (www.martinkeitel.net) describing the book of Revelation:

A book from almost 2000 years in the past...Yet it contains detailed information about

- The Iraq War
- The New York terrorist strike, Sept 11, 2001
- Modern war technology
- The global political situation in the beginning of the 3rd millennium
- The natural disasters of 2003 - 2005 and onward
- The fall of Capitalism and materialism

The complete fallacy of such an opinion of the Revelation should be so apparent that it would be dismissed without consideration. If the above were true, no Christian prior to this century, especially those to whom this book was addressed, could have possibly understood what John wrote. Of course, in virtually every generation for the past few centuries, one could have read very similar statements, only the events have been continually updated to match current news. This would be laughable if it were not for the fact that it is God's word being maligned and so many people, because of their own lack of knowledge, actually believe these fabricated stories.

Was it possible for the Christians in Corinth to understand the letters Paul wrote to them? Did Theophilus understand the Gospel of Luke? How can anyone seriously claim the Holy Spirit directed the writers of the New Testament to specifically address letters to people who had no chance of understanding their meaning? The doctrine that we are living in the "last days" and the Lord will return at any moment is perhaps the most illogical and misguided interpretation of Scripture imaginable. If this teaching is true it means the Holy Spirit deliberately deceived those first century Christians, and every succeeding generation, into believing the Lord's coming was soon. It also means Revelation, as well as large parts of other letters, could not possibly have been understood by the people to whom they were addressed.

The "**soon** coming of Jesus" teaching gets more absurd with every passing generation. To any people of any generation, 2,000 years and counting is not *soon*. If Jesus lied in Matthew 24:34, why should anyone believe John 3:16? If the Bible has deceived Christians of every generation into believing something that did not happen, why believe any of it? And what has this doctrine done to the credibility of preachers of the Gospel? Every one of them espousing this message has been proven to be a false teacher. Not a single Christian teacher before us who confidently taught this message understood Bible prophecy. And…since the same message will still be taught twenty-five years from now and a hundred years from then, only applied to a new set of world events, that means every Christian teaching about this subject today is wrong.

Please consider the following inescapable reality. If the prophesies in Revelation concern some future events, there is no possible way of understanding these Scriptures. Time will prove this generation, and every succeeding generation wrong. Eventually, to every sound-thinking individual, the Christian message becomes nothing more than rehashed delusions. The modern message of the soon coming of Jesus is perhaps the most damaging false doctrine afflicting the church because it destroys the credibility of the Scriptures and undermines the faithfulness of God. The Bible is not a book of false prophesies. The Holy Spirit did not delude the apostles and writers of the New Testament. The Revelation of Jesus Christ was understood by the first century Christians, and it can be understood today.

So what is this book about? When did (or will) the events described in this book happen? Can we really understand it? The answer to those and other questions depend, to a large extent, on how we view the Scriptures and whether or not we are willing to spend the necessary time and effort to comprehend them. The purpose of this writing is to encourage the study of God's Revelation and is based on the absolute belief that the Bible is the complete, infallible, divinely revealed word of God. It is also based on the belief that, through a careful examination of his divine will, we can understand not only the overall meaning of John's Revelation but also the time in history to which it is referring.

As we look in depth at the Revelation of Jesus Christ, let's remember the three fundamental rules of interpretation:

1. **Let the Bible interpret itself.**
2. **Keep Scripture in its context.**
3. **Understand the historical time frame.**

Before we begin the actual study of the text of the Revelation it is important to understand the significance of the time in history that John lived. He, along with Jesus and the other apostles, lived during the Biblical "last days" of the nation of Israel just prior to its destruction in A. D. 70. He was sitting with Jesus on the Mount of Olives and heard the Master's explanation of the impending calamities that were going to befall Jerusalem and its sacred temple (Matthew 24-25, Mark 13, Luke 21). Approximately thirty-five years later, John was the last surviving apostle and was given, by divine revelation, the final chapter of God's will for mankind; the last word on the end time events and the consummation of the ages.

As we shall soon discover, the book of Revelation is about the judgment. Since the Almighty is a just God, his divine nature demands an accounting of those who are subject to him. The very essence of law demands judgment and consequences. Sin is a transgression of God's law (Romans 4:15) and the consequence of sin is eternal death (Romans 6:23). Since every person sins, we are all subject to his judgment and wrath. That is why the Hebrew writer said we are all destined to die and then face the judgment (Hebrews 9:27). Yet God, in his infinite mercy, had a plan that would meet the demands of justice and provide a way of redemption for fallen mankind. After thousands of years of preparation, at the time of John's writing the stage is finally set for this final scene. As with everything else in God's plan, it was all contingent upon the atonement sacrifice of his only begotten Son.

In the very first chapter of Revelation we learn the purpose of John's letter was to explain how Jesus fulfilled all the prophesies of Scripture to accomplish the great mystery of God to redeem mankind. Perhaps the biggest problem facing people today in studying Revelation is our lack of knowledge of these very prophesies the book was written to explain. For that reason, we will begin with a brief review of four of the books in the Old Testament that contain many of these prophesies.

CHAPTER 12

The Prophecy of Isaiah

Isaiah lived and prophesied from 740-681 B.C. during the days of the expansion of the Assyrian Empire and approximately 125 years before the Babylonians destroyed Jerusalem in 586 B.C. His prophesies concerned the future of Judah and Jerusalem and how God would ultimately deliver on his promise of salvation through their descendants. He predicted events that were to happen over the next 800 years that would culminate in the establishment of the eternal kingdom of heaven with Jesus Christ sitting on David's throne forever.

The major theme throughout the book is the sin of mankind, resulting in the judgment of God, followed by the promise of redemption. This is the story of the Bible from Genesis through Revelation. How God was going to bring about eternal redemption was the great mystery of the ages. The kingdom of Israel was set up by God to serve as a prototype of the coming kingdom of heaven. Comprehending how the major events of the kingdom of Israel, Jerusalem, and the temple were prefigures to the eventual establishment of the kingdom of heaven is absolutely crucial to properly understanding and interpreting the New Testament, especially the book of Revelation.

Isaiah spoke of three catastrophic events in Israel's history as it related to the kingdom of Israel and accomplishing of the mystery of God. The first was the time during which he lived. Although the kingdom began with King Saul from the tribe of Benjamin, he was selected because of the people's rejection of God's will. He failed to follow God's laws and the throne was taken from him and given to David, a descendant of Judah. From that time on it was known in Scripture as the throne of David. After the death of Solomon the kingdom was divided between Israel and Judah. At the beginning of Isaiah's ministry all of Israel was threatened by the advancing Assyrian Empire. God's call for repentance was ignored by the Northern kingdom and in 722 B.C. it fell into the hands of the Assyrians, never to be restored (Isaiah 8).

Seemingly faced with a similar fate as their brothers to the north, the southern King Hezekiah remained faithful to God and prayed for the Lord's deliverance and God answered his prayer and spared the kingdom of Judah (Isaiah 36-37). This was a graphic demonstration of the judgment of God against the unfaithful and his divine forgiveness and mercy extended to those who repent and trust in him.

But Judah would not remain faithful forever. Isaiah also predicted a second catastrophe that would befall what was left of the kingdom of Israel. This would come at the hands of the Babylonians.

> *"Then Isaiah said to Hezekiah, 'Hear the word of the Lord Almighty: The time will surely come when everything in your palace, and all that your fathers have stored up until this day, will be carried off to Babylon. Nothing will be left, says the Lord. And some of your descendants, your own flesh and blood who will be born to you, will be taken away, and they will become eunuchs in the palace of the king of Babylon' "* (Isaiah 39:5-7).

However, God would not abandon Israel or forget his promise that the throne of David would be established forever in an everlasting kingdom. Israel would eventually be resettled in

Jerusalem and Judea in three stages beginning under the leadership of Zerubbabel in 538 B.C., a second group coming with Ezra in 458 B.C. and the last group with Nehemiah in 432 B.C. The Jews were hopeful that this would be followed by the coming of the Messiah and the establishment of an eternal kingdom of Israel. They were both right…and very wrong.

Woven throughout Isaiah's prophesies of these first two major events in Israel's history was a third time the physical nation would be faced with catastrophic destruction by a foreign invader. This would come at the hands of the Roman Empire and result in the final destruction of Jerusalem, the total annihilation of the temple and the earthly kingdom of Israel from the planet. What the Jews did not understand was the spiritual nature of their kingdom. The Messiah would come, but not to set up an earthly reign on an earthly throne in the physical city of Jerusalem as they thought. He would come to make atonement for sin after which the headquarters of the kingdom would be in heaven. David's throne would finally be secure forever where no foreign army could invade. This would be the final event in the consummation of the ages, the establishment of the kingdom of heaven, where Jesus, a descendant of David, the Lion of the Tribe of Judah, would reign as King of Kings and Lord of Lords forever. This eternal kingdom would include all nations of the earth, not just Israel. This was Israel's calling from the time of Abraham forward.

This overriding theme of redemption in Jesus Christ is clearly seen in all of Isaiah's prophesies. Isaiah 1:1 says:

> *"The vision concerning Judah and Jerusalem that Isaiah son of Amoz saw during the reigns of Uzziah, Jotham, Ahaz and Hezekiah, kings of Judah. Hear, O heavens! Listen, O earth! For the Lord has spoken: I reared children and brought them up, but they have rebelled against me."*

He began by stating his vision concerned Judah and Jerusalem. As a nation they had been born and raised up by God, but had rebelled. In verses 6-7 he described the extent of their sin.

> *"From the sole of your foot to the top of your head there is no soundness— only wounds and welts and open sores, not cleansed or bandaged or soothed with oil. Your country is desolate, your cities burned with fire; your fields are being stripped by foreigners right before you, laid waste as when overthrown by strangers."*

As is typical in Old Testament prophesies, the results of sin were described both in personal terms and in symbolic language that related to the physical nation itself: desolate country, cities burned, fields bare, overthrown by foreigners.

In verse 18 of this first chapter we see the promise of redemption.

> *"Come now, let us reason together, says the Lord. Though your sins are like scarlet, they shall be as white as snow; though they are red as crimson, they shall be like wool."*

God would not forsake his people, regardless of the extent of their sin, but would eventually provide forgiveness. He would also not forget his promise that their kingdom would be an everlasting one. In the closing two verses he said,

> *"Afterward you will be called the City of Righteousness, the Faithful City. Zion will be redeemed with justice, her penitent ones with righteousness."*

The second chapter further underscores God's ultimate faithfulness to his promise of an eternal kingdom and looks toward its fulfillment.

> *"This is what Isaiah son of Amoz saw concerning Judah and Jerusalem: In the last days the mountain of the Lord's temple will be established as chief among the mountains; it will be raised above the hills, and all nations will stream to it. Many peoples will come and say, 'Come, let us go up to the mountain of the Lord, to the house of the God of Jacob. He will teach us his ways, so that we may walk in his paths.' The law will go out from Zion, the word of the Lord from Jerusalem. He will judge between the nations and will settle disputes for many peoples. They will beat their swords into plowshares and their spears into pruning hooks. Nation will not take up sword against nation, nor will they train for war anymore. Come, O house of Jacob, let us walk in the light of the Lord"* (Isaiah 2:1-5).

The physical kingdom was not going to last forever. It would be eventually destroyed. But during its "last days" God would establish a "new" kingdom that would never end. It would not be subject to earthly wars, famine, pestilence, etc. because it would be a heavenly kingdom. The plague of sin would not afflict this kingdom because there would be no more sin. He warned that this glorious day of atonement and salvation would also be a day of judgment and wrath on the disobedient as well as a time of trial for all who lived on the earth. The "day of the Lord" was a major theme throughout the prophesies, indicating a time when God would bring his divine judgment against nations.

> *"The Lord Almighty has a day in store for all the proud and lofty, for all that is exalted…The arrogance of man will be brought low and the pride of men humbled; the Lord alone will be exalted in*

> *that day, and the idols will totally disappear. Men will flee to caves in the rocks and to holes in the ground from dread of the Lord and the splendor of his majesty, when he rises to shake the earth"* (Isaiah 2:12-22).

The shaking of the earth was also a figure of speech referring to the results of God's judgment. Isaiah predicted the first "shaking of the earth" when God brought about the destruction of Jerusalem in 586 B.C. by the Babylonians. This event prefigured the final destruction of Jerusalem and its temple which was also predicted by Haggai and the writer of Hebrews (Haggai 2:6, Hebrews 12:26-29). Jesus also discussed with his apostles in Matthew 24, Mark 13, and Luke 21 this coming time when God would "shake the earth". He cautioned those who were watching and recognized the signs to run to the hills and take cover in the rocks to escape the destruction that would come on Jerusalem. Jesus used the same language found in Isaiah and the other prophesies of this event.

As Isaiah predicted hardships that were coming on Judah and Jerusalem because of their rebellion against God, he continually reminded them of a coming Redeemer.

> *"In that day the Branch of the Lord will be beautiful and glorious, and the fruit of the land will be the pride and glory of the survivors in Israel. Those who are left in Zion, who remain in Jerusalem, will be called holy, all who are recorded among the living in Jerusalem. The Lord will wash away the filth of the women of Zion; he will cleanse the bloodstains from Jerusalem by a spirit of judgment and a spirit of fire. Then the Lord will create over all of Mount Zion and over those who assemble there a cloud of smoke by day and a glow of flaming fire by night; over all the*

> *glory will be a canopy. It will be a shelter and shade from the heat of the day, and a refuge and hiding place from the storm and rain"* (Isaiah 4:2-6).

The concept of Jesus as the "Branch" is seen in a number of places. Jeremiah 23:5 says, *"The days are coming, declares the Lord, when I will raise up to David a righteous Branch, a King who will reign wisely and do what is just and right in the land."*

That God would not forsake his promise to Israel is seen over and over again in Isaiah. One of the most familiar prophesies is found in Isaiah 9.

> *"For to us a child is born, to us a son is given, and the government will be on his shoulders. And he will be called Wonderful Counselor, Mighty God, Everlasting Father, Prince of Peace. Of the increase of his government and peace there will be no end. He will reign on David's throne and over his kingdom, establishing and upholding it with justice and righteousness from that time on and forever. The zeal of the Lord Almighty will accomplish this."*

Isaiah promised that when the eternal kingdom of heaven would finally be established the Lord would assemble all the faithful of Israel, as well as other nations, and welcome them into their promised rest.

> *"In that day the Root of Jesse will stand as a banner for the peoples; the nations will rally to him, and his place of rest will be glorious. In that day the Lord will reach out his hand a second time to reclaim the remnant that is left of his people from Assyria, from Lower Egypt, from Upper Egypt, from Cush, from Elam, from Babylonia, from Hamath and from the islands of the sea. He will raise a banner for the*

nations and gather the exiles of Israel; he will assemble the scattered people of Judah from the four quarters of the earth" (Isaiah 11:10-12).

Isaiah also used very graphic, apocalyptic language to describe God's judgment on nations. There are dozens of examples in the book. One of many such descriptions occurs in Isaiah 13. Speaking of the coming overthrow of the Babylonian Empire by the Medes, he says,

> *"Listen, a noise on the mountains, like that of a great multitude! Listen, an uproar among the kingdoms, like nations massing together! The Lord Almighty is mustering an army for war. They come from faraway lands, from the ends of the heavens— the Lord and the weapons of his wrath— to destroy the whole country. Wail, for the day of the Lord is near; it will come like destruction from the Almighty...The stars of heaven and their constellations will not show their light. The rising sun will be darkened and the moon will not give its light... Therefore I will make the heavens tremble; and the earth will shake from its place at the wrath of the Lord Almighty, in the day of his burning anger."*

This language was used to describe what would happen to the Babylonians at the hands of the Medes. Notice he said it was the Lord who directed the army. Nobody in the battle at that time knew they were doing God's bidding, but they were. He said in verses 17-18,

> *"See, I will stir up against them the Medes, who do not care for silver and have no delight in gold. Their bows will strike down the young men; they will have no mercy on infants nor will they look with*

compassion on children. Babylon, the jewel of kingdoms, the glory of the Babylonians' pride, will be overthrown by God like Sodom and Gomorrah."

Many people today are confused by the apocalyptic language used in the Revelation given to John. John's own explanation of his writing was to show how Jesus fulfilled the Scriptures to accomplish the mystery of God. Rather than make up some explanation of passages found in Revelation, all one has to do is find the origin of what John was explaining in the Scriptures that had already been recorded. That John used the same graphic language and images found in the prophesies he was explaining should surprise or confuse no one. As we shall see, Isaiah, Jeremiah, Ezekiel, Daniel, Zechariah, Jesus, Peter, Paul, and John all used the same language to describe the very same events leading to the same culminating event: the establishment of the kingdom of heaven and accomplishing of the mystery of God.

Time after time we see God working through physical nations to bring his eternal kingdom into existence. History says the northern kingdom of Israel was overthrown by the Assyrians. The Bible says it was overthrown by God. History says the Assyrians were overthrown by the Babylonians. The Bible says God did it. History says the Babylonians destroyed Jerusalem in 586 A.D. The Bible says God sent the Israelites into Babylon. History says the Babylonian Empire was destroyed by the Medes. The Bible says God was the one responsible. History says the Roman army destroyed Jerusalem and its temple in 70 A.D. The Bible says it was another "God-directed" war. We should not discount the eternal significance of these God-directed events in human history.

These were all part of a chain of events that would result in establishing the throne of David forever. Isaiah 16:5, *"In love a throne will be established; in faithfulness a man will sit on it— one from the house of David— one who in judging seeks justice and speeds the cause of righteousness."* And in Isaiah 25:1-9,

> *"O Lord, you are my God; I will exalt you and praise your name, for in perfect faithfulness you have done marvelous things, things planned long ago...On this mountain the Lord Almighty will prepare a feast of rich food for all peoples, a banquet of aged wine— the best of meats and the finest of wines. On this mountain he will destroy the shroud that enfolds all peoples, the sheet that covers all nations; he will swallow up death forever. The Sovereign Lord will wipe away the tears from all faces; he will remove the disgrace of his people from all the earth. The Lord has spoken. In that day they will say, 'Surely this is our God; we trusted in him, and he saved us. This is the Lord, we trusted in him; let us rejoice and be glad in his salvation.' "*

Isaiah said in this coming kingdom death would be no more and the Lord would wipe away all tears. He does not mean death and sadness would vanish from the earth, but they would not exist in the kingdom of heaven, the church. In Christ there is no more death, no more war, no more tears like there was in the earthly kingdom. Jesus said, *"I tell you the truth, whoever hears my word and believes him who sent me has eternal life and will not be condemned; he has crossed over from death to life"* (John 5:24).

As we continue to read through Isaiah, we see over and over his graphic descriptions of God's judgment on nations. In Isaiah 34:8-10,

> *"For the Lord has a day of vengeance, a year of retribution, to uphold Zion's cause. Edom's streams will be turned into pitch, her dust into burning sulfur; her land will become blazing pitch! It will not be quenched night and day; its smoke will rise forever. From generation to generation it will lie desolate; no one will*

ever pass through it again."

This same apocalyptic language appears again in John's Revelation. Remember from where it came.

In contrast, Isaiah also describes the new kingdom, the heavenly Jerusalem (the church) in similar language.

> *"And a highway will be there; it will be called the Way of Holiness. The unclean will not journey on it; it will be for those who walk in that Way; wicked fools will not go about on it. No lion will be there, nor will any ferocious beast get up on it; they will not be found there. But only the redeemed will walk there, and the ransomed of the Lord will return. They will enter Zion with singing; everlasting joy will crown their heads. Gladness and joy will overtake them, and sorrow and sighing will flee away"* (Isaiah 35:8-10).

Another theme found in several places in Isaiah is that the Gentiles were also to be included in the promise of the new kingdom. Isaiah 49:6-16, *"It is too small a thing for you to be my servant to restore the tribes of Jacob and bring back those of Israel I have kept. I will also make you a light for the Gentiles, that you may bring my salvation to the ends of the earth."* Simeon quoted this prophesy when he finally saw the baby Jesus at the temple. Taking the little boy in his arms he praised God saying, *"Sovereign Lord, as you have promised, you now dismiss your servant in peace. For my eyes have seen your salvation, which you have prepared in the sight of all people, a light for revelation to the Gentiles and for glory to your people Israel"* (Luke 2:29-32).

Another such passage is found in Isaiah 56:3-8:

> *"Let no foreigner who has bound himself to the Lord say, 'The Lord will surely exclude me from his people.' And let not any eunuch complain, 'I am only*

> *a dry tree.' For this is what the Lord says: To the eunuchs who keep my Sabbaths, who choose what pleases me and hold fast to my covenant- to them I will give within my temple and its walls a memorial and a name better than sons and daughters; I will give them an everlasting name that will not be cut off. And foreigners who bind themselves to the Lord to serve him, to love the name of the Lord, and to worship him, all who keep the Sabbath without desecrating it and who hold fast to my covenant- these I will bring to my holy mountain and give them joy in my house of prayer. Their burnt offerings and sacrifices will be accepted on my altar; for my house will be called a house of prayer for all nations. The Sovereign Lord declares— he who gathers the exiles of Israel: I will gather still others to them besides those already gathered."*

The promise of salvation *through* the Jews was not only *for* the Jews, but for all nations. Jesus was not just the hope of Israel, he was the hope of the world!

Isaiah's description of the heavenly Jerusalem (the church) is seen again in John's Revelation. *"O afflicted city, lashed by storms and not comforted, I will build you with stones of turquoise, your foundations with sapphires. I will make your battlements of rubies, your gates of sparkling jewels, and all your walls of precious stones. All your sons will be taught by the Lord, and great will be your children's peace. In righteousness you will be established: Tyranny will be far from you; you will have nothing to fear. Terror will be far removed; it will not come near you"* (Isaiah 54:11-14, Revelation 21).

Everything in the prophesies concerning the restoration of Israel, the redemption of mankind, and the establishment of the kingdom of heaven was totally dependent upon a solution to the problem of sin.

> *"Surely the arm of the Lord is not too short to save, nor his ear too dull to hear. But your iniquities have separated you from your God; your sins have hidden his face from you, so that he will not hear"* (Isaiah 59:1-2).

Because of sin mankind was eternally separated from God's presence.

Isaiah not only identified the problem, he also knew there was no one to intervene. Continuing in verses 17-20:

> *"He saw that there was no one, he was appalled that there was no one to intervene; so his own arm worked salvation for him, and his own righteousness sustained him…'The Redeemer will come to Zion, to those in Jacob who repent of their sins,' declares the Lord."*

The creation of the nation of Israel was described in Isaiah 51 as the Lord "creating the heavens and earth." The term "heaven and earth" is often used in prophetic language referring to a nation or people. Their destruction, as we have already seen, is often described as the stars falling, the sun darkened, the moon not giving light, etc. The prophet also consistently described the establishment of the new Jerusalem, the kingdom of heaven, in these same terms.

> *"Behold, I will create* ***new heavens and a new earth****. The former things will not be remembered, nor will they come to mind. But be glad and rejoice forever in what I will create, for* ***I will create Jerusalem*** *to be a delight and its people a joy. I will rejoice over Jerusalem and take delight in my people; the sound of weeping and of crying will be heard in it*

no more" (Isaiah 65:17-19).

This is the same "new Jerusalem" we see in John's Revelation coming down from heaven (Revelation 21).

Three times Isaiah described the nation of Israel as a pregnant woman about to give birth. The first time is in Isaiah 26:17-19:

> *"As a woman with child and about to give birth writhes and cries out in her pain, so were we in your presence, O Lord. We were with child, we writhed in pain, but we gave birth to wind. We have not brought salvation to the earth; we have not given birth to people of the world. But your dead will live; their bodies will rise. You who dwell in the dust, wake up and shout for joy. Your dew is like the dew of the morning; the earth will give birth to her dead."*

Isaiah, through the Holy Spirit, recognized Israel's responsibility to bring salvation to the earth, but he also knew she had failed to do so. Israel had not even been a very good influence on the nations around her because of her own sins and rebellion against God.

Then, speaking of the coming of Jesus in Isaiah 42:1-7:

> *"Here is my servant, whom I uphold, my chosen one in whom I delight; I will put my Spirit on him and he will bring justice to the nations...A bruised reed he will not break, and a smoldering wick he will not snuff out. In faithfulness he will bring forth justice; he will not falter or be discouraged till he establishes justice on earth...I, the Lord, have called you in righteousness; I will take hold of your hand. I will keep you and will make you to be a covenant for the people and a light for the Gentiles, to open eyes that are blind, to free captives from prison and to release from the dungeon those who sit in darkness."*

He then returns to his analogy of a woman giving birth in verses 14-16:

> *"For a long time I have kept silent, I have been quiet and held myself back. But now, like a woman in childbirth, I cry out, I gasp and pant. I will lay waste the mountains and hills and dry up all their vegetation; I will turn rivers into islands and dry up the pools. I will lead the blind by ways they have not known, along unfamiliar paths I will guide them; I will turn the darkness into light before them and make the rough places smooth. These are the things I will do; I will not forsake them."*

Jesus was going to be born of Israel, but not by her own doing. The Lord would bring this about.

> *"Hear that uproar from the city, hear that noise from the temple! It is the sound of the Lord repaying his enemies all they deserve. Before she goes into labor, she gives birth; before the pains come upon her, she delivers a son. Who has ever heard of such a thing? Who has ever seen such things? Can a country be born in a day or a nation be brought forth in a moment? Yet no sooner is Zion in labor than she gives birth to her children. 'Do I bring to the moment of birth and not give delivery?' says the Lord. 'Do I close up the womb when I bring to delivery?' says your God. Rejoice with Jerusalem and be glad for her, all you who love her; rejoice greatly with her, all you who mourn over her. For you will nurse and be satisfied at her comforting breasts; you will drink deeply and delight in her overflowing abundance. For this is what the Lord says: 'I will extend peace to her like a*

river, and the wealth of nations like a flooding stream; you will nurse and be carried on her arm and dandled on her knees. As a mother comforts her child, so will I comfort you; and you will be comforted over Jerusalem.' When you see this, your heart will rejoice and you will flourish like grass; the hand of the Lord will be made known to his servants, but his fury will be shown to his foes. See, the Lord is coming with fire, and his chariots are like a whirlwind; he will bring down his anger with fury, and his rebuke with flames of fire. For with fire and with his sword the Lord will execute judgment upon all men, and many will be those slain by the Lord" (Isaiah 66:6-16).

Isaiah concludes his prophesies with this very unusual picture of Israel giving birth, through the power of Almighty God, to her own new kingdom. In his final comments he says,

> *"And I, because of their actions and their imaginations, am about to come and gather all nations and tongues, and they will come and see my glory… 'As the new heavens and the new earth that I make will endure before me,' declares the Lord, 'so will your name and descendants endure. From one New Moon to another and from one Sabbath to another, all mankind will come and bow down before me,' says the Lord. 'And they will go out and look upon the dead bodies of those who rebelled against me; their worm will not die, nor will their fire be quenched, and they will be loathsome to all mankind"* (Isaiah 66:18-24).

We find the fulfillment and explanation of this prophesy in Revelation chapter 12.

CHAPTER 13

The Prophecy of Ezekiel

Ezekiel was both a prophet and a priest whose ministry spanned just over twenty years from 593-571 B.C. He was among the Jews exiled to Babylon in 597, and predicted Jerusalem's destruction in 586. Ezekiel lived during a time of international upheaval. The Assyrian Empire had destroyed the northern kingdom of Israel about 125 years earlier. As we learned in Isaiah, the southern kingdom of Judah had been spared following King Hezekiah's intercession. In spite of this earlier reprieve, Judah and Jerusalem were also destined for destruction.

The Babylonians eventually displaced the Assyrians as the new world empire and Ezekiel and his fellow countrymen were exiled to Babylon by King Nebuchadnezzar. Ezekiel's prophetic book is divided into two major sections. The first 33 chapters contain prophesies of the destruction of Judah and Jerusalem and God's pronounced judgment, not only on the remainder of Israel, but on the surrounding nations. Jerusalem was destroyed and the temple burned by the Babylonians in 586 B.C. Once news of this event reached the exiled Jews, Ezekiel's message turned to one of hope in the future restoration of Israel. In the remainder of the book, chapters 34-48, he described this future kingdom as the glorious and perfect kingdom of God. Major portions of John's revelation explain how Jesus fulfilled Ezekiel's visions and prophesies.

In the first chapter of Ezekiel we read about an *"immense cloud with flashing lightning and surrounded by brilliant light."* The prophet goes on to describe in great detail four living creatures which were in the presence of God. Ezekiel explained his vision in the last verse of the first chapter. *"This was the appearance of the likeness of the glory of the Lord. When I saw it, I fell facedown, and I heard the voice of one speaking."* In Ezekiel 10 he saw the same creatures again and identified them in verse 20 as cherubim. *"These were the living creatures I had seen beneath the God of Israel by the Kebar River, and I realized that they were cherubim."* In Isaiah 6:2 they are described as "Seraphim," which literally means "burning ones." Moses was instructed to have two gold replicas of these celestial beings fashioned and place one at each end of the Mercy Seat on top of the Ark of the Covenant. In each case they represented the place where the presence of God dwelt.

In chapter 2:3 God told Ezekiel, *"Son of man, I am sending you to the Israelites, to a rebellious nation that has rebelled against me; they and their fathers have been in revolt against me to this very day."* In verse 9-10 he saw, *"a hand stretched out to me. In it was a scroll, which he unrolled before me. On both sides of it were written words of lament and mourning and woe."* Continuing in chapter 3 Ezekiel was told to eat the scroll which represented what God wanted him to tell the nation of Israel. It tasted sweet in his mouth, but the message was a very bitter one for his fellow countrymen. He was instructed to go to the people of Israel and warn them of the coming destruction of their city and temple. His message, complete with apocalyptic symbolism and graphic demonstrations, was indeed "words of lament and mourning and woe." Ezekiel's message had immediate significance to the Jews of his day, but also served to predict Israel's ultimate demise at the hands of the Romans in A.D. 70. Jesus and his apostles used this same symbolism in their descriptions of this final destruction in the New Testament, especially the Revelation.

> *"Therefore this is what the Sovereign Lord says: I myself am against you, Jerusalem, and I will inflict*

> *punishment on you in the sight of the nations. Because of all your detestable idols, I will do to you what I have never done before and will never do again. Therefore in your midst fathers will eat their children, and children will eat their fathers. I will inflict punishment on you and will scatter all your survivors to the winds. Therefore as surely as I live, declares the Sovereign Lord, because you have defiled my sanctuary with all your vile images and detestable practices, I myself will withdraw my favor; I will not look on you with pity or spare you. A third of your people will die of the plague or perish by famine inside you; a third will fall by the sword outside your walls; and a third I will scatter to the winds and pursue with drawn sword"* (Ezekiel 5:8-12).

Ezekiel's apocalyptic language not only described what was soon to happen to Jerusalem at the hands of the Babylonians, it also foreshadowed another future destruction that would be far worse. At that time things would happen that had never happened before or since. Daniel used this same language when he predicted the tribulation that would precede the destruction of Jerusalem by the Romans. *"There will be a time of distress such as has not happened from the beginning of nations until then"* (Daniel 12:1). Jesus repeated the same in Matthew 24:21, *"For then there will be great distress, unequaled from the beginning of the world until now—and never to be equaled again."* John also referred back to this same prophecy in his Revelation of Jesus Christ. Josephus' historical account of the destruction of Jerusalem by the Romans in A.D.70 described the literal fulfillment of the events Ezekiel predicted, including people eating their own children.

> *"This is what the Sovereign Lord says: Disaster! An unheard-of disaster is coming. The end has come!*

The end has come! It has roused itself against you. It has come! Doom has come upon you—you who dwell in the land. The time has come, the day is near; there is panic, not joy, upon the mountains. I am about to pour out my wrath on you and spend my anger against you; I will judge you according to your conduct and repay you for all your detestable practices. I will not look on you with pity or spare you; I will repay you in accordance with your conduct and the detestable practices among you. Then you will know that it is I the Lord who strikes the blow.

The day is here! It has come! Doom has burst forth, the rod has budded, arrogance has blossomed! Violence has grown into a rod to punish wickedness; none of the people will be left, none of that crowd—no wealth, nothing of value. The time has come, the day has arrived…Outside is the sword, inside are plague and famine; those in the country will die by the sword, and those in the city will be devoured by famine and plague. All who survive and escape will be in the mountains, moaning like doves of the valleys, each because of his sins…They will throw their silver into the streets, and their gold will be an unclean thing. Their silver and gold will not be able to save them in the day of the Lord's wrath. They will not satisfy their hunger or fill their stomachs with it, for it has made them stumble into sin. They were proud of their beautiful jewelry and used it to make their detestable idols and vile images. Therefore I will turn these into an unclean thing for them. I will hand it all over as plunder to foreigners and as loot to the wicked of the earth, and they will defile it. I will turn my face away from them, and they will desecrate my

> *treasured place; robbers will enter it and desecrate it.*
>
> *Prepare chains, because the land is full of bloodshed and the city is full of violence. I will bring the most wicked of the nations to take possession of their houses; I will put an end to the pride of the mighty, and their sanctuaries will be desecrated. When terror comes, they will seek peace, but there will be none. Calamity upon calamity will come, and rumor upon rumor. They will try to get a vision from the prophet; the teaching of the law by the priest will be lost, as will the counsel of the elders. The king will mourn, the prince will be clothed with despair, and the hands of the people of the land will tremble. I will deal with them according to their conduct, and by their own standards I will judge them. Then they will know that I am the Lord"* (Ezekiel 7:5-27).

Over and over Ezekiel depicted the coming judgment of God and destruction of their beloved City of Jerusalem. Israel was condemned for her idolatry, for her spiritual adultery with other gods. The glory of the Lord was going to be removed from the temple. Israel had been unfaithful and God's judgment was inescapable. In chapter 21 he identified Babylon as the nation God would use for the destruction of his day. One should note in this description the prophet specifically said the throne would not be reestablished until Jesus comes. There can be no doubt about the meaning of this, the fact that his prophecy also concerned another future event.

> *"The word of the Lord came to me: Son of man, mark out two roads for the sword of the king of Babylon to take, both starting from the same country. Make a signpost where the road branches off to the city. Mark out one road for the sword to come against*

> *Rabbah of the Ammonites and another against Judah and fortified Jerusalem. For the king of Babylon will stop at the fork in the road, at the junction of the two roads, to seek an omen: He will cast lots with arrows, he will consult his idols, he will examine the liver. Into his right hand will come the lot for Jerusalem, where he is to set up battering rams, to give the command to slaughter, to sound the battle cry, to set battering rams against the gates, to build a ramp and to erect siege works. It will seem like a false omen to those who have sworn allegiance to him, but he will remind them of their guilt and take them captive.*
>
> *Therefore this is what the Sovereign Lord says: 'Because you people have brought to mind your guilt by your open rebellion, revealing your sins in all that you do—because you have done this, you will be taken captive.'*
>
> *O profane and wicked prince of Israel, whose day has come, whose time of punishment has reached its climax, this is what the Sovereign Lord says: Take off the turban, remove the crown. It will not be as it was: The lowly will be exalted and the exalted will be brought low. A ruin! A ruin! I will make it a ruin!* ***It will not be restored until he comes to whom it rightfully belongs; to him I will give it*"** (Ezekiel 21:19-27).

Not only did Ezekiel prophesy against Israel, but all the surrounding nations were also included in God's judgment decrees. The last one to be singled out was Egypt in chapter 32. It is important to see and understand the symbolic language used to describe God's judgment if we are to understand the New Testament passages that refer to these same prophesies.

"In the twelfth year, in the twelfth month on the first day, the word of the Lord came to me: Son of man, take up a lament concerning Pharaoh king of Egypt and say to him: 'You are like a lion among the nations; you are like a monster in the seas thrashing about in your streams, churning the water with your feet and muddying the streams.' This is what the Sovereign Lord says: 'With a great throng of people I will cast my net over you, and they will haul you up in my net. I will throw you on the land and hurl you on the open field. I will let all the birds of the air settle on you and all the beasts of the earth gorge themselves on you. I will spread your flesh on the mountains and fill the valleys with your remains. I will drench the land with your flowing blood all the way to the mountains, and the ravines will be filled with your flesh. When I snuff you out, ***I will cover the heavens and darken their stars; I will cover the sun with a cloud, and the moon will not give its light. All the shining lights in the heavens I will darken over you****; I will bring darkness over your land, declares the Sovereign Lord…The sword of* ***the king of Babylon will come against you****. I will cause your hordes to fall by the swords of mighty men— the most ruthless of all nations. They will shatter the pride of Egypt, and all her hordes will be overthrown. I will destroy all her cattle from beside abundant waters no longer to be stirred by the foot of man or muddied by the hoofs of cattle. Then I will let her waters settle and make her streams flow like oil, declares the Sovereign Lord. When I make Egypt desolate and strip the land of everything in it, when I strike down all who live there, then they will know*

that I am the Lord' " (Ezekiel 32:1-15).

This is typical language used by all the Old Testament prophets concerning God's judgment on a nation. Egypt's sun would be covered with a cloud, the stars would be darkened, the moon would not give its light. This was Ezekiel's description of the time when the Babylonian Empire would overthrow the Egyptians. We should not be surprised to see this same language used in reference to the Roman army's advance against Jerusalem in A.D. 70. The biggest problem most people today have understanding Jesus' teaching in Matthew 24, Mark 13, and Luke 21, as well as the book of Revelation, is a gross lack of knowledge of Old Testament prophesies concerning this very event.

Beginning in chapter 34 Ezekiel changed his message from doom and destruction to the future hope of a new restored kingdom. He condemned the shepherds of Israel for not tending the flock, then prophesied of one who was coming who would be the true Shepherd of Israel.

> *"Therefore this is what the Sovereign Lord says to them: See, I myself will judge between the fat sheep and the lean sheep. Because you shove with flank and shoulder, butting all the weak sheep with your horns until you have driven them away, I will save my flock, and they will no longer be plundered. I will judge between one sheep and another.* ***I will place over them one shepherd, my servant David, and he will tend them; he will tend them and be their shepherd.*** *I the Lord will be their God, and* ***my servant David will be prince among them.*** *I the Lord have spoken.*
>
> *I will make a covenant of peace with them and rid the land of wild beasts so that they may live in the desert and sleep in the forests in safety. I will bless*

them and the places surrounding my hill. I will send down showers in season; there will be showers of blessing. The trees of the field will yield their fruit and the ground will yield its crops; the people will be secure in their land. They will know that I am the Lord, when I break the bars of their yoke and rescue them from the hands of those who enslaved them. They will no longer be plundered by the nations, nor will wild animals devour them. They will live in safety, and no one will make them afraid. I will provide for them a land renowned for its crops, and they will no longer be victims of famine in the land or bear the scorn of the nations. Then they will know that I, the Lord their God, am with them and that they, the house of Israel, are my people, declares the Sovereign Lord. You my sheep, the sheep of my pasture, are people, and I am your God, declares the Sovereign Lord" (Ezekiel 34:20-31).

Remember back in chapter 21 the Lord had said the throne would not be restored until he to whom it rightfully belongs comes. We know from a host of other prophesies this would be the King of Kings who would sit on David's throne forever. Here Ezekiel referred to the coming Christ as "my servant David." A more beautiful picture of the coming kingdom of heaven would be difficult to find. This was fulfilled when the "mystery of God" was accomplished, which is what John explained in his Revelation of Jesus Christ. Ezekiel also identified the timing of this coming kingdom with the time when they would be cleansed from sin.

"This is what the Sovereign Lord says: ***On the day I cleanse you from all your sins,*** *I will resettle your towns, and the ruins will be rebuilt. The desolate land will be cultivated instead of lying desolate in the*

> *sight of all who pass through it. They will say, 'This land that was laid waste has become like the garden of Eden; the cities that were lying in ruins, desolate and destroyed, are now fortified and inhabited.' Then the nations around you that remain will know that I the Lord have rebuilt what was destroyed and have replanted what was desolate. I the Lord have spoken, and I will do it' "* (Ezekiel 36:33-36).

Not until the atonement sacrifice of Jesus did the Israelites, or anyone else, receive cleansing for their sins. Also, from the time of Ezekiel forward, no king sat on the throne of David in the physical city of Jerusalem. The Israelites were allowed to return to Judea beginning in 538 B.C. under the leadership of Zerubbabel and rebuild the city. Reconstruction of the temple began in 520 B.C. and was finished in 516 B.C. It was later remodeled by Herod the Great in 20 B.C., but no Jewish king ever sat on the throne again until Jesus.

> *"This is what the Sovereign Lord says: I will take the Israelites out of the nations where they have gone. I will gather them from all around and bring them back into their own land. I will make them* ***one nation*** *in the land, on the mountains of Israel. There will be* ***one king*** *over all of them and they will* ***never again be two nations or be divided into two kingdoms****. They will no longer defile themselves with their idols and vile images or with any of their offenses, for I will save them from all their sinful backsliding, and* ***I will cleanse them****. They will be my people, and I will be their God"* (Ezekiel 37:21-23).

The future hope of Israel was inseparably linked to the coming of Jesus, the completion of the atonement sacrifice, and the final destruction of Jerusalem and its temple when the everlasting temple would be established in heaven. This new kingdom would reunite Israel, never to be divided again. This "new Jerusalem" was what Ezekiel and the other prophets saw beyond the physical destruction of the earthly city. He spent the final several chapters describing his vision of this new city with its temple which was once again measured in minute detail.

Ezekiel, like Isaiah before him and John many years later, was shown visions of the eternal plan of Almighty God to bring to fruition his promise of redemption in the kingdom of heaven. Jesus came to finish the plan and John explained how he fulfilled all Scripture in doing so. The final book of the Bible is the testimony of Jesus in accomplishing this great mystery of the ages.

CHAPTER 14

The Six Kingdoms of Daniel

The book of Daniel not only sheds a lot of light on the "last days" of Israel as it predicts the "time of the end," but also further explains the consummation of the ages. It is the most straight forward and comprehensive Old Testament book on Biblical eschatology. A good understanding of Daniel is crucial to much of what Jesus and the apostles taught as their teaching is based on the soon (in their day) fulfillment of these prophesies.

There are six kingdoms in the book of Daniel. Five of these are physical, earthly kingdoms: Israel, Babylon, Mede and Persian, Greek and Roman. The sixth kingdom of Daniel is one that would be *"...set up by the God of heaven...not by human hands... that will never be destroyed nor left to another people"* (Dan. 2:44-45).

The book is about the history of Israel from the time of Nebuchadnezzar's reign in Babylon to the end of Israel as a physical nation in A. D. 70 and the ultimate fulfillment of God's promise to Abraham that is seen in the final kingdom...the kingdom of heaven, the church. The purpose of the calling of Abraham and the establishment of the nation of Israel was always to bring the Redeemer into the world to set up his eternal kingdom. Daniel shows us how God also used the other earthly kingdoms to help bring about his plan.

The kingdoms are first introduced beginning in chapter two with the interpretation of Nebuchadnezzar's dream. Here Daniel speaks of four successive earthly kingdoms, other than Israel. These kingdoms are not specifically identified in this chapter, but it is clearly stated that it would be during the fourth one the God of heaven would set up his kingdom.

In chapter seven Daniel has a similar dream of four kingdoms that would play a major role in Israel's future. These kingdoms are clearly the same as the ones in Nebuchadnezzar's earlier dream. Daniel was extremely troubled by his dream because of the obvious calamity that was to befall the physical nation of Israel. He specifically inquired into the nature of the fourth kingdom, since it was this one that would bring to an end the physical nation of Israel. The angel briefly explained to Daniel how this kingdom would be given power to besiege God's people and bring terrible oppression against the Jews. These kingdoms of Daniel chapters 2 and 7 are clearly understood to be the Babylonians, Medes and Persians, Greeks, and Romans.

Beginning in chapter eight and going through the end of the book the Lord begins to carefully and methodically outline what would take place throughout this historical period and identifies by name the Medo-Persian Empire that followed the Babylonian, as well as the Greek empire including the Ptolemies and Seleucids. We pick up this history in chapter 11 with the Persian rulers Cambyses (530-522), Gaumata (522) and Darius (522-486) who attempted to conquer Greece in 480 B.C. The mighty king of 11:3 is Alexander the Great, whose empire was eventually broken up and divided among several lesser rulers. Several interesting historical figures are clearly identified in this chapter, including Bernice, daughter of Ptolemy II who married Antiochus in a political alliance that came to an end when Antiochus' former wife Laodice conspired to have them put to death.

We follow this sordid history through the marriage of Cleopatra to Ptolemy V in 11:17 to the eventual takeover of the entire region by Rome. In verse 31, 32 we have the prediction of the "abomination that causes desolation" that Jesus mentioned in Matthew 24:15. Jesus clearly identifies this time with the coming destruction of Jerusalem that was to occur in A. D. 70 at the hands of the Romans under the leadership of Titus. Daniel 11:41 predicts this invasion of the "Beautiful Land" by the Romans.

Chapter twelve of Daniel begins by describing this time of distress, when the beautiful land would be invaded, as such that has never been seen from the beginning of nations until then. Jesus describes it in Matthew 24:21 as a time of *"...distress unequaled from the beginning of the world until now...and never to be equaled again."*

Daniel is then told to *"...close up and seal the words of the scroll until the time of the end."* This time of the end was the end of the nation of Israel as a physical kingdom. At this time the God of heaven would have another kingdom in place into which all nations would be welcomed. This kingdom would not be built by human hands and not be subject to the invasion of physical armies. There would be no fear of an overthrow of this kingdom, and it would never come to an end. We know this eternal kingdom to be the same one John the Baptist said was "at hand" when he preached, and of which Jesus said, *"I will build my church and the gates of Hell shall not prevail against it."*

There are six kingdoms in the book of Daniel. One is the nation of Israel whose history is revealed as it relates to the other four physical kingdoms that invaded, occupied and played a major role in Israel's existence. These four earthly kingdoms are the kingdoms of the Babylonians, Medes and Persians, Greeks and Romans. It was during the fourth kingdom (Roman) that the final kingdom in Daniel was established. This is the kingdom of heaven. There are no other kingdoms discussed in Daniel...and there are no prophecies in Daniel that have not been fulfilled by Jesus and the establishment of his eternal kingdom.

Some people want to bring at least part of Daniel's prophecies into the history of today's world and teach that the fourth kingdom of Daniel is still in the future. If this is true, then the kingdom of God has not yet been established since Daniel clearly tells us it will be established *"...in the time of those kings"* (fourth kingdom) (Dan. 2:44). This would mean that Jesus was NOT the promised Messiah and we are still waiting for him to come and establish God's eternal kingdom. There are six kingdoms in Daniel. Israel and the four other kingdoms were a prelude to the kingdom that would be *"...set up by the God of heaven."* They ALL (including God's) stand or fall together. If we are still living in the "last days" and awaiting the "time of the end" then we are also still awaiting the fourth kingdom of Daniel...and are also still awaiting a Savior and for God's eternal kingdom to be established.

With this overview in mind, let us examine more closely Daniel's visions and specifically the timing of their fulfillment. One thing is unmistakable in his revelations from God. What is being revealed to him concerns "the time of the end." Daniel is a book almost wholly devoted to teachings about eschatology, the study of the end times. It is worth noting that the Bible speaks often about the "time of the end," it never mentions the "end of time." Note the following verses from Daniel.

> Daniel 8:17, *"As he came near the place where I was standing, I was terrified and fell prostrate. 'Son of man,' he said to me, 'understand that the vision concerns* **the time of the end***.' "*

> Daniel 8:19, *"He said: "I am going to tell you what will happen later in the time of wrath, because the vision concerns* **the appointed time of the end***."*

> Daniel 9:26-27, *"After the sixty-two 'sevens,' the Anointed One will be cut off and will have nothing. The people of the ruler who will come will destroy the*

city and the sanctuary. ***The end*** *will come like a flood: War will continue until* ***the end,*** *and desolations have been decreed. He will confirm a covenant with many for one 'seven.' In the middle of the 'seven' he will put an end to sacrifice and offering. And on a wing of the temple he will set up an abomination that causes desolation, until* ***the end that is decreed*** *is poured out on him. "*

Daniel 11:27, *"The two kings, with their hearts bent on evil, will sit at the same table and lie to each other, but to no avail, because* ***the end will still come at the appointed time.****"*

Daniel 11:35, *"Some of the wise will stumble, so that they may be refined, purified and made spotless until* ***the time of the end,*** *for it will still come at the appointed time."*

Daniel 11:40, *"At* ***the time of the end*** *the king of the South will engage him in battle, and the king of the North will storm out against him with chariots and cavalry and a great fleet of ships. He will invade many countries and sweep through them like a flood."*

Daniel 12:4, *"But you, Daniel, close up and seal the words of the scroll until* ***the time of the end.*** *Many will go here and there to increase knowledge."*

Daniel 12:9, *"He replied, Go your way, Daniel, because the words are closed up and sealed until* ***the time of the end.****"*

> Daniel 12:13, *"As for you, go your way till* ***the end****. You will rest, and then at* ***the end of the days*** *you will rise to receive your allotted inheritance."*

Numerous other Scriptures in both the Old and New Testaments speak of this same time of the end. Habakkuk 2:3 says, *"For the revelation awaits an appointed time; it speaks of the end and will not prove false. Though it linger, wait for it; it will certainly come and will not delay."*

This time was a specific day in history known in Scripture as the "day of the Lord" when he would reveal his divine mystery of salvation at the consummation of the ages. Daniel is given two specific revelations that allow us to pinpoint with historical accuracy the exact timing of these events.

In Daniel 9 we read that the angel Gabriel was sent to give him insight and understanding into what he had seen. In verses 24-27 we read:

> *"Seventy 'sevens' are decreed for your people and your holy city to finish transgression, to put an end to sin, to atone for wickedness, to bring in everlasting righteousness, to seal up vision and prophecy and to anoint the most holy.*
>
> *Know and understand this: From the issuing of the decree to restore and rebuild Jerusalem until the Anointed One, the ruler, comes, there will be seven 'sevens,' and sixty-two 'sevens.' It will be rebuilt with streets and a trench, but in times of trouble. After the sixty-two 'sevens,' the Anointed One will be cut off and will have nothing. The people of the ruler who will come will destroy the city and the sanctuary. The end will come like a flood: War will continue until the end, and desolations have been decreed. He will confirm a covenant with many for one 'seven.' In the*

middle of the 'seven' he will put an end to sacrifice and offering. And on a wing of the temple he will set up an abomination that causes desolation, until the end that is decreed is poured out on him."

The Hebrew word for "sevens" (translated "weeks" in some versions) means a unit of seven of something, much like the English word "dozen" means twelve of something. In this case, the prophecy concerns seventy seven-year periods of time, divided into three groups. The angel says there will be seven "sevens," or a period of 49 years, followed by sixty-two "sevens," or 434 years, followed by one 'seven,' or 7 years.

The time begins with *"...the issuing of the decree to restore and rebuild Jerusalem"* by Artaxerxes in 457 B.C. (Ezra 7:11-26). We read in Nehemiah how the rebuilding began with the wall of Jerusalem being completed in 52 days. The work was done in times of trouble, just as the angel had said to Daniel, with the workers carrying supplies in one hand and a sword in the other. Over the next 49 years the people of Israel rebuilt the city and surrounding communities and were resettled there.

According to the angel there would be a second period of 434 years, during which nothing specific was foretold. It was simply the time between the resettlement of Israel in and around Jerusalem and the beginning of the final 'seven'. He describes things that will happen "after the sixty-two sevens." Some of these occur during this final seven year period, and others are "decreed" during this time frame. When all of these events will have occurred, including the destruction of the "...city (Jerusalem) and the sanctuary (temple)," then "...the end will come like a flood."

According to Daniel, the events of this time frame leading up to "the end" would accomplish all of the following:

1. Finish transgression
2. Put an end to sin

3. Atone for wickedness
4. Bring in everlasting righteousness
5. Seal up vision and prophecy
6. Anoint the Most Holy

If this list does not cause one to see the importance of understanding Biblical eschatology, something is dreadfully wrong. None of these appear to this writer to be irrelevant or "disputable" matters.

The final 'seven' in Gabriel's revelation to Daniel is divided into two segments. *"He will confirm a covenant with many for one 'seven.' In the middle of the 'seven' he will put an end to sacrifice and offering."* This seven year period begins with the "anointing" of Jesus at his baptism and ends with the dispersion of the Jewish Christians following the stoning of Stephen. In the middle of this period Jesus is crucified, putting an end to sacrifice and offering.

Jesus had emptied himself of his heavenly glory and authority and had become human (Philippians 2:6-8, Hebrews 2:17) and was publicly declared to be the Son of God and "anointed" with the Holy Spirit at his baptism. Following his temptation by the Devil for forty days, he went to Nazareth where he had lived as a child, stood up in the synagogue and read from Isaiah 61:1-2, " *'The Spirit of the Lord is on me, because he has anointed me to preach good news to the poor. He has sent me to proclaim freedom for the prisoners and recovery of sight for the blind, to release the oppressed, to proclaim the year of the Lord's favor.' Then he rolled up the scroll, gave it back to the attendant and sat down. The eyes of everyone in the synagogue were fastened on him, and he began by saying to them, 'Today this Scripture is fulfilled in your hearing' "* (Luke 4:18-21).

Beginning with his anointing, Jesus spent the next 3 ½ years teaching and "confirming" a new covenant with the people. His earthly ministry was confined to the people of Israel. During this time he not only taught about the coming kingdom of heaven, the church which he would build, but also carefully and in great detail explained (decreed) future events that would happen in that generation leading up to "the time of the end."

In the middle of this seven year period he was crucified. Following his death and resurrection the disciples were told to wait in Jerusalem for the Holy Spirit. For the next 3 ½ years their ministry was confined to Jerusalem and Judea, to the people of Israel. It was not until the stoning of Stephen that the gospel was taken to the Gentile world. This was to fulfill what had been prophesied that the word of the Lord would go out from Jerusalem. Jesus told the apostles they would be witnesses, beginning in Jerusalem, then Judea, then to the rest of the world. The covenant was confirmed with the Jews for a period of seven years and the "time of the end" had been decreed, just as Gabriel had explained to Daniel.

In the last three chapters of Daniel he is shown revelations and given explanations about the final events leading up to the "time of the end." In chapter 10 he is shown a vision of an astonishing man who said, *"I have come to explain to you what will happen to your people in the future, for the vision concerns a time yet to come."* Through chapter 11 he once again takes Daniel through the coming, earthly kingdoms that will rise and fall before the final one that will destroy Jerusalem and its temple.

Speaking of this fourth kingdom (Roman) Daniel 11:31-32 says, *"His armed forces will rise up to desecrate the temple fortress and will abolish the daily sacrifice. Then they will set up the abomination that causes desolation."* Verse 35 says, *"Some of the wise will stumble so that they may be refined, purified and made spotless until the time of the end, for it will still come at the appointed time."*

"At the time of the end the king of the South will engage him in battle and the king of the North will storm out against him with chariots and cavalry and a great fleet of ships. He will invade many countries and sweep through them like a flood. He will invade the

Beautiful Land" (Daniel 11:40-41). A study of the history of the Roman Jewish Wars between A.D. 66 and A.D. 70 shows a precise fulfillment of Daniel's prophesies.

> *"At that time Michael, the great prince who protects your people, will arise. There will be a time of distress such as has not happened from the beginning of nations until then. But at that time your people—everyone whose name is found written in the book—will be delivered. Multitudes who sleep in the dust of the earth will awake: some to everlasting life, others to shame and everlasting contempt. Those who are wise will shine like the brightness of the heavens, and those who lead many to righteousness, like the stars forever and ever. But you, Daniel, close up and seal the words of the scroll until the time of the end"* (Daniel 12:1-4).

When is this "time of the end"? Daniel identifies it as the time when the nation that rises to power following the Babylonians, Medes and Persians, and the Greeks invades the Beautiful Land, the home of his people, and sets up "the abomination that causes desolation" in the temple. He further describes it as *"...a time of distress such as has not happened from the beginning of nations until then."* As we will see, Jesus clearly identifies these very same things as he "decrees" the signs that will precede the destruction of Jerusalem in his generation. The invading nation was Rome; the time was A. D. 70.

As Daniel looked up, he saw two more men standing on opposite banks of the Tigris River. One of them asked, *"How long will it be before these astonishing things are fulfilled?"* In the same figurative language used earlier in Daniel 7:25-28 the man answered, *"It will be for a time, times and half a time. When the power of the holy people has been finally broken, all these things will be completed."* Translated into years that would be 3 ½ years or

1,290 days.

We now have another 3 ½ year period during which there would be terrible times like never before or after leading up to the "time of the end." Exactly when would these days begin and end? Daniel gives us the answer.

"From the time that the daily sacrifice is abolished and the abomination that causes desolation is set up, there will be 1,290 days. Blessed is the one who waits for and reaches the end of the 1,335 days" (Daniel 12:11-12). Jesus confirmed this prophecy to be one of the signs of the impending destruction of Jerusalem and its temple and that it would happen during that generation.

From a historical standpoint we have the writings of Josephus, who witnessed these actual events. While not inspired Scripture, they give us an accurate historical account of what happened. Just as we can compare historical records with Daniel's prophesies about the four kingdoms with uncanny accuracy, so we see the same accuracy between the Scripture and the historical record of the Roman conquest of Judea and Jerusalem.

Josephus recorded in July of A.D. 66, in their rebellion against Rome, Jewish Zealots stormed Jerusalem, burned the palace of Agrippa and Bernice, killed Ananias, the High Priest, and killed a garrison of Roman soldiers. They stopped the twice-daily sacrifices that were being offered in the temple. Josephus identified the cessation of the daily sacrifices as the true beginning of the Roman-Jewish War.

Three-and-one-half years later (1290 days), in A.D. 70 Josephus records a major abomination in the temple. While the Roman army was encamped outside the city, three rival Jewish groups got embroiled in a bloody fight inside the temple for control. The temple was a battleground, and the carnage filled every corner of the sacred building. Worshippers coming to offer sacrifices were murdered. Blood literally flowed out of the temple. Nothing like this had ever occurred before.

Forty-five days later, 1,335 days after the cessation of the daily sacrifice, the Roman army advanced into Jerusalem and began the final siege. The "time of the end" had come. By September of A.D. 70 not one stone was left on another.

The Bible speaks of the "time of the end." It never speaks of the "end of time." God does not "trick" us with his time statements. He means exactly what he says in every instance. His will is revealed for our understanding. We are the ones who confuse the time issue.

Hal Lindsey was wrong. Pat Robertson, Paul Crouch and the other "end time prophets" have all been proven wrong. The *Left Behind* series is fiction. The Apostle Paul describes such teachers in 1 Timothy 1:5-7, *"The goal of this command is love, which comes from a pure heart and a good conscience and a sincere faith. Some have wandered away from these and turned to meaningless talk. They want to be teachers of the law, but they do not know what they are talking about or what they so confidently affirm."*

CHAPTER 15

The Prophecy of Zechariah

Zechariah, a prophet and priest in Israel who ministered from about 520-480 B.C., was born during the Babylonian captivity and returned to Jerusalem in 538 B.C. under the leadership of Zerubbabel and Joshua the High Priest. The visions of Zechariah began in 520 B.C., which was the same year the Jews started reconstruction of the temple. He encouraged his fellow Israelites to remain faithful to the Lord and finish the rebuilding of the temple in Jerusalem. Following the exact same theology of his predecessors, he not only prophesied about God's mercy extended to Judah in allowing them to return to their home country and rebuild their precious city and temple, but looked beyond to a future, more glorious city and temple that would be built by God.

Much of the symbolic and apocalyptic language used by Zechariah is found again in New Testament passages which refer to the final destruction of Jerusalem and its temple and the establishment of God's eternal kingdom of heaven. John, in his Revelation of Jesus Christ, draws on several of these images in his explanation of how Jesus accomplished the mystery of God. Zechariah's first vision concerned God's judgment on surrounding nations which had brought misery and desolation to his people.

> *"During the night I had a vision—and there before me was a man riding a red horse! He was standing among the myrtle trees in a ravine. Behind him were red, brown and white horses. I asked,*

'What are these, my lord?' The angel who was talking with me answered, 'I will show you what they are.' Then the man standing among the myrtle trees explained, 'They are the ones the Lord has sent to go throughout the earth.' And they reported to the angel of the Lord, who was standing among the myrtle trees, 'We have gone throughout the earth and found the whole world at rest and in peace.'

Then the angel of the Lord said, 'Lord Almighty, how long will you withhold mercy from Jerusalem and from the towns of Judah, which you have been angry with these seventy years?' So the Lord spoke kind and comforting words to the angel who talked with me. Then the angel who was speaking to me said, 'Proclaim this word: This is what the Lord Almighty says: I am very jealous for Jerusalem and Zion, but I am very angry with the nations that feel secure. I was only a little angry, but they added to the calamity.' Therefore, this is what the Lord says: 'I will return to Jerusalem with mercy, and there my house will be rebuilt. And the measuring line will be stretched out over Jerusalem,' declares the Lord Almighty. Proclaim further: This is what the Lord Almighty says: 'My towns will again overflow with prosperity, and the Lord will again comfort Zion and choose Jerusalem' " (Zechariah 1:8-17).

Riders on horses are seen in many of the prophetic writings and always represent God's messengers being sent into the world for a specific purpose. In this instance they reported the peaceful condition of the nations surrounding Judah. One of the angels asked the Lord how long he would withhold his judgment against these nations. God answered the question with another vision.

"Then I looked up—and there before me were four horns! I asked the angel who was speaking to me, 'What are these?' He answered me, 'These are the horns that scattered Judah, Israel and Jerusalem.' Then the Lord showed me four craftsmen. I asked, 'What are these coming to do?' He answered, 'These are the horns that scattered Judah so that no one could raise his head, but the craftsmen have come to terrify them and throw down these horns of the nations who lifted up their horns against the land of Judah to scatter its people' " (Zechariah 1:18-21).

Physical nations in Old Testament prophesies were often referred to as beasts and the succeeding kingdoms within those nations as horns. Zechariah followed this same pattern. The four horns he saw represented four kingdoms within the empires that had scattered the Jews. These four kingdoms were the Babylonians, Medo-Persians, Egyptians, and Assyrians. God assured Zechariah through this vision that he would bring justice for Judah against these nations.

In chapter 2 Zechariah saw an angel of the Lord proclaiming Jerusalem would again be a holy city and the Lord would be a wall of fire around it for protection. Beginning in verse seven he described God's judgment against Judah's enemies.

"Come, O Zion! Escape, you who live in the Daughter of Babylon! For this is what the Lord Almighty says: After he has honored me and has sent me against the nations that have plundered you—for whoever touches you touches the apple of his eye- I will surely raise my hand against them so that their slaves will plunder them. Then you will know that the Lord Almighty has sent me. Shout and be glad, O Daughter of Zion. For I am coming, and I will live

> *among you, declares the Lord. Many nations will be joined with the Lord in that day and will become my people. I will live among you and you will know that the Lord Almighty has sent me to you. The Lord will inherit Judah as his portion in the holy land and will again choose Jerusalem. Be still before the Lord, all mankind, because he has roused himself from his holy dwelling"* (Zechariah 2:7-13).

The rebuilding of the temple in Jerusalem meant the resumption of the responsibilities of priests, and most important, the role of the High Priest. It is in this context Zechariah's prophesy went beyond the time of his writing and looked to a future High Priest he identified as "the Branch." He said the Jewish priesthood was symbolic of "things to come."

> *"Listen, O high priest Joshua and your associates seated before you, who are men symbolic of things to come: I am going to bring my servant,* ***the Branch****. See, the stone I have set in front of Joshua! There are seven eyes on that one stone, and I will engrave an inscription on it, says the Lord Almighty,* ***and I will remove the sin of this land in a single day****. In that day each of you will invite his neighbor to sit under his vine and fig tree, declares the Lord Almighty"* (Zechariah 3:8-10).

This Branch who would remove the sin of the people in a single day was the same Branch found in Isaiah 11:1, *"A shoot will come up from the stump of Jesse; from his roots a Branch will bear fruit."* It is seen again in Jeremiah 23:5, *"The days are coming, declares the Lord, when I will raise up to David a righteous Branch, a King who will reign wisely and do what is just and right in the land."* This can only refer to Jesus, the Great High Priest who was to come. His coming was associated in Zechariah's prophecy with the building of the temple. Zechariah, like the other prophets, was guided by the Spirit of God to clearly establish this correlation between the physical temple in Jerusalem and a future spiritual one in heaven. But the role of High Priest was not the only role this coming Branch would fill.

> *"Then the angel who talked with me returned and wakened me, as a man is wakened from his sleep. He asked me, 'What do you see?' I answered, 'I see a solid gold lampstand with a bowl at the top and seven lights on it, with seven channels to the lights. Also there are two olive trees by it, one on the right of the bowl and the other on its left.'*
>
> *I asked the angel who talked with me, 'What are these, my lord?' He answered, 'Do you not know what these are?' 'No, my lord,' I replied. So he said to me, 'This is the word of the Lord to Zerubbabel: Not by might nor by power, but by my Spirit,' says the Lord Almighty. What are you, O mighty mountain? Before Zerubbabel you will become level ground. Then he will bring out the capstone to shouts of 'God bless it! God bless it!' Then the word of the Lord came to me: The hands of Zerubbabel have laid the foundation of this temple; his hands will also complete it. Then you will know that the Lord Almighty has sent me to you. Who despises the day of small things? Men will rejoice when they see the plumb line in the hand of Zerubbabel. (These seven are the eyes of the Lord, which range throughout the earth.)*
>
> *Then I asked the angel, 'What are these two olive trees on the right and the left of the lampstand?' Again I asked him, 'What are these two olive branches beside the two gold pipes that pour out*

golden oil?' He replied, 'Do you not know what these are?' 'No, my lord,' I said. So he said, 'These are the two who are anointed to serve the Lord of all the earth' " (Zechariah 4).

In Zechariah's visions he saw the rebuilding of the temple. The High Priest, Joshua would serve at this rebuilt temple. The temple itself would be built by Zerubbabel. The Lord showed the prophet that the construction of the temple would not be accomplished simply by the might and strength of men, but by the power of the Holy Spirit of God. The seven lights on the bowl at the top of the golden lampstand represented the eyes of the Lord that watch over the affairs of the earth. God knew exactly what he was doing in leading all the armies of the world to come to this particular point in history when Zerubbabel would rebuild the temple. The many events of this period of history from the exile into Babylon to the time of Zechariah may have seemed like ordinary happenings in the world at that time. But they were actually carefully orchestrated by an all-seeing God who was working his divine plan.

The fact that Zerubbabel was selected by God as the one to rebuild the temple was no accident either. On each side of the lampstand in his vision Zachariah saw **two olive trees**. When he asked what these were, he was told they were the two who were anointed to serve the Lord. Two people were "anointed" to serve the Lord in the construction and operation of the original tabernacle in the wilderness that served to house the Ark of the Covenant in the Holy of Holies where the presence of God lived and atonement for sin was made. The man chosen to oversee its construction was Bezalel. *"Then the Lord said to Moses, See, I have chosen Bezalel son of Uri, the son of Hur, **of the tribe of Judah**, and **I have filled him with the Spirit of God**, with skill, ability and knowledge in all kinds of crafts- to make artistic designs for work in* *gold, silver and bronze, to cut and set stones, to work in wood, and to engage in all kinds of craftsmanship"* (Exodus 31:1-4). The head of the Tribe of Judah was "anointed" to build the tabernacle and Aaron, **the High Priest**, was "anointed" to serve in its operation offering blood sacrifices for the atonement of sin.

Once Israel settled in the Promised Land, Jerusalem was chosen as the permanent place for a permanent temple. King Solomon, **the head of the Tribe of Judah** was "anointed" to construct this house of God and **the High Priest** continued to be God's "anointed" one to make atonement for the people. Two people were also "anointed" by God to serve in the construction and operation of the rebuilt the temple in Jerusalem following its destruction by the Babylonians, Zerubbabel, **the head of the Tribe of Judah**, and Joshua **the High Priest**. There would be a final destruction of this temple by the Romans in A.D. 70 and a final, everlasting temple would be built, once again by the "anointed" **head of the Tribe of Judah** and again the "anointed" **High Priest** would make atonement for sin. The difference in this final temple in the kingdom of heaven is the same person would serve as both king and priest. In Revelation 11 John sees these same two olive trees and shows through an incredible vision how Jesus was the ultimate fulfillment of Zechariah's prophecy.

Another prophetic vision of how Jesus will be both builder and High Priest of the future temple is recorded in chapter 6. In this vision we see not only the future of Judah, but how it will also reunite the kingdom.

> *"I looked up again—and there before me were four chariots coming out from between two mountains—mountains of bronze! The first chariot had red horses, the second black, the third white, and the fourth dappled—all of them powerful. I asked the angel who was speaking to me, 'What are these, my lord?' The angel answered me, 'These are the four*

> *spirits of heaven, going out from standing in the presence of the Lord of the whole world. The one with the black horses is going toward the north country, the one with the white horses toward the west, and the one with the dappled horses toward the south.'*
>
> *When the powerful horses went out, they were straining to go throughout the earth. And he said, 'Go throughout the earth!' So they went throughout the earth. Then he called to me, 'Look, those going toward the north country have given my Spirit rest in the land of the north' "* (Zechariah 6:1-8).

Again Zechariah saw horses, this time pulling chariots that went out from the presence of the Lord. They represented the spirits of heaven as they went into the earth. The ones that were specifically singled out were those that went to the North Country and brought peace to that land. After the reign of Solomon, the kingdom of Israel was divided between the kingdom of Israel to the north and the kingdom of Judah in the south. These two factions among the Jews fought each other for many years. Two hundred years before the time of Zechariah, the Northern kingdom had been destroyed and was never rebuilt. Although some of the displaced Jews from the north eventually made their way back to Judea, the kingdom was never truly reunited. Yet, in Zechariah's vision he sees rest in the land of the north.

> *"The word of the Lord came to me: Take silver and gold from the exiles Heldai, Tobijah and Jedaiah, who have arrived from Babylon. Go the same day to the house of Josiah son of Zephaniah. Take the silver and gold and make a crown, and set it on the head of the high priest, Joshua son of Jehozadak. Tell him this is what the Lord Almighty says: 'Here is the man whose name is the Branch, and*

> *he will branch out from his place and build the temple of the Lord. It is he who will build the temple of the Lord, and he will be clothed with majesty and will sit and rule on his throne. And he will be a priest on his throne.* ***And there will be harmony between the two.*** *' The crown will be given to Heldai, Tobijah, Jedaiah and Hen son of Zephaniah as a memorial in the temple of the Lord. Those who are far away will come and help to build the temple of the Lord, and you will know that the Lord Almighty has sent me to you. This will happen if you diligently obey the Lord your God"* (Zechariah 6:9-15).

The Hebrew for the crown in this text is not that which described the turban made for the High Priest, but one for a king. This was a symbolic gesture to show that Joshua represented a future High Priest that would also be crowned king. He clearly stated that the Branch would be a **High Priest on a throne** and the only person who fulfilled that prophecy was Jesus. The prophet also said when that time will have come, there would be harmony between the two. In the context of the former passage about rest in the North Country, this would suggest that God's rest would be for the entire kingdom, not just Judah. Remember what Ezekiel had said, *"I will make them* ***one nation*** *in the land, on the mountains of Israel. There will be* ***one king*** *over all of them and they will* ***never again be two nations or be divided into two kingdoms****"* (Ezekiel 37:21-23). In Christ, the kingdom was finally reunited and there was peace. That both Zechariah and Ezekiel saw Israel's ultimate fulfillment in a future heavenly kingdom cannot be questioned.

> *"Rejoice greatly, O Daughter of Zion! Shout, Daughter of Jerusalem! See, your king comes to you, righteous and having salvation, gentle and riding on*

a donkey, on a colt, the foal of a donkey. I will take away the chariots from Ephraim and the war-horses from Jerusalem, and the battle bow will be broken. He will proclaim peace to the nations. His rule will extend from sea to sea and from the River to the ends of the earth. As for you, because of the blood of my covenant with you, I will free your prisoners from the waterless pit" (Zechariah 9:9-11).

"And I will pour out on the house of David and the inhabitants of Jerusalem a spirit of grace and supplication. They will look on me, the one they have pierced, and they will mourn for him as one mourns for an only child, and grieve bitterly for him as one grieves for a firstborn son" (Zechariah 12:10).

"On that day a fountain will be opened to the house of David and the inhabitants of Jerusalem, to cleanse them from sin and impurity" (Zechariah 13:1).

"Awake, O sword, against my shepherd, against the man who is close to me, declares the Lord Almighty. Strike the shepherd, and the sheep will be scattered, and I will turn my hand against the little ones. In the whole land, declares the Lord, two-thirds will be struck down and perish; yet one-third will be left in it. This third I will bring into the fire; I will refine them like silver and test them like gold. They will call on my name and I will answer them; I will say, 'They are my people,' and they will say, 'The Lord is our God' " (Zechariah 13:7-9, Matthew 26:31, Mark 14:27).

In his final chapter Zechariah predicted a future destruction of

Jerusalem. Since there was only one such event in Israel's future at the time of his writing, he could have only been speaking of that brought about by the Romans in A.D. 70. This was going to be a catastrophic event that was to happen on "the day of the Lord."

> *"A day of the Lord is coming when your plunder will be divided among you. I will gather all the nations to Jerusalem to fight against it; the city will be captured, the houses ransacked, and the women raped. Half of the city will go into exile, but the rest of the people will not be taken from the city. Then the Lord will go out and fight against those nations, as he fights in the day of battle.* **On that day** *his feet will stand on the Mount of Olives, east of Jerusalem, and the Mount of Olives will be split in two from east to west, forming a great valley, with half of the mountain moving north and half moving south. You will flee by my mountain valley, for it will extend to Azel. You will flee as you fled from the earthquake in the days of Uzziah king of Judah.* **Then the Lord my God will come, and all the holy ones with him. On that day** *there will be no light, no cold or frost. It will be a unique day, without daytime or nighttime—a day known to the Lord. When evening comes, there will be light.* **On that day** *living water will flow out from Jerusalem, half to the eastern sea and half to the western sea, in summer and in winter"* (Zechariah 14:1-8).

At the time of that destruction the Lord would come as both king and High Priest to accomplish the mystery of God. He would finish God's plan for redemption and reign as king over the whole world. Jerusalem would then be established forever as an eternal City of God. From this eternal city living water would flow to the east and the west to all who would accept it. Zechariah predicted the Lord would come on that day and bring all the righteous who had gone before with him. It would be a day that would bring about the judgment of the unrighteous as well as atonement for those who were faithful to the Lord. Zechariah's prophesy was totally consistent with that of all the other prophets before and after him. He was prophesying about the time when the physical kingdom of God (Israel) would finally be replaced with the spiritual kingdom of heaven.

> *"The Lord will be king over the whole earth.* ***On that day*** *there will be one Lord, and his name the only name. The whole land, from Geba to Rimmon, south of Jerusalem, will become like the Arabah. But Jerusalem will be raised up and remain in its place, from the Benjamin Gate to the site of the First Gate, to the Corner Gate, and from the Tower of Hananel to the royal winepresses. It will be inhabited;* ***never again will it be destroyed.***
>
> *This is the plague with which the Lord will strike all the nations that fought against Jerusalem: Their flesh will rot while they are still standing on their feet, their eyes will rot in their sockets, and their tongues will rot in their mouths.* ***On that day*** *men will be stricken by the Lord with great panic. Each man will seize the hand of another, and they will attack each other. Judah too will fight at Jerusalem. The wealth of all the surrounding nations will be collected—great quantities of gold and silver and clothing. A similar plague will strike the horses and mules, the camels and donkeys, and all the animals in those camps...* ***On that day*** *HOLY TO THE Lord will be inscribed on the bells of the horses, and the cooking pots in the Lord's house will be like the sacred bowls*

> *in front of the altar. Every pot in Jerusalem and Judah will be holy to the Lord Almighty, and all who come to sacrifice will take some of the pots and cook in them. And* **on that day** *there will no longer be a Canaanite in the house of the Lord Almighty"* (Zechariah 14:9-21).

Following his resurrection and before he ascended back into heaven, Jesus made sure his apostles understood the prophesies about his coming and what would follow. In Luke 24:44-45 he told them, *"This is what I told you while I was still with you: Everything must be fulfilled that is written about me in the Law of Moses, the Prophets and the Psalms. Then he opened their minds so they could understand the Scriptures."* The mission of Jesus was not finished when he ascended. If, as he said, everything written in the Law, the Prophets, and the Psalms had to be fulfilled, he still had work to do. Virtually all the prophets clearly stated the final destruction of Jerusalem was associated with the coming king who would sit on David's throne forever. This changing of the kingdom from earthly to heavenly was not finished, nor were all the prophesies fulfilled, until Jerusalem was destroyed in A.D. 70. Before Christians today can understand how these prophesies were fulfilled, we must first spend the time and effort to study the Old Testament and learn what was prophesied. Once we understand the prophets, we will be able to understand the fulfillment of them…including Revelation.

The more time one spends in studying the Old Testament prophesies, the easier it becomes to understand Revelation. As we attempt to unlock the mysteries of this great book, the reader is encouraged to look for answers in the word of God, not in the modern theories and philosophies of man. Let us now turn our attention to the Revelation of Jesus Christ.

CHAPTER 16

Mystery Accomplished

Revelation 1

"The revelation of Jesus Christ, which God gave him to show his servants what must soon take place. He made it known by sending his angel to his servant John, who testifies to everything he saw—that is, the word of God and the testimony of Jesus Christ. Blessed is the one who reads the words of this prophecy, and blessed are those who hear it and take to heart what is written in it, because the time is near" (1:1-3).

The opening three verses tell us the author as well as the subject and framework of his book. John is identified as the writer to whom this Revelation is given. He was also the author of the fourth gospel as well as three letters included in the New Testament. He had a very close relationship with Jesus and is referred to in Scripture as *"the disciple whom Jesus loved."* It is important to remember, as has been previously noted, that John was the one about whom Jesus said to Peter in John 21:15-23, *"If I want him to remain alive until I return, what is that to you?"* John was to remain alive until Jesus returned because he was the one selected to witness the great day of the Lord and record how Jesus had fulfilled all Scripture. The time had come.

In addition to identifying himself as the author, John's introduction gives major clues to the remainder of the book. The first five words tell us what this book is all about. It is **The Revelation of Jesus Christ**. The Greek word translated revelation is *"apokalupsis,"* which means "an uncovering." Literally it means to make something known that was hidden. Far from the modern notion that Revelation is a book of unfathomable mysteries, it is exactly the opposite. This is the revealing, or uncovering, of the mystery of God that was hidden for generations. This mystery was how Almighty God was going to redeem mankind from the curse of sin and unite all believers of every nation in one eternal kingdom. **The accomplishment of that mystery was the mission of Jesus Christ.** The book of Revelation (not Revelations) is the explanation of how Jesus fulfilled centuries of prophesies and brought to fruition this great mystery of God. As the Apostle Paul wrote in Romans 16:25-27, *"Now to him who is able to establish you by my gospel and the proclamation of Jesus Christ, according to the revelation of the mystery hidden for long ages past, but now revealed and made known through the prophetic writings by the command of the eternal God, so that all nations might believe and obey him— to the only wise God be glory forever through Jesus Christ! Amen."* Let us begin by understanding the title; **THE REVELATION OF JESUS CHIRST**. There is only ONE revelation and it is the revealing (uncovering) of Jesus Christ. Simply believing the name of the book will go a long way toward helping us understand its contents. Everything in this book will relate somehow to "uncovering" how Jesus accomplished the mystery of God. Revelation is the ultimate "this is that" explanation found in the Bible.

The next thing we learn from the introduction is the book of Revelation concerns ***"things that must soon take place, because the time is near."*** If we can simply believe what the Bible says, everything John was going to write about was about to happen during his generation. It was so very important to John, and the Holy Spirit, that readers understand the Revelation was about events of that day that he says twice in the opening three verses and then repeats FIVE TIMES in the closing verses of the book that these things were going to happen SOON. Revelation 22:6, *"The angel said to me, 'These words are trustworthy and true. The Lord, the God of the spirits of the prophets, sent his angel* ***to show his servants the things that must soon take place.'"*** Revelation 22:7, *"Behold,* ***I am coming soon!*** *Blessed is he who keeps the words of the prophecy in this book."* Revelation 22:10, *"Then he told me, 'Do not seal up the words of the prophecy of this book, because* ***the time is near.'*** *"* Revelation 22:12-13, *"Behold,* ***I am coming soon!*** *My reward is with me, and I will give to everyone according to what he has done. I am the Alpha and the Omega, the First and the Last, the Beginning and the End."* Revelation 22:20, *"He who testifies to these things says,* ***'Yes, I am coming soon.'*** *Amen. Come, Lord Jesus."*

By simply reading (and believing) the first verse we already know two things that will help us understand the entire book. First, the Revelation is about Jesus and second it concerns things that were soon going to happen, not things that would happen thousands of years into the future. Most of the modern myths about this book are shattered in the very first verse. Rule number one...**let the Bible interpret itself.**

John then tells us what he saw, which would be described in detail in the book. He said what he saw was *"**the word of God and the testimony of Jesus Christ.**"* One can know from this brief introduction the Revelation is about Jesus Christ as revealed in the word of God, the Scriptures, regarding things that were going to happen very soon. It will be very helpful to keep this introduction in mind as we move forward into the text. The inspired apostle clearly set the framework for the book. If we are willing to accept the Holy Spirit's definition of what this final Revelation is about, we will see how the details fit into the puzzle and unravel the mystery of God.

> *"John, to the seven churches in the province of Asia: Grace and peace to you from him who is, and who was, and who is to come, and from the seven spirits before his throne, and from Jesus Christ, who is the faithful witness, the firstborn from the dead, and the ruler of the kings of the earth. To him who loves us and has freed us from our sins by his blood, and has made us to be a kingdom and priests to serve his God and Father—to him be glory and power for ever and ever! Amen"* (1:4-6).

The salutation is similar to what one sees in other New Testament letters. Although "ground zero" for the events described in Revelation that were soon going to happen was the city of Jerusalem, the book was addressed to first century Christians living hundreds of miles away in what is now Turkey. This underscores the global impact of those age-changing events and the importance of Christians everywhere understanding their significance.

> *"Look, he is coming with the clouds, and every eye will see him, even those who pierced him; and all the peoples of the earth will mourn because of him. So shall it be! Amen. 'I am the Alpha and the Omega,' says the Lord God, 'who is, and who was, and who is to come, the Almighty' "* (1:7-8).

The Revelation begins with the promised return of Jesus. Everything that follows is contingent upon the fulfillment of this promise. Remember, the first verse said John was going to be shown things that **must soon take place**. John was present when Jesus said in Matthew 24:30-34, *"At that time the sign of the Son of Man will appear in the sky, and all the nations of the earth will* *mourn. They will see the Son of Man coming on the clouds of the sky, with power and great glory. And he will send his angels with a loud trumpet call, and they will gather his elect from the four winds, from one end of the heavens to the other…Even so, when you see all these things, you know that it is near, right at the door. I tell you the truth,* ***this generation will certainly not pass away until all these things have happened."***

This concept of his coming in the clouds was not new with Jesus. He was quoting from Daniel 7:13, *"In my vision at night I looked, and there before me was one like a son of man, coming with the clouds of heaven. He approached the Ancient of Days and was led into his presence. He was given authority, glory and sovereign power; all peoples, nations and men of every language worshiped him. His dominion is an everlasting dominion that will not pass away, and his kingdom is one that will never be destroyed."*

Daniel's prophecy concerned the establishment of God's eternal kingdom which would be accomplished during the reign of a "fourth kingdom" that would appear on the earth. One does not have to guess about this kingdom or the time of its existence. The book of Daniel specifically identifies the four kingdoms as the Babylon Empire, followed by the Medes and Persians, the Greeks, and finally the Roman Empire, during which time the God of heaven would establish his kingdom that would never be destroyed.

Describing this time Daniel 2:44-45 says, *"In the time of those kings (fourth kingdom-Roman Empire), the God of heaven will set up a kingdom that will never be destroyed, nor will it be left to another people. It will crush all those kingdoms and bring them to an end, but it will itself endure forever. This is the meaning of the vision of the rock cut out of a mountain, but not by human hands—a rock that broke the iron, the bronze, the clay, the silver and the gold to pieces. The great God has shown the king what will take place in the future. The dream is true and the interpretation is trustworthy."*

John was not only knowledgeable of what Jesus had said about his "coming in the clouds" during that generation, he was also a witness to his ascension into heaven, at which time the angels told the apostles, *"Men of Galilee, why do you stand here looking into the sky? This same Jesus, who has been taken from you into heaven, will come back in the same way you have seen him go into heaven"* (Acts 2:11). They had seen him go "in the clouds," he would return "in the clouds." So John's revealing of Jesus Christ starts with his second appearing "in the clouds." As was explained in greater detail in the discussion of what Jesus said in Matthew 24, Mark 13, and Luke 21, the expression that the Lord would "come in the clouds" was never used in the Bible to describe a literal sighting of God. It was used throughout Old Testament prophesies to refer to God's coming in judgment via an invading foreign army. The context has not changed.

> *"I, John, your brother and companion in the suffering and kingdom and patient endurance that are ours in Jesus, was on the island of Patmos because of the word of God and the testimony of Jesus"* (1:9).

John was on the island of Patmos when he wrote Revelation. Why he was there has been the subject of speculation. He says it was *"because of the word of God and the testimony of Jesus."* Whether he was led by the Spirit to this island to receive God's Revelation, as Moses was led up on Mt. Sinai to receive the Law, or was exiled there by the Romans because of his teaching, we don't know.

> *"On the Lord's Day I was in the Spirit, and I heard behind me a loud voice like a trumpet, which said: 'Write on a scroll what you see and send it to the seven churches: to Ephesus, Smyrna, Pergamum, Thyatira, Sardis, Philadelphia, and Laodicea' "* (1:10-11).

A casual modern observance of these verses might lead one to assume John was worshipping on Sunday when he saw a vision. John was not making a casual observation. He was laying the foundation for everything that was to follow, and understanding the long-anticipated Biblical "Lord's Day" is critical to comprehending the visions contained in the book. The concept of "the Lord's Day" or "the Day of the Lord" was firmly established in Scripture. The Old Testament contains numerous such phrases. Isaiah 13:6 says, *"Wail, for the* ***day of the Lord*** *is near; it will come like destruction from the Almighty."* Joel 2:31, a verse quoted by the Apostle Peter in the first sermon in Acts 2 about the things that would happen in the "last days" said, *"The sun itself will be turned into darkness, and the moon into blood, before the coming of the great and awesome* ***day of the Lord.****"* Predicting the coming of John the Baptist, whom Jesus identified as the fulfillment of the prophecy, Malachi 4:5 says, *"See, I will send you the prophet Elijah before that great and dreadful* ***day of the Lord*** *comes."* How could the coming of John the Baptist been a relevant precedent to the "day of the Lord" if it were not going to come for thousands of years after John lived? And the Apostle Peter in 2 Peter 3:10 uses this same phrase when he says, *"But the* ***day of the Lord*** *will come like a thief. The heavens will disappear with a roar; the elements will be destroyed by fire, and the earth and everything in it will be laid bare."*

Vines Expository Dictionary of New Testament Words has the following to say about this phrase. " 'The Lord's Day,' (Rev 1:10) or 'the Day of the Lord' (where an adjective, kuriakos, is used), is the Day of his manifested judgment on the world." Today's English Version translates this verse, *"On the Lord's day the Spirit took control of me."* And the New World Translation says, *"By inspiration I came to be in the Lord's Day."*

Paul mentions a similar experience he had in 2 Corinthians 12:2, *"I know a man in Christ who fourteen years ago was caught up to the third heaven. Whether it was in the body or out of the body I do not know—God knows."* Paul goes on to say he was not permitted to write about the things he saw. John was caught up "in the Spirit" on "the Lord's Day" and shown things he was instructed to write. He was literally shown what would happen on "that Day" which was soon coming on the earth.

> *"I turned around to see the voice that was speaking to me. And when I turned I saw seven golden lampstands, and among the lampstands was someone 'like a son of man,' dressed in a robe reaching down to his feet and with a golden sash around his chest. His head and hair were white like wool, as white as snow, and his eyes were like blazing fire. His feet were like bronze glowing in a furnace, and his voice was like the sound of rushing waters. In his right hand he held seven stars, and out of his mouth came a sharp double-edged sword. His face was like the sun shining in all its brilliance"* (1:12-16).

This first vision John saw gives us major clues as to how this book should be interpreted. The language is very graphic as well as symbolic and has its origin in the Scriptures. Remember John said in the introduction he was going to reveal how the word of God testifies to Jesus Christ. The concept of Jesus as a "Son of Man" is established throughout the Bible. In the previously noted vision of the fourth beast (Roman Empire) during which time the kingdom of heaven would be established, Daniel said, *"In my vision at night I looked, and there before me was one like a* **son of man**, *coming with the clouds of heaven. He approached the Ancient of Days and was led into his presence. He was given authority, glory and sovereign power; all peoples, nations and men of every language worshiped him. His dominion is an everlasting dominion that will not pass away, and his kingdom is one that will never be destroyed"* (Daniel 7:13-14).

Jesus is identified as this Son of Man at least seventy eight times in the four gospels. In many of these passages his identity as the Son of Man is connected with his coming kingdom. Matthew 16:28 says, *"I tell you the truth, some who are standing here will not taste death before they see the* ***Son of Man coming in his kingdom.****"* In his description of events surrounding the destruction of Jerusalem in Matthew 24:30 he said, *"****At that time*** *the sign of the* ***Son of Man*** *will appear in the sky, and all the nations of the earth will mourn. They will see the* ***Son of Man*** *coming on the clouds of the sky, with power and great glory."* John's description of Jesus in his vision is most certainly one of "power and great glory."

> *"When I saw him, I fell at his feet as though dead. Then he placed his right hand on me and said: 'Do not be afraid. I am the First and the Last. I am the Living One; I was dead, and behold I am alive forever and ever! And I hold the keys of death and Hades' "* (1:17-18).

Not only was John living, through the Spirit, the events of "the Lord's Day," he was about to witness Jesus unlock death and Hades and set the captives free. One does not have to guess what the remainder of the vision means because it is explained for us.

> *"Write, therefore, what you have seen, what is now and what will take place later. The mystery of the seven stars that you saw in my right hand and of the seven golden lampstands is this: The seven stars are the angels of the seven churches, and the seven lampstands are the seven churches"* (1:19-20).

Revelation 2 & 3

In the opening chapter John saw a glorious vision of Jesus portrayed as the Son of Man. Before showing John the things that were soon going to happen, he addressed each of the seven churches. The message to each church was very similar. He encouraged them to remain faithful, or repent if they had already become unfaithful, and persevere until the end, at which time they will receive their reward. It is helpful to notice how he addressed and how he concluded his remarks to each church.

Let us first look at the salutations:

- *"To the angel of the church in Ephesus write: These are the words of him who holds the seven stars in his right hand and walks among the seven golden lampstands"* (2:1).
- *"To the angel of the church in Smyrna write: These are the words of him who is the First and the Last, who died and came to life again"* (2:8).
- *"To the angel of the church in Pergamum write: These are the words of him who has the sharp, double-edged sword"* (2:12).
- *"To the angel of the church in Thyatira write: These are the words of the Son of God, whose eyes are like blazing fire and whose feet are like burnished bronze"* (2:18).
- *"To the angel of the church in Sardis write: These are the words of him who holds the seven spirits of God and the seven stars"* (3:1).
- *"To the angel of the church in Philadelphia write: These are the words of him who is holy and true, who holds the key of David. What he opens no one can shut, and what he shuts no one can open"* (3:7).
- *"To the angel of the church in Laodicea write: These are the words of the Amen, the faithful and true witness, the ruler of God's creation"* (3:14).

Jesus is the person addressing the church in each of these seven salutations. Every one of them could read, "These are the words of Jesus." Instead, each one is a different description of the very same Jesus. Understanding why so many different descriptions are used in the book of Revelation for the same thing is key to our comprehension of the message. Keep in mind the framework laid out in the first chapter. The book is the testimony, or revealing (uncovering), of Jesus as seen in the word of God. These descriptions, and many others which follow, are all taken from quotations or concepts that had been long established throughout the Old Testament as well as the teachings of Jesus and his apostles.

He is described as the first and the last. Isaiah 44:6 says, *"This is what the Lord says— Israel's King and Redeemer, the Lord Almighty:* ***I am the first and I am the last****; apart from me there is no God."* This will be seen again at the close of this book in Revelation 22:13. *"I am the Alpha and the Omega,* ***the First and the Last****, the Beginning and the End."*

He is described as the one who has the sharp, double-edged sword. Hebrews 4:12 says, *"For the* ***word of God*** *is living and active.* ***Sharper than any double-edged sword****, it penetrates even to dividing soul and spirit, joints and marrow; it judges the thoughts and attitudes of the heart."* In John 1:1 this same Apostle John wrote, *"In the beginning was* ***the Word****, and* ***the Word was with God****, and* ***the Word was God****. He was with God in the beginning."* And in verse 14 of that same chapter, *"****The Word became flesh and made his dwelling among us****. We have seen his glory, the glory of the one and only, who came from the Father, full of grace and truth."*

He is described as the Son of God, whose eyes are like blazing fire and whose feet are like burnished bronze. In Daniel 10:5-6 the prophet said, *"I looked up and there before me was a man dressed in linen, with a belt of the finest gold around his waist. His body was like chrysolite, his face like lightning, his* ***eyes like flaming torches****, his* ***arms and legs like the gleam of burnished bronze****, and his voice* *like the sound of a multitude."* In verse 14 of that same chapter the Lord told Daniel, *"I have come to explain to you what will happen to your people* (Israel) *in the future, for the vision concerns a time yet to come."* When John wrote Revelation, that time had finally come.

To the church in Philadelphia he said, *"These are the words of him who is holy and true, who holds the key of David. What he opens no one can shut, and what he shuts no one can open."* Speaking of one who would save a remnant of Israel, Isaiah 22:22 says, *"I will place on his shoulder the* ***key to the house of David; what he opens no one can shut, and what he shuts no one can open.****"*

Finally, he is described as the true and faithful witness and ruler of creation. Jeremiah 42:5-6 employs this same terminology. *"May the Lord be* **a true and faithful witness** *against us if we do not act in accordance with everything the Lord your God sends you to tell us. Whether it is favorable or unfavorable, we will obey the Lord our God, to whom we are sending you, so that it will go well with us, for we will obey the Lord our God."*

The Book of Revelation is the ultimate explanation of everything that has been written before and how the great mystery of God's redemptive plan is finally and completely fulfilled in the person and work of Jesus. The same can be seen in the closing words of each message to these seven churches.

- Ephesus: *"Repent and do the things you did at first. If you do not repent, I will come to you and remove your lampstand from its place"* (2:5).
- Smyrna: *"Be faithful, even to the point of death, and I will give you the crown of life"* (2:10).
- Pergamum: *"To him who overcomes, I will give some of the hidden manna. I will also give him a white stone with a new name written on it, known only to him who receives it"* (2:17).
- Thyatira: *"To him who overcomes and does my will to the end, I will give authority over the*

nations— he will rule them with an iron scepter; he will dash them to pieces like pottery— just as I have received authority from my Father. I will also give him the morning star" (2:26-28).

- Sardis: *"He who overcomes will, like them, be dressed in white. I will never blot out his name from the book of life, but will acknowledge his name before my Father and his angels"* (3:5).
- Philadelphia: *"Him who overcomes I will make a pillar in the temple of my God. Never again will he leave it. I will write on him the name of my God and the name of the city of my God, the new Jerusalem, which is coming down out of heaven from my God; and I will also write on him my new name"* (3:12).
- Laodicea: *"To him who overcomes, I will give the right to sit with me on my throne, just as I overcame and sat down with my Father on his throne"* (3:21).

These do not represent different promises to each church. Rather we see the exact same promise described in different terminology. The basic message is eternal life for the faithful and eternal condemnation for the unfaithful. And, just as in the greetings, the concepts are taken from other Scriptures to show how they are all fulfilled in Jesus.

Revelation 4

"After this I looked, and there before me was a door standing open in heaven. And the voice I had first heard speaking to me like a trumpet said, 'Come up here, and I will show you what must take place

after this' " (4:1).

Beginning with chapter four we get to the actual visions John saw concerning the "soon coming" events that were about to unfold. What John saw in heaven would set the stage for the remainder of the Revelation which had to do with "the word of God," the "testimony of Jesus Christ," and things that "must soon (during his generation) take place."

> *"At once I was in the Spirit, and there before me was a throne in heaven with someone sitting on it. And the one who sat there had the appearance of jasper and carnelian. A rainbow, resembling an emerald, encircled the throne. Surrounding the throne were twenty-four other thrones, and seated on them were twenty-four elders. They were dressed in white and had crowns of gold on their heads. From the throne came flashes of lightning, rumblings and peals of thunder. Before the throne, seven lamps were blazing. These are the seven spirits of God. Also before the throne there was what looked like a sea of glass, clear as crystal.*
>
> *In the center, around the throne, were four living creatures, and they were covered with eyes, in front and in back. The first living creature was like a lion, the second was like an ox, the third had a face like a man, the fourth was like a flying eagle. Each of the four living creatures had six wings and was covered with eyes all around, even under his wings. Day and night they never stop saying: 'Holy, holy, holy is the Lord God Almighty, who was, and is, and is to come.' Whenever the living creatures give glory, honor and thanks to him who sits on the throne and who lives for ever and ever, the twenty-four elders fall down*

> *before him who sits on the throne, and worship him who lives for ever and ever. They lay their crowns before the throne and say: 'You are worthy, our Lord and God, to receive glory and honor and power, for you created all things, and by your will they were created and have their being'* " (4:2-11).

If the Revelation is the "testimony of Jesus Christ" as seen in "the word of God," then what John saw must have some relationship to what had been previously written through the inspiration of the Holy Spirit and the redemptive mission of Jesus. The relationship between the physical kingdom of Israel (old Jerusalem) and the spiritual kingdom of heaven (new Jerusalem) cannot be overstated. The purpose of the physical kingdom was to bring the Messiah into the world to establish the spiritual kingdom. The first kingdom was a prototype of the second. The events of the first were foreshadows of what was to come.

This is clearly seen in the writings of the Old Testament prophets. The prophets described in very graphic images and symbolic language what would happen to the physical nation of Israel. Isaiah, Jeremiah, and Ezekiel all prophesied about the destruction of Jerusalem and its temple by the Babylonians in 586 B.C. They each predicted the return of the Jews to their homeland and the rebuilding of the temple. But their prophesies also clearly described a future destruction that would bring an end to the physical kingdom on the earth and make way for the ultimate promise to Israel, which was an eternal heavenly kingdom. Daniel lived during the days of Babylonian captivity and wrote of these same "end time" events.

The culmination of the eternal plan of redemption, promised since the sin of Adam and Eve, would be fulfilled in the eternal kingdom, not the physical one. This would happen at the "time of the end" during the "last days of Judah and Jerusalem" on the "great day of the Lord" as prophesied throughout the Old Testament. This is also described in Scripture as the "consummation of the ages" when the "mystery of God" would be accomplished. John was taken by the Spirit of God into heaven to witness and record the events of this "great day of the Lord." The Revelation of those events is given in the very same graphic images and the same symbolic language of the Old Testament prophets to show how they were all fulfilled.

The prophet Ezekiel was twice shown a vision of the Lord's presence which serves as a forerunner to John's vision in Revelation. In the first chapter of Ezekiel we read about an *"immense cloud with flashing lightning and surrounded by brilliant light."* The prophet went on to describe, in much greater detail than John, the four living creatures which were in the presence of God. Ezekiel explained his vision in the last verse of the first chapter. *"**This was the appearance of the likeness of the glory of the Lord.** When I saw it, I fell facedown, and I heard the voice of one speaking."* In Ezekiel 10 he saw the same creatures again and identified them in verse 20 as cherubim. *"These were the living creatures I had seen beneath the God of Israel by the Kebar River, and I realized that they were cherubim."* In Isaiah 6:2 they are described as "Seraphim," which literally means "burning ones." Moses was instructed to have two gold replicas of these celestial beings fashioned and to place one at each end of the Mercy Seat on top of the Ark of the Covenant. In each case they represented the place where the presence of God dwelt.

Ezekiel was given a scroll to eat which represented what God wanted him to tell the nation of Israel. It was as sweet as honey in his mouth, but the message was a bitter prediction of Israel's demise. The prophet then proceeded to pronounce God's judgment against Israel and predict not only the impending destruction by the Babylonians, but the ultimate destruction of their kingdom. As with all the Old Testament prophets, Ezekiel also had words of hope for Israel. Ultimately God was going to restore the kingdom of David as an eternal one which would have no end. At that time Israel would receive forgiveness for her sins.

Ezekiel 36:33-36, *"This is what the Sovereign Lord says:* ***On the day I cleanse you from all your sins,*** *I will resettle your towns, and the ruins will be rebuilt. The desolate land will be cultivated instead of lying desolate in the sight of all who pass through it. They will say, 'This land that was laid waste has become like the garden of Eden; the cities that were lying in ruins, desolate and destroyed, are now fortified and inhabited.' Then the nations around you that remain will know that I the Lord have rebuilt what was destroyed and have replanted what was desolate. I the Lord have spoken, and I will do it."* Not until the atonement sacrifice of Jesus did the Israelites, or anyone else, receive cleansing for their sins.

What John saw in heaven was the same "appearance of the likeness of the glory of the Lord" Ezekiel and Isaiah saw. His description is an abbreviated version of the first chapter of Ezekiel. In John's vision, in addition to the four living creatures, he also saw twenty-four elders sitting on thrones around the throne of God. They laid their crowns before the Almighty and bowed down to worship him.

This image has its roots in Isaiah. The prophet pronounced God's judgment against the nations, including Israel, in chapter 22. In chapter 24 he described a day when God would bring devastation on the earth and in verse 22 said, *"The moon will be abashed, the sun ashamed; for the Lord Almighty will reign on Mount Zion and in Jerusalem, and* ***before its elders, gloriously.****"* He continued in the next chapter to describe how the city will have been destroyed, but then said, *"On this mountain the Lord Almighty will prepare a feast of rich food for all peoples, a banquet of aged wine— the best of meats and the finest of wines. On this mountain he will destroy the shroud that enfolds all peoples, the sheet that covers all nations;* ***he will swallow up death forever.*** *The*

Sovereign Lord will wipe away the tears from all faces; he will remove the disgrace of his people from all the earth. The Lord has spoken" (Isaiah 25:6-8).

The specific identity of these twenty-four elders in Revelation is not revealed in the text, but that John saw the Lord reigning on Mt. Zion "before its elders, **gloriously,**" as Isaiah had prophesied, cannot be denied. Many scholars have suggested these elders represent the twelve patriarchs of Israel and the twelve apostles, which is consistent with the overall theme of the book. John was being shown how the great mystery of God would be accomplished. That mystery was how the kingdom of heaven, first represented on earth by the physical kingdom of Israel, was going to provide redemption from sin and include the saved from all generations and nations of mankind at the consummation of the ages. The physical kingdom of Israel began with twelve patriarchs or elders. Jesus began his earthly ministry by selecting twelve apostles who became the founding patriarchs or elders of the kingdom of heaven. John saw all twenty four encircling the throne, casting their crowns before the Almighty demonstrating there is but one kingdom…the kingdom of God.

That some of them represented Israel seems to be confirmed by comments two of them made later in the Revelation text. In Revelation 5:5, *"Then one of the elders said to me, 'Do not weep! See, the Lion of the tribe of Judah, the Root of David, has triumphed. He is able to open the scroll and its seven seals.' "* We will get to the explanation of the scroll and its seals later, but the elders recognized the *"Lion of the tribe of Judah."* However, Revelation 7:13 says, *"Then one of the elders asked me, 'These in white robes—who are they, and where did they come from?' "* This elder did not recognize or understand the non-Jewish redeemed ones, so he asked John (who would have been one of the other "apostle" elders represented) who they were. In John's answer we see the inclusion of all other nations into the kingdom of heaven by the atonement blood of Jesus, which is the answer to the mystery (Ephesians 3:6).

Regardless of the identity of the elders, John saw in heaven *"the appearance of the likeness of the glory of the Lord,"* just as Ezekiel had seen hundreds of years before. A mistake many people make when studying Revelation is to try to assign some meaning or analogy to every detail and every description in the text. Many times the details are simply John's attempt to put into words the grandeur of what he saw. If we allow ourselves to get too bogged down trying to explain details that are not clearly revealed we will miss the overall message. Chapter four sets the stage. The scene is the throne of God in heaven.

Revelation 5

> *"Then I saw in the right hand of him who sat on the throne a scroll with writing on both sides and sealed with seven seals. And I saw a mighty angel proclaiming in a loud voice, 'Who is worthy to break the seals and open the scroll?' But no one in heaven or on earth or under the earth could open the scroll or even look inside it. I wept and wept because no one was found who was worthy to open the scroll or look inside. Then one of the elders said to me, 'Do not weep! See, the Lion of the tribe of Judah, the Root of David, has triumphed. He is able to open the scroll and its seven seals.'*
>
> *Then I saw a Lamb, looking as if it had been slain, standing in the center of the throne, encircled by the four living creatures and the elders. He had seven horns and seven eyes, which are the seven spirits of God sent out into all the earth. He came and took the scroll from the right hand of him who sat on the*

> *throne. And when he had taken it, the four living creatures and the twenty-four elders fell down before the Lamb. Each one had a harp and they were holding golden bowls full of incense, which are the prayers of the saints"* (5:1-8).

Everything John was shown from this point forward had to do with the opening of the seven seals that bound the scroll and the resulting events and consequences. The scroll is identified in Scripture as the word of God. Isaiah 34:16 calls God's word *"**the scroll of the Lord**."* One time when Jesus went to the temple, *"The **scroll** of the prophet Isaiah was handed to him. Unrolling it, he found the place where it is written: The Spirit of the Lord is on me, because he has anointed me to preach good news to the poor. He has sent me to proclaim freedom for the prisoners and recovery of sight for the blind, to release the oppressed, to proclaim the year of the Lord's favor. Then he rolled up the **scroll**, gave it back to the attendant and sat down"* (Luke 4:17-20).

Jesus also said in Luke 24:44, *"All things must be fulfilled which were written in the Law of Moses, and the prophets, and in the Psalms concerning me."* And Hebrews 10:7 quotes Jesus as saying, *"Here I am—**it is written about me in the scroll**— I have come to do your will, O God."* The scroll John saw in heaven was the word of God...which was what he said at the beginning of his writing would be the subject of his Revelation.

What were the seven seals that bound the scroll? The overall purpose of the Scroll (God's word) was to reveal the mystery of his eternal plan by which he determined to redeem mankind from the penalty of sin and establish a way by which the righteous of every generation could be saved. We know from verses we will study in future chapters of Revelation that the opening of the seven seals and the resulting seven trumpets heralded the final accomplishment of the "mystery of God" and the establishment of his eternal kingdom. Revelation 10:7 says, *"But in the days when the seventh angel is about to sound his trumpet,* ***the mystery of God will be accomplished, just as he announced to his servants the prophets.****"* And in Revelation 11:15 we read, *"The seventh angel sounded his trumpet, and there were loud voices in heaven, which said: 'The kingdom of the world has become the kingdom of our Lord and of his Christ, and he will reign for ever and ever.' "* The opening of the seals resulted in the accomplishment of the mystery and the establishment of the kingdom of heaven, just as the Old Testament prophets had foretold. Once again, as John said in his introduction, he saw the revealing (uncovering) of Jesus and just how he fulfilled everything written in the word of God.

The concept of God's covenants being sealed is confirmed in Scripture. When Moses assembled the nation of Israel to review the Law God had given them, in Deuteronomy 29:12-15 he said, *"You are standing here in order to enter into a covenant with the Lord your God,* ***a covenant the Lord is making with you this day and sealing with an oath****, to confirm you this day as his people, that he may be your God as he promised you and as he swore to your fathers, Abraham, Isaac and Jacob. I am making this covenant, with its oath, not only with you who are standing here with us today in the presence of the Lord our God but also with those who are not here today."* In the Bible we find the following covenants, each sealed with the promise or oath of God, that would have to be loosed (opened) before people of every generation could experience divine redemption and be granted eternal life.

1. **Covenant with Adam:** God established his first covenant with Adam and Eve in the Garden. In short, **"You sin, you die."** All who lived under that covenant came under the penalty of death.
2. **Covenant with Noah:** After the flood God made a covenant with Noah and his

descendants. Their inability to keep his covenant resulted in the same consequence for the people of his day…death. The rule was still the same; **"You sin, you die."**

3. **Covenant with Abraham:** God's covenant with Abraham and his descendants contained the promise of a "seed" through which all nations would be blessed. But they still were unable to keep God's laws without sin, so they also suffered spiritual death. **"You sin, you die."**
4. **Covenant with Moses:** Moses was given the Ten Commandments and yet another covenant from God. As Paul said, the law which could have brought life actually resulted in death because they could not keep it. **"You sin, you die."**
5. **Covenant with Death:** The Old Testament clearly revealed the covenant relationship between sin and death. Since by God's decree, the penalty of sin was spiritual death, unless something could be done about sin, death would have dominion over mankind forever. Even though death and the grave were misunderstood by the people of Ephraim who thought they could escape God's judgment by entering into a covenant with them, Isaiah recognized that only when Jesus made atonement for sin could their seal be broken. Isaiah 28:16-18, *"So this is what the Sovereign Lord says: 'See, I lay a stone in Zion, a tested stone, a precious cornerstone for a sure foundation; the one who trusts will never be*

dismayed...Your ***covenant with death*** *will be annulled;* ***your agreement with the grave will not stand.****"*

6. **Covenant with Hades (Grave):** Also by God's own decree, there existed a resulting covenant with the grave (Hades) as also seen in Isaiah's prophecy. Unless atonement for sin could be made, the grave was the eternal "holding place" for both the righteous and unrighteous. It was the Devil's stronghold. Because of sin, nobody could return from the grave.
7. **Covenant of Judgment:** The final oath or covenant God made concerning man and his redemption was one of final judgment. Because sin had consequences, for God to be true to his word, there must be an accounting; a judgment. Jesus discussed the coming judgment in John 5:22-30. *"Moreover, the Father judges no one, but has entrusted all judgment to the Son, that all may honor the Son just as they honor the Father...I tell you the truth, whoever hears my word and believes him who sent me has eternal life and will not be condemned; he has crossed over from death to life...a time is coming when all who are in their graves will hear his voice and come out—those who have done good will rise to live, and those who have done evil will rise to be condemned."* And in John 9:39 he said, *"For judgment I have come into this world..."* In Hebrews 9:27 it says, *"It is appointed for man to die once, and after that to face judgment."* Judgment was the

> final event Jesus would fulfill, the final binding seal he would lose, in accomplishing the mystery of God.

Once all seven seals had been fulfilled or opened, God would have a new covenant with man. This one would be based on grace, not law. There had to be atonement for sin. Without the blood of the perfect sacrifice, someone who could live without sin, there was no hope for redemption. Hebrews 9:15 says, *"Christ is the mediator of a new covenant, that those who are called may receive the promised eternal inheritance—now that he has died as a ransom to set them free from the sins committed under the first covenant."* And in verse 22, *"In fact, the law requires that nearly everything be cleansed with blood, and* ***without the shedding of blood there is no forgiveness.****"* With the atonement of Jesus we finally see a change in the rule; **"You sin…I DIED!"**

In John's vision the only being in all of heaven and earth who could open the scroll, fulfill every covenant and loose every seal was Jesus Christ, the Lamb of God who takes away the sins of the world!

> *"And they sang a new song: 'You are worthy to take the scroll and to open its seals, because you were slain, and with your blood you purchased men for God from every tribe and language and people and nation. You have made them to be a kingdom and priests to serve our God, and they will reign on the earth.'*
>
> *Then I looked and heard the voice of many angels, numbering thousands upon thousands, and ten thousand times ten thousand. They encircled the throne and the living creatures and the elders. In a loud voice they sang: 'Worthy is the Lamb, who was*

> *slain, to receive power and wealth and wisdom and strength and honor and glory and praise!'*
>
> *Then I heard every creature in heaven and on earth and under the earth and on the sea, and all that is in them, singing: 'To him who sits on the throne and to the Lamb be praise and honor and glory and power, for ever and ever!' The four living creatures said, 'Amen,' and the elders fell down and worshiped"* (5:9-14).

With the atonement for sin complete, the great day of the Lord had come and all mankind in every generation could now be judged by one criteria: does a person receive the benefits of the atonement blood sacrifice of Jesus Christ? Those who are declared righteous because of their faithfulness to God's commands, even though they could not keep his laws perfectly, are saved by grace. Those who reject God and his will for their lives receive eternal condemnation. It does not matter under which law or covenant one lived (or lives). The same blood that forgives us our sin today also forgave Adam and Eve for eating that forbidden fruit, and forgave Noah for getting drunk, and forgave Abraham, and Moses…and everyone who ever has or will live.

Revelation 6

Beginning in chapter six and continuing for the next several chapters we will see the opening of the seven seals that bound the scroll, the word of God. One must remember that the only being in heaven or earth who was able to unlock these seals was Jesus, the Lion of the tribe of Judah. This means that whatever the seals were, their opening and the subsequent events that followed were only possible because of Jesus' sacrifice as the *"Lamb of God who takes away the sins of the world."*

There were not only seven seals on the Scroll, but the opening of the seventh seal released seven angels with seven trumpets. There were also seven thunders whose message John was forbidden to write, and there were seven bowls of God's wrath. As we shall soon discover, these are all related and must be considered with each other. The first trumpet and the first bowl of wrath are related to the first seal but could not be released until the seal was opened. The same is true of the others.

> *"I watched as the Lamb opened the first of the seven seals. Then I heard one of the four living creatures say in a voice like thunder, "Come!" I looked, and there before me was a white horse! Its rider held a bow, and he was given a crown, and he rode out as a conqueror bent on conquest"* (6:1-2).

This first covenant which God "sealed" was the one he made with Adam and Eve. The white horse symbolized the sinless state of mankind when this covenant was made. Its rider wore a crown and was sent out to conquer, which is consistent with God's blessing and command to Adam and Eve when he said, *"Be fruitful and increase in number; fill the earth and subdue it. Rule over the fish of the sea and the birds of the air and over every living creature that moves on the ground"* (Genesis 1:28).

> *"When the Lamb opened the second seal, I heard the second living creature say, 'Come!' Then another horse came out, a fiery red one. Its rider was given power to take peace from the earth and to make men slay each other. To him was given a large sword"* (6:3-4).

The second covenant was with Noah and his descendants. The red horse and its rider symbolized the extent to which sin had engulfed the entire world and led to its destruction in the flood. In

Genesis 6:5 the Bible says, *"The Lord saw how great man's wickedness on the earth had become, and that every inclination of the thoughts of his heart was only evil all the time."* In God's covenant with Noah we see for the first time his law of capital punishment for those who "slay each other." Genesis 9:5-6, *"And from each man, too, I will demand an accounting for the life of his fellow man. Whoever sheds the blood of man, by man shall his blood be shed; for in the image of God has God made man."*

> *"When the Lamb opened the third seal, I heard the third living creature say, 'Come!' I looked, and there before me was a black horse! Its rider was holding a pair of scales in his hand. Then I heard what sounded like a voice among the four living creatures, saying, 'A quart of wheat for a day's wages, and three quarts of barley for a day's wages, and do not damage the oil and the wine' "* (6:5-6)!

God's third sealed covenant was the one he made with Abraham. The black horse most likely symbolized the utter hopelessness of mankind without a redeemer. It was to Abraham that the first specific promise of a redeemer was made. Despite the fact that at the time there was no remedy for sin, God promised through Abraham and his seed all nations of the earth would be blessed. The descendants of Abraham also spent 450 years in Egypt where the concepts of weights and measurements, such as the ephah and hin, originated. These became a part of the laws of the Israelites after they emerged from Egypt and traveled across the wilderness. In Leviticus 19:35-37 we read, *"Do not use dishonest standards when measuring length, weight or quantity. Use honest scales and honest weights, an honest ephah and an honest hin. I am the Lord your God, who brought you out of Egypt. Keep all my decrees and all my laws and follow them. I am the Lord."*

> *"When the Lamb opened the fourth seal, I heard*

the voice of the fourth living creature say, 'Come!' I looked, and there before me was a pale horse! Its rider was named Death, and Hades was following close behind him. They were given power over a fourth of the earth to kill by sword, famine and plague, and by the wild beasts of the earth" (6:7-8).

The fourth sealed covenant was the Law of Moses given on Mt. Sinai. This one was represented by a pale horse, the color of death. The Law of Moses was described by the Apostle Paul as that which led to death. In Romans 7:11 he said, *"For sin, seizing the opportunity afforded by the commandment, deceived me, and through the commandment put me to death."* Again in Romans 8:1-2, *"Therefore, there is now no condemnation for those who are in Christ Jesus, because through Christ Jesus the law of the Spirit of life set me free from the* ***law of sin and death.****"*

"When he opened the fifth seal, I saw under the altar the souls of those who had been slain because of the word of God and the testimony they had maintained. They called out in a loud voice, 'How long, Sovereign Lord, holy and true, until you judge the inhabitants of the earth and avenge our blood?' Then each of them was given a white robe, and they were told to wait a little longer, until the number of their fellow servants and brothers who were to be killed as they had been was completed" (6:9-11).

The fifth and sixth sealed covenants we read about in the Old Testament were with death and the grave. With the opening of the fifth seal the righteous dead asked how much longer they would have to wait. The penalty of sin was spiritual death, eternal separation from the presence of God. Until the sacrifice of Jesus and the completion of the atonement ritual, death had absolute control over everyone who lived. Hebrews 2:14-15 says, *"Since the children have flesh and blood, he too* (Jesus) *shared in their humanity so that by his death he might destroy him who holds the power of death—that is, the devil— and free those who all their lives were held in slavery by their fear of death."* In John's Revelation they were told to wait just a little longer until everything was completed.

The opening of the sixth seal will encompass the remainder of chapter six and all of chapter seven.

> *"I watched as he opened the sixth seal. There was a great earthquake. The sun turned black like sackcloth made of goat hair, the whole moon turned blood red, and the stars in the sky fell to earth, as late figs drop from a fig tree when shaken by a strong wind. The sky receded like a scroll, rolling up, and every mountain and island was removed from its place.*
>
> *Then the kings of the earth, the princes, the generals, the rich, the mighty, and every slave and every free man hid in caves and among the rocks of the mountains. They called to the mountains and the rocks, 'Fall on us and hide us from the face of him who sits on the throne and from the wrath of the Lamb! For the great day of their wrath has come, and who can stand' "* (6:12-17)?

Revelation 7

> *"After this I saw four angels standing at the four corners of the earth, holding back the four winds of the earth to prevent any wind from blowing on the land or on the sea or on any tree. Then I saw another angel coming up from the east, having the seal of the living God. He called out in a loud voice to the four*

angels who had been given power to harm the land and the sea: 'Do not harm the land or the sea or the trees until we put a seal on the foreheads of the servants of our God.' Then I heard the number of those who were sealed: 144,000 from all the tribes of Israel.

From the tribe of Judah 12,000 were sealed,
from the tribe of Reuben 12,000,
from the tribe of Gad 12,000,
from the tribe of Asher 12,000,
from the tribe of Naphtali 12,000,
from the tribe of Manasseh 12,000,
from the tribe of Simeon 12,000,
from the tribe of Levi 12,000,
from the tribe of Issachar 12,000,
from the tribe of Zebulun 12,000,
from the tribe of Joseph 12,000,
from the tribe of Benjamin 12,000.

After this I looked and there before me was a great multitude that no one could count, from every nation, tribe, people and language, standing before the throne and in front of the Lamb. They were wearing white robes and were holding palm branches in their hands. And they cried out in a loud voice: 'Salvation belongs to our God, who sits on the throne, and to the Lamb.' All the angels were standing around the throne and around the elders and the four living creatures. They fell down on their faces before the throne and worshiped God, saying: 'Amen! Praise and glory and wisdom and thanks and honor and power and strength be to our God for ever and ever. Amen' "

(7:1-12)!

Once death had been destroyed, the sixth seal with the grave could be released. We see in this glorious scene the assembling of all the saved of the earth before the throne of God. They were marked with God's seal and assembled in his presence prior to the opening of the seventh and final seal of judgment. In Revelation 6:17 John said, *"For the great day of their wrath has come, and who can stand?"* The symbolism for this comes from Ezekiel 9:3-4, *"Now the glory of the God of Israel went up from above the cherubim, where it had been, and moved to the threshold of the temple. Then the Lord called to the man clothed in linen who had the writing kit at his side and said to him, 'Go throughout the city of Jerusalem and put a mark on the foreheads of those who grieve and lament over all the detestable things that are done in it.' "* And in verse six, *"Slaughter old men, young men and maidens, women and children, but do not touch anyone who has the mark."* This marking began with the twelve tribes of Israel and extended to every righteous person on earth. Those who are marked with God's seal escape the judgment and wrath that was about to come on the earth.

> *"Then one of the elders asked me, 'These in white robes—who are they, and where did they come from?' I answered, 'Sir, you know.' And he said, 'These are they who have come out of the great tribulation; they have washed their robes and made them white in the blood of the Lamb. Therefore, they are before the throne of God and serve him day and night in his temple; and he who sits on the throne will spread his tent over them. Never again will they hunger; never again will they thirst. The sun will not beat upon them, nor any scorching heat. For the Lamb at the center of the throne will be their shepherd; he will lead them to springs of living water. And God will wipe away every tear from their eyes"* (7:13-17).

John was not describing life in heaven after we die physically. While that will certainly be the case throughout all eternity, it was a symbolic description of eternal life which we have in Jesus, and begins now, the minute we accept his blood for our atonement. Jesus told the woman at the well in the fourth chapter of John's gospel that she should have asked him and he would have given her "living water." And in John 7:38 Jesus said, *"Whoever believes in me, as the Scripture has said, streams of living water will flow from within him."*

John's Revelation is about the redemptive plan of God, the mystery of the ages, which finds its fulfillment in the atonement sacrifice of Jesus' blood for sin. That was what fulfilled and made possible the opening of these seven seals. Only those who were cleansed by the blood of the Lamb could stand before the Lord of Hosts! They were finally restored to his presence by the atonement of Jesus Christ. He was the only one in heaven or on earth who could open these seals. The saved were given white robes, indicating their forgiveness, and invited into the presence of God...ETERNAL LIFE!

The great tribulation, out of which these saints had come, was sin. God's deliverance of the Israelites from Egyptian slavery was a prototype of mankind's deliverance from sin. Everything about the Exodus was symbolic of our salvation in Christ Jesus. Physical bondage and tribulation, so often suffered by the people of God, was always a result of their rebellion against his will. These physical times of trial represented the greatest tribulation that has plagued mankind since creation; the bondage of sin. In John's Revelation it was the blood of Jesus that finally delivered God's people from this great tribulation.

We see in the above passage the fulfillment of a host of Old Testament prophesies. As John said in his introduction, this is the story of how Jesus fulfilled the Scriptures in accomplishing the mystery of God. Consider the following excerpts from Isaiah in light of what John is saying.

Isaiah 4:4-6, *"The Lord will wash away the filth of the women of Zion;* ***he will cleanse the bloodstains from Jerusalem by a spirit of judgment and a spirit of fire.*** *Then the Lord will create over all of Mount Zion and over those who assemble there a cloud of smoke by day and a glow of flaming fire by night; over all the glory will be a canopy.* ***It will be a shelter and shade from the heat of the day, and a refuge and hiding place from the storm and rain."***

Isaiah 25:6-8, *"On this mountain the Lord Almighty will prepare a feast of rich food for all peoples, a banquet of aged wine— the best of meats and the finest of wines. On this mountain he will destroy the shroud that enfolds all peoples, the sheet that covers all nations;* ***he will swallow up death forever. The Sovereign Lord will wipe away the tears from all faces;*** *he will remove the disgrace of his people from all the earth. The Lord has spoken."*

Isaiah 35:8-10, *"And a highway will be there; it will be called the Way of Holiness. The unclean will not journey on it; it will be for those who walk in that Way; wicked fools will not go about on it. No lion will be there, nor will any ferocious beast get up on it; they will not be found there. But only the redeemed will walk there, and the ransomed of the Lord will return.* ***They will enter Zion with singing; everlasting joy will crown their heads. Gladness and joy will overtake them, and sorrow and sighing will flee away."***

Isaiah 49:8-10, *"This is what the Lord says: In*

> *the time of my favor I will answer you, and* ***in the day of salvation*** *I will help you; I will keep you and will make you to be a covenant for the people, to restore the land and to reassign its desolate inheritances, to say to the captives, 'Come out,' and to those in darkness, 'Be free!' They will feed beside the roads and find pasture on every barren hill.* ***They will neither hunger nor thirst, nor will the desert heat or the sun beat upon them.*** *He who has compassion on them will guide them and lead them beside springs of water."*

> Isaiah 65:17-19, *"Behold, I will create new heavens and a new earth. The former things will not be remembered, nor will they come to mind. But be glad and rejoice forever in what I will create, for I will create Jerusalem to be a delight and its people a joy. I will rejoice over Jerusalem and take delight in my people;* ***the sound of weeping and of crying will be heard in it no more.****"*

With the opening of the sixth seal and the releasing of those who had been held captive by death and the grave, they could now enter the heavenly Jerusalem, the eternal City of God. All of these prophesied blessings are true in the spiritual kingdom of heaven, the church. Remember, John said the events he would describe in this book were things that would soon (in his day) happen. If we are still waiting for this sealing of the redeemed and the judgment, we are also still waiting for the cleansing from sin by the blood of Jesus. These events all happened with the opening of the sixth seal. This was something the Bible said would happen at the "time of the end" on the "great day of the Lord" when Jerusalem would be destroyed.

Revelation 8

> *"When he opened the seventh seal, there was silence in heaven for about half an hour. And I saw the seven angels who stand before God, and to them were given seven trumpets.*
>
> *Another angel, who had a golden censer, came and stood at the altar. He was given much incense to offer, with the prayers of all the saints, on the golden altar before the throne. The smoke of the incense, together with the prayers of the saints, went up before God from the angel's hand. Then the angel took the censer, filled it with fire from the altar, and hurled it on the earth; and there came peals of thunder, rumblings, flashes of lightning and an earthquake.*
>
> *Then the seven angels who had the seven trumpets prepared to sound them"* (8:1-6).

The opening of the seventh seal of judgment began with a period of silence. Since it is not specifically revealed, what this silence represents is the subject of speculation. It may represent the period of time between the last prophesies of the Old Testament and the coming of John the Baptist heralding the kingdom of heaven. It could refer to the period between the ascension of Jesus and the preaching of the first gospel sermon on the day of Pentecost, which was the beginning of the establishment of the kingdom. More likely, since it immediately precedes the judgment of the seventh seal, it represents the time between the ascension of Jesus and his completion of the atonement ritual in heaven. Regardless, it is a time of reverence in light of God's impending judgment as declared in Amos 8:3, *"In that day, declares the Sovereign Lord, the songs in the temple will turn to wailing. Many, many bodies—flung everywhere!* ***Silence!****"*

Following the silence the angel took a censor, filled it with fire from the altar, and hurled it on the earth. Judgment had begun! This would be a judgment of fire. In Isaiah 4:4 the prophet said, *"The Lord will wash away the filth of the women of Zion; he will cleanse the bloodstains from Jerusalem by a spirit of judgment and a spirit of fire."* The Apostle Peter described the coming destruction of Jerusalem and accompanying judgment in the same terms. In 2 Peter 3:7 he said, *"By the same word the present heavens and earth are reserved for fire, being kept for the day of judgment and destruction of ungodly men."* Judgment was the final event on the "great day of the Lord."

From chapter 8 verse seven through chapter 20 everything in the book of Revelation is about the judgment. The seven trumpets and seven bowls of God's wrath resulted from the opening of the seventh seal. To comprehend this lengthy explanation of judgment in Revelation one must understand, as John said in the introduction about everything in his book, it is the explanation of what has already been written in the Scroll, the word of God. The judgment of the world coincides with the judgment of the kingdom of Israel. The fate of the entire world from creation forward is intrinsically linked to the kingdom of Israel. God withheld judgment until the atonement sacrifice was complete. Once that had been accomplished, death was destroyed and judgment was decreed. Salvation and judgment are inseparable in Scripture. They both are directly tied to the fate of Israel. Speaking to a Samaritan woman, Jesus said *"salvation is from the Jews"* (John 4:22).

God's judgment on the physical nation of Israel, which he brought about by the Babylonians, served as the foreshadowing event of his final judgment on the entire world. John's language and symbolism came from the Old Testament prophesies. As we read about the sounding of the trumpets, which herald God's impending judgment, we must understand its historical Biblical background and remember John was explaining (revealing) what was spoken by the prophets concerning the coming king and kingdom.

> Ezekiel 5:8-12, *"Therefore this is what the Sovereign Lord says: I myself am against you, Jerusalem, and I will inflict punishment on you in the sight of the nations. Because of all your detestable idols, I will do to you what I have never done before and will never do again. Therefore in your midst fathers will eat their children, and children will eat their fathers. I will inflict punishment on you and will scatter all your survivors to the winds. Therefore as surely as I live, declares the Sovereign Lord, because you have defiled my sanctuary with all your vile images and detestable practices, I myself will withdraw my favor; I will not look on you with pity or spare you.* ***A third*** *of your people will die of the plague or perish by famine inside you;* ***a third*** *will fall by the sword outside your walls; and* ***a third*** *I will scatter to the winds and pursue with drawn sword."*
>
> Ezekiel 7:1-12, *"The word of the Lord came to me: Son of man, this is what the Sovereign Lord says to the land of Israel: The end! The end has come upon the four corners of the land. The end is now upon you and I will unleash my anger against you. I will judge you according to your conduct and repay you for all your detestable practices. I will not look on you with pity or spare you; I will surely repay you for your conduct and the detestable practices among you. Then you will know that I am the Lord.*
>
> *This is what the Sovereign Lord says: Disaster! An unheard-of disaster is coming. The end has come! The end has come! It has roused itself against you. It has come! Doom has come upon you—you who dwell in the*

> *land. The time has come, the day is near; there is panic, not joy, upon the mountains. I am about to pour out my wrath on you and spend my anger against you; I will judge you according to your conduct and repay you for all your detestable practices. I will not look on you with pity or spare you; I will repay you in accordance with your conduct and the detestable practices among you. Then you will know that it is I the Lord who strikes the blow.*
>
> *The day is here! It has come! Doom has burst forth, the rod has budded, arrogance has blossomed! Violence has grown into a rod to punish wickedness; none of the people will be left, none of that crowd—no wealth, nothing of value. The time has come, the day has arrived."*

We see these same symbolic images and language repeated several times in the coming judgment described in Revelation. As we learned from Ezekiel, we know he was not only speaking of the physical nation of Israel in which he was living. His prophesies were directly aimed at the ultimate destruction of the physical kingdom and the establishment of the eternal City of Jerusalem and the kingdom of heaven.

> Ezekiel 37:22-37, *"I will make them one nation in the land, on the mountains of Israel. There will be one king over all of them and they will never again be two nations or be divided into two kingdoms. They will no longer defile themselves with their idols and vile images or with any of their offenses, for I will save them from all their sinful backsliding, and* ***I will cleanse them. They will be my people, and I will be their God.***
>
> ***My servant David will be king over them, and they will all have one shepherd.*** *They will follow*

> *my laws and be careful to keep my decrees. They will live in the land I gave to my servant Jacob, the land where your fathers lived. They and their children and their children's children will live there forever, and* **David my servant will be their prince forever**. *I will make a covenant of peace with them; it will be an* **everlasting covenant**. *I will establish them and increase their numbers, and I will put my sanctuary among them forever.* **My dwelling place will be with them; I will be their God, and they will be my people**. *Then the nations will know that I the Lord make Israel holy, when* **my sanctuary is among them forever**.*"*

Obviously the prophet could not have literally been referring to David coming back from the dead and reigning in Jerusalem. This was a prophecy of Jesus, the coming prince, who would occupy David's throne forever. Psalm 89:3-4, *"You said, 'I have made a covenant with my chosen one, I have sworn to David my servant, I will establish your line forever and make your throne firm through all generations.' "* And in Isaiah 9:6-7 the prophet foretold, *"For to us a child is born, to us a son is given, and the government will be on his shoulders. And he will be called Wonderful Counselor, Mighty God, Everlasting Father, Prince of Peace. Of the increase of his government and peace there will be no end.* **He will reign on David's throne and over his kingdom**, *establishing and upholding it with justice and righteousness from that time on and forever."*

Before we get back to the text in Revelation, let us recall some of the things the prophet Zechariah said concerning this same time of the end. Like Ezekiel, he was prophesying about the ultimate fate of Israel and how the Lord was going to fulfill his promises to her in the eternal kingdom which was coming to fruition as John was writing the Revelation.

Zechariah 12:1-4, *"This is the word of the Lord concerning Israel. The Lord, who stretches out the heavens, who lays the foundation of the earth, and who forms the spirit of man within him, declares: I am going to make Jerusalem a cup that sends all the surrounding peoples reeling. Judah will be besieged as well as Jerusalem. On that day, when all the nations of the earth are gathered against her, I will make Jerusalem an immovable rock for all the nations."*

Physical Jerusalem and Judah were completely destroyed, never to be rebuilt on earth. The "immovable rock" was the spiritual kingdom of Israel, the heavenly Jerusalem, the church.

Zechariah 12:10-11, *"And I will pour out on the house of David and the inhabitants of Jerusalem a spirit of grace and supplication. They will look on me, the one they have pierced, and they will mourn for him as one mourns for an only child, and grieve bitterly for him as one grieves for a firstborn son. On that day the weeping in Jerusalem will be great, like the weeping of Hadad Rimmon in the plain of Megiddo."*

Zechariah 13:1, *"On that day a fountain will be opened to the house of David and the inhabitants of Jerusalem, to cleanse them from sin and impurity."*

Zechariah 13:7-9, *"Awake, O sword, against my shepherd, against the man who is close to me! declares the Lord Almighty.* **Strike the shepherd, and the sheep will be scattered,** *and I will turn my hand against the little ones. In the whole land, declares the Lord,* **two-thirds** *will be struck down and perish; yet*

> **one-third** *will be left in it. This third I will bring into the fire; I will refine them like silver and test them like gold. They will call on my name and I will answer them; I will say, 'They are my people,' and they will say, 'The Lord is our God.' "*

We know for certain this was a prophecy of Jesus because he quoted this same Scripture and said he was its fulfillment (Matthew 26:31, Mark 14:27). Once we understand God's judgment of the physical nation of Israel was a prototype of his coming judgment of the world, we will be able to understand the judgment depicted by John in Revelation. As we get back to the sounding of the trumpets we shall see the use of similar symbolic language used by Ezekiel and Zechariah. One third is a symbolic term borrowed from the Old Testament prophets, not a literal number.

> *"The first angel sounded his trumpet, and there came hail and fire mixed with blood, and it was hurled down upon the earth. A third of the earth was burned up, a third of the trees were burned up, and all the green grass was burned up"* (8:7).

There were seven trumpets, each corresponding to its respective seal that Jesus has just opened. The first trumpet sounded the judgment of God upon the earth. The pronouncement included the grass and trees, which is indicative of the curse pronounced against Adam with the introduction of sin into the world. *"To Adam he said, 'Because you listened to your wife and ate from the tree about which I commanded you, you must not eat of it, cursed is the ground because of you; through painful toil you will eat of it all the days of your life. It will produce thorns and thistles for you, and you will eat the plants of the field"* (Genesis 3:17-18).

> *"The second angel sounded his trumpet, and*

> *something like a huge mountain, all ablaze, was thrown into the sea. A third of the sea turned into blood, a third of the living creatures in the sea died, and a third of the ships were destroyed"* (8:8-9).

The second trumpet heralded the judgment due under the second seal. The fact this destruction came by water would suggest the flood of Noah's age.

> *"The third angel sounded his trumpet, and a great star, blazing like a torch, fell from the sky on a third of the rivers and on the springs of water— the name of the star is Wormwood. A third of the waters turned bitter, and many people died from the waters that had become bitter"* (8:10-11).

The third trumpet resulted in a star named Wormwood falling from the sky and people being afflicted and dying from its bitterness. Wormwood was an ancient plant that was extremely bitter suggesting the hardship of Egyptian slavery during this period.

> *"The fourth angel sounded his trumpet, and a third of the sun was struck, a third of the moon, and a third of the stars, so that a third of them turned dark. A third of the day was without light, and also a third of the night"* (8:12).

The fourth trumpet sounded God's judgment against those living under the Law of Moses. It was directed at the heavenly bodies, which corresponds to how the prophet Isaiah had described Israel's creation by God as the creation of the Heavens and earth (Isaiah 51:15-16).

> *"As I watched, I heard an eagle that was flying in midair call out in a loud voice: 'Woe! Woe! Woe to*

> *the inhabitants of the earth, because of the trumpet blasts about to be sounded by the other three angels'* " (8:13)!

There were three woes which accompanied the final three trumpets. Because these judgments had to do with the overcoming of death, the grave, and God's final judgment on the entire world, they had an enormous impact, both physically and spiritually, in heaven and on earth. The final woe includes the seven bowls of God's wrath and extends through chapter 20 of Revelation.

Revelation 9

> *"The fifth angel sounded his trumpet, and I saw a star that had fallen from the sky to the earth. The star was given the key to the shaft of the Abyss. When he opened the Abyss, smoke rose from it like the smoke from a gigantic furnace. The sun and sky were darkened by the smoke from the Abyss. And out of the smoke locusts came down upon the earth and were given power like that of scorpions of the earth. They were told not to harm the grass of the earth or any plant or tree, but only those people who did not have the seal of God on their foreheads. They were not given power to kill them, but only to torture them for five months. And the agony they suffered was like that of the sting of a scorpion when it strikes a man. During those days men will seek death, but will not find it; they will long to die, but death will elude them.*
>
> *The locusts looked like horses prepared for battle. On their heads they wore something like crowns of gold, and their faces resembled human faces. Their hair was like women's hair, and their teeth were like*

> *lions' teeth. They had breastplates like breastplates of iron, and the sound of their wings was like the thundering of many horses and chariots rushing into battle. They had tails and stings like scorpions, and in their tails they had power to torment people for five months. They had as king over them the angel of the Abyss, whose name in Hebrew is Abaddon, and in Greek, Apollyon. The first woe is past; two other woes are yet to come"* (9:1-12).

The abyss is the eternal home of the Devil and his angels and will be the home of all those who refuse to accept the atonement of Jesus for their sin. It is a place of eternal separation from the presence of God, which is spiritual death. It is the consequence of sin. During the time of Jesus, demons were allowed to roam the earth and possess people. In Matthew 8:28-32, *"When he* (Jesus) *arrived at the other side in the region of the Gadarenes, two demon-possessed men coming from the tombs met him. They were so violent that no one could pass that way. 'What do you want with us, Son of God?' they shouted. 'Have you come here to torture us before the appointed time?' Some distance from them a large herd of pigs was feeding. The demons begged Jesus, 'If you drive us out, send us into the herd of pigs.' He said to them, 'Go!' So they came out and went into the pigs, and the whole herd rushed down the steep bank into the lake and died in the water."*

These demons understood a time was coming when they would not be allowed to roam free but would be locked in the abyss forever. They also recognized Jesus as the Son of God who had come to do just that. The star coming from heaven, going into the abyss, signified Jesus entering the realm of death to overcome the devil. In a discussion about casting out demons in Matthew 12:29 he said, *"How can anyone enter a strong man's house and carry off his possessions unless he first ties up the strong man? Then he can rob his house.*" Until Jesus resurrection and atonement for sin, death had complete control over everyone, good or bad. Not until the atonement were the righteous freed from the hold of death.

Not only did this fifth trumpet sound the demise of death, it also brought destruction to those who did not have the mark of God. With his triumph over death, Jesus not only freed the righteous, he also sealed the eternal fate of the unrighteous. He was the only hope for the dead. The plague of locusts were allowed to destroy the unsaved.

We must also remember this "time of the end" was also a time of terrible persecution on the earth. Daniel, Ezekiel, and Jesus had all described the persecution of this time as something that had not happened before nor would happen again. Cornelius Gallus was a Roman poet who lived during the first century. He wrote, "Worse than any wound is the wish to die and yet not be able to do so." The first woe is passed.

> *"The sixth angel sounded his trumpet, and I heard a voice coming from the horns of the golden altar that is before God. It said to the sixth angel who had the trumpet, 'Release the four angels who are bound at the great river Euphrates.' And the four angels who had been kept ready for this very hour and day and month and year were released to kill a third of mankind. The number of the mounted troops was two hundred million. I heard their number.*
>
> *The horses and riders I saw in my vision looked like this: Their breastplates were fiery red, dark blue, and yellow as sulfur. The heads of the horses resembled the heads of lions, and out of their mouths came fire, smoke and sulfur. A third of mankind was killed by the three plagues of fire, smoke and sulfur that came out of their mouths. The power of the horses was in their mouths and in their tails; for their*

> *tails were like snakes, having heads with which they inflict injury.*
>
> *The rest of mankind that were not killed by these plagues still did not repent of the work of their hands; they did not stop worshiping demons, and idols of gold, silver, bronze, stone and wood—idols that cannot see or hear or walk. Nor did they repent of their murders, their magic arts, their sexual immorality or their thefts"* (9:13-21).

The sixth trumpet sounded God's judgment for all who were in the grave. With the resurrection of Jesus, the Devil's stronghold had been invaded and his power crushed. It was time to free the captives. As Isaiah 28:16-18 predicted, *"So this is what the Sovereign Lord says: 'See, I lay a stone in Zion, a tested stone, a precious cornerstone for a sure foundation; the one who trusts will never be dismayed...Your* ***covenant with death*** *will be annulled;* ***your agreement with the grave will not stand.****"* We see in John's vision the preparation for a battle of eternal proportions and significance. There were also fierce battles going on in the physical realm in Jerusalem and Judea with the Jewish Roman Wars. This is exactly what Jesus had predicted in Matthew 24, Mark 13 and Luke 21. At that time Jesus had told his disciples they would be able to read signs to know the time was approaching, but would not know the exact day or hour. Here John was shown "the rest of the story." The four angels who had been kept ready for **this very hour and day and month and year** were released. The time for the consummation of the ages had come. John witnessed the "great day of the Lord" and saw the ultimate triumph of Jesus as the spiritual, eternal kingdom of heaven replaced the old physical kingdom of Israel. This was also the signal to all the saints that the atonement was a reality! It was the second appearance of the High Priest from behind the veil. But it was a time of terrible persecution. Those who had listened to Jesus had left the city, escaping into the hills.

Revelation 10

> *"Then I saw another mighty angel coming down from heaven. He was robed in a cloud, with a rainbow above his head; his face was like the sun, and his legs were like fiery pillars. He was holding a little scroll, which lay open in his hand. He planted his right foot on the sea and his left foot on the land, and he gave a loud shout like the roar of a lion. When he shouted, the voices of the seven thunders spoke. And when the seven thunders spoke, I was about to write; but I heard a voice from heaven say, 'Seal up what the seven thunders have said and do not write it down'"* (10:1-4).

As has been previously stated, God does not choose to reveal everything to us. Based on the structure of the book we can surmise these thunders would have spoken about each of the seven seals. What they actually said will remain a mystery.

> *"Then the angel I had seen standing on the sea and on the land raised his right hand to heaven. And he swore by him who lives for ever and ever, who created the heavens and all that is in them, the earth and all that is in it, and the sea and all that is in it, and said, 'There will be no more delay! But in the days when the seventh angel is about to sound his trumpet, the mystery of God will be accomplished, just as he announced to his servants the prophets'"* (10:5-7).

The announcement by the angel of what would happen when the seventh angel sounded his trumpet is critical to understanding the Book of Revelation. Everything that had happened up to this point and everything that happens after the sounding of this last trumpet had to do with accomplishing the mystery of God. The mystery of God is clearly defined in Scripture. In Ephesians 1:9-10 Paul said, *"And he (God) made known to us the* ***mystery of his will*** *according to his good pleasure, which he purposed in Christ, to be put into effect when the times will have reached their fulfillment—****to bring all things in heaven and on earth together under one head, even Christ.****"* And in chapter 3:4-6, *"In reading this, then, you will be able to understand my insight into the* ***mystery of Christ,*** *which was not made known to men in other generations as it has now been revealed by the Spirit to God's holy apostles and prophets.* ***This mystery is that through the gospel the Gentiles are heirs together with Israel, members together of one body, and sharers together in the promise in Christ Jesus.****"* He further identified that body as the church in verses 10-11, *"His intent was that now, through the church, the manifold wisdom of God should be made known to the rulers and authorities in the heavenly realms, according to his eternal purpose which he accomplished in Christ Jesus our Lord."*

He wrote the same thing in Colossians 1:26-27 where he spoke again of "*...****the mystery that has been kept hidden for ages and generations,*** *but is now disclosed to the saints. To them God has chosen to make known among the Gentiles* ***the glorious riches of this mystery, which is Christ in you, the hope of glory.****"*

In 1 Peter 1:12 Peter referred to the same revealing of this mystery when he wrote of the message of the prophets of the Old Testament. *"It was revealed to them that they were not serving themselves but you, when they spoke of the things that have now been told you by those who have preached the gospel to you by the Holy Spirit sent from heaven. Even angels long to look into these things."*

When the seventh angel sounded his trumpet all things in

heaven and on earth were brought together under one head, Christ. The Gentiles became heirs together with Israel, members together of one body, the kingdom of heaven, the church. The things in Revelation that were to shortly come to pass had to do with the completion of the kingdom. This included the judgment because that was what the seventh trumpet heralded with the opening of the seventh seal. This becomes very clear by the end of the book.

> *"Then the voice that I had heard from heaven spoke to me once more: 'Go, take the scroll that lies open in the hand of the angel who is standing on the sea and on the land.' So I went to the angel and asked him to give me the little scroll. He said to me, 'Take it and eat it. It will turn your stomach sour, but in your mouth it will be as sweet as honey.' I took the little scroll from the angel's hand and ate it. It tasted as sweet as honey in my mouth, but when I had eaten it, my stomach turned sour. Then I was told, 'You must prophesy again about many peoples, nations, languages and kings' "* (10:8-11).

This scene in Revelation also came from Ezekiel. The prophet was chosen to prophesy against the nation of Israel for her sins against God. He was given a little scroll, just as John was. The scroll tasted sweet but its message was a very bitter one for his fellow countrymen. Ezekiel 2:9-3:3, *"Then I looked, and I saw a hand stretched out to me. In it was a scroll, which he unrolled before me. On both sides of it were written words of lament and mourning and woe. And he said to me, 'Son of man, eat what is before you, eat this scroll; then go and speak to the house of Israel.' So I opened my mouth, and he gave me the scroll to eat. Then he said to me, 'Son of man, eat this scroll I am giving you and fill your stomach with it.' So I ate it, and it tasted as sweet as honey in my mouth."*

For the next thirty-seven chapters Ezekiel was sent throughout the land to prophesy against Israel. He graphically predicted the complete destruction of Jerusalem and its temple, then predicted a day when the Lord world rebuild it as an eternal sanctuary for his people. Beginning in chapter forty he was told to measure the new temple. Following the measuring of the temple he said in Ezekiel 43:5-9, *"Then the Spirit lifted me up and brought me into the inner court, and the glory of the Lord filled the temple. While the man was standing beside me, I heard someone speaking to me from inside the temple. He said: 'Son of man, this is the place of my throne and the place for the soles of my feet.* ***This is where I will live among the Israelites forever****. The house of Israel will never again defile my holy name—neither they nor their kings—by their prostitution and the lifeless idols of their kings at their high places. When they placed their threshold next to my threshold and their doorposts beside my doorposts, with only a wall between me and them, they defiled my holy name by their detestable practices. So I destroyed them in my anger. Now let them put away from me their prostitution and the lifeless idols of their kings, and I will live among them forever."*

Just as Peter had said on the Day of Pentecost in Acts 2, *"...this is that which was spoken by the prophet Joel,"* John, in Revelation 10, saw in person the fulfillment of the prophecy of Ezekiel. He was given a little scroll to eat that was sweet to the taste, but contained some bitter prophesies regarding the physical nation of Israel and the persecution that would lead up to its final destruction in the very near future by the Roman Empire.

Revelation 11

> *"I was given a reed like a measuring rod and was told, 'Go and measure the temple of God and the altar, and count the worshipers there. But exclude the outer court; do not measure it, because it has been*

given to the Gentiles. They will trample on the holy city for 42 months. And I will give power to my two witnesses, and they will prophesy for 1,260 days, clothed in sackcloth. These are the two olive trees and the two lampstands that stand before the Lord of the earth. If anyone tries to harm them, fire comes from their mouths and devours their enemies. This is how anyone who wants to harm them must die. These men have power to shut up the sky so that it will not rain during the time they are prophesying; and they have power to turn the waters into blood and to strike the earth with every kind of plague as often as they want' "(11:1-6).

Ezekiel measured the newly rebuilt temple in anticipation of the restoration of Israel. John was told to measure this same rebuilt temple in view of its impending final destruction. It was going to be trampled by the Gentiles. Before that would happen, God would give power to his two witnesses to prophesy for three-and-one-half years. These are the same two witnesses, or olive trees, Zechariah saw. Therefore we know they are, "*...the two who are anointed to serve the Lord of all the earth*" (Zechariah 4:14). These two are identified by Zechariah as the anointed king, or head, of the tribe of Judah and the High Priest.

Every High Priest who ever served at the temple was a prototype of the coming Christ. Every king who sat on the throne of David was also a prototype of the same coming King of Kings. Both the anointed king and High Priest would find their eventual fulfillment in the person and work of Jesus. Jesus was the incarnate word of God. John, in his Gospel, said, "*In the beginning was the Word, and the Word was with God, and the Word was God...the Word became flesh and dwelt with men*" (John 1). The Word of God is all powerful, having the power to destroy enemies, to control nature, to work wonders, and bring plagues on the earth. God gave power to him as both king and High Priest and he prophesied for three-and-one-half years before being crucified. Everything these two anointed ones stood for throughout the history of Israel died with Jesus.

> *"Now when they have finished their testimony, the beast that comes up from the Abyss will attack them, and overpower and kill them. Their bodies will lie in the street of the great city, which is figuratively called Sodom and Egypt, where also their Lord was crucified. For three and a half days men from every people, tribe, language and nation will gaze on their bodies and refuse them burial. The inhabitants of the earth will gloat over them and will celebrate by sending each other gifts, because these two prophets had tormented those who live on the earth. But after the three and a half days a breath of life from God entered them, and they stood on their feet, and terror struck those who saw them. Then they heard a loud voice from heaven saying to them, 'Come up here.' And they went up to heaven in a cloud, while their enemies looked on. At that very hour there was a severe earthquake and a tenth of the city collapsed. Seven thousand people were killed in the earthquake, and the survivors were terrified and gave glory to the God of heaven. The second woe has passed; the third woe is coming soon"* (11:7-14).

For three days and nights the powers of Satan rejoiced over their seeming victory. Then these two witnesses, king (head of the Tribe of Judah) and High Priest, both now represented in the person of Jesus, came back to life by the Spirit of God and were called back up to heaven. Their mission was to reestablish one final time the temple of God and heavenly City of Jerusalem. At the resurrection of Jesus there was a great earthquake, the power of the grave had been overcome. The sixth seal had been broken.

With the sounding of the seventh trumpet, judgment was proclaimed on the earth. As the angel had said, *"There will be no more delay! But in the days when the seventh angel is about to sound his trumpet,* **the mystery of God will be accomplished***, just as he announced to his servants the prophets."*

> *"The seventh angel sounded his trumpet, and there were loud voices in heaven, which said: 'The kingdom of the world has become the kingdom of our Lord and of his Christ, and he will reign for ever and ever.' And the twenty-four elders, who were seated on their thrones before God, fell on their faces and worshiped God, saying: 'We give thanks to you, Lord God Almighty, the one who is and who was, because you have taken your great power and have begun to reign. The nations were angry; and your wrath has come. The time has come for judging the dead, and for rewarding your servants the prophets and your saints and those who reverence your name, both small and great— and for destroying those who destroy the earth.' Then God's temple in heaven was opened, and within his temple was seen the ark of his covenant. And there came flashes of lightning, rumblings, peals of thunder, an earthquake and a great hailstorm"* (11:15-19).

With the sounding of the seventh trumpet the time had come for judging the dead. This is the same time Daniel saw in his vision. Daniel 12:1-4, *"There will be a time of distress such as has not happened from the beginning of nations until then. But at that time your people—everyone whose name is found written in the book—will be delivered. Multitudes who sleep in the dust of the earth will awake: some to everlasting life, others to shame and everlasting contempt. Those who are wise will shine like the brightness of the heavens, and those who lead many to righteousness, like the stars for ever and ever. But you, Daniel, close up and seal the words of the scroll until the time of the end."*

This would also be the time when the kingdom of the world, the physical kingdom of Israel which had served as the prototype of the church for so many years, would finally become the kingdom of our Lord Jesus Christ. This kingdom will have no end. Jesus will reign forever and ever. As he said, *"Upon this rock I will build my church and the gates of Hell shall not prevail against it"* (Matthew 16:18). In Matthew 25:31-33 Jesus said, *"When the Son of Man comes in his glory, and all the angels with him, he will sit on his throne in heavenly glory. All the nations will be gathered before him, and he will separate the people one from another as a shepherd separates the sheep from the goats. He will put the sheep on his right and the goats on his left."* Jesus continued, *"Then he will say to those on his left, 'Depart from me, you who are cursed, into the eternal fire prepared for the devil and his angels."* (vs. 41)

Again in the Gospel of John (12:30-33), Jesus spoke of how his death would result in judgment, the destruction of Satan's power, and salvation. *" 'Now is the time for judgment on this world; now the prince of this world will be driven out. But I, when I am lifted up from the earth, will draw all men to myself.' He said this to show the kind of death he was going to die."* John saw in his vision the temple in heaven and in it was the Ark of the Covenant. It was on this Altar, not the one in the physical temple in Jerusalem, that Jesus took his blood sacrifice to make atonement for our sins.

At the time of the writing of the New Testament the "day of the Lord" and the judgment was still in their future. Paul said in Romans 2:5, *"But because of your stubbornness and your unrepentant heart, you are storing up wrath against yourself for the day of God's wrath, when his righteous judgment will be revealed."* And Peter said in 2 Peter 2:9, *"...the Lord knows how to rescue godly men from trials and to hold the unrighteous for the day of judgment, while continuing their punishment."* Both of these apostles wrote a few years before John's Revelation and both of them explained this day was not centuries away, but coming soon, right at the door. John was witnessing first hand this great day.

Revelation 12

> *"A great and wondrous sign appeared in heaven: a woman clothed with the sun, with the moon under her feet and a crown of twelve stars on her head. She was pregnant and cried out in pain as she was about to give birth. Then another sign appeared in heaven: an enormous red dragon with seven heads and ten horns and seven crowns on his heads. His tail swept a third of the stars out of the sky and flung them to the earth. The dragon stood in front of the woman who was about to give birth, so that he might devour her child the moment it was born. She gave birth to a son, a male child, who will rule all the nations with an iron scepter. And her child was snatched up to God and to his throne. The woman fled into the desert to a place prepared for her by God, where she might be taken care of for 1,260 days"* (12:1-6).

Three times the prophet Isaiah described Israel as a mother who was to give birth to a male child who would fulfill God's promise to build his everlasting kingdom. The coming of this male child and the kingdom he would establish would also result in the judgment. In Isaiah 66:6-16, *"Hear that uproar from the city, hear that noise from the temple! It is the sound of the Lord repaying his enemies all they deserve. Before she goes into labor, she gives birth; before the pains come upon her, she delivers a son. Who has ever heard of such a thing? Who has ever seen such things? Can a country be born in a day or a nation be brought forth in a moment? Yet no sooner is Zion in labor than she gives birth to her children. 'Do I bring to the moment of birth and not give delivery?' says the Lord. 'Do I close up the womb when I bring to delivery?' says your God. Rejoice with Jerusalem and be glad for her, all you who love her; rejoice greatly with her, all you who mourn over her...As a mother comforts her child, so will I comfort you; and you will be comforted over Jerusalem. When you see this, your heart will rejoice and you will flourish like grass; the hand of the Lord will be made known to his servants, but his fury will be shown to his foes. See, the Lord is coming with fire, and his chariots are like a whirlwind; he will bring down his anger with fury, and his rebuke with flames of fire. For with fire and with his sword the Lord will execute judgment upon all men, and many will be those slain by the Lord."*

The woman and the child in John's Revelation were the same woman and child of Isaiah's prophecy. John was writing the Revelation of Jesus Christ as seen by the prophets. His stated purpose from the beginning was to explain how Jesus fulfilled these prophesies. That he would come as a king who would rule with an iron scepter was prophesied in Psalm 2:6-9, *"I have installed my king on Zion, my holy hill. I will proclaim the decree of the Lord: He said to me, 'You are my Son; today I have become your Father. Ask of me, and I will make the nations your inheritance, the ends of the earth your possession. You will rule them with an iron scepter; you will dash them to pieces like pottery."* Three times in Revelation John referred to this Psalm (Revelation 2:27, 12:5, 19:15). Because of sin, Satan had dominion over God's creation and he would not give up without a fight.

> *"And there was war in heaven. Michael and his angels fought against the dragon, and the dragon and*

> *his angels fought back. But he was not strong enough, and they lost their place in heaven. The great dragon was hurled down—that ancient serpent called the devil, or Satan, who leads the whole world astray. He was hurled to the earth, and his angels with him. Then I heard a loud voice in heaven say: Now have come the salvation and the power and the kingdom of our God, and the authority of his Christ. For the accuser of our brothers, who accuses them before our God day and night, has been hurled down. They overcame him by the blood of the Lamb and by the word of their testimony; they did not love their lives so much as to shrink from death. Therefore rejoice, you heavens and you who dwell in them! But woe to the earth and the sea, because the devil has gone down to you! He is filled with fury, because he knows that his time is short"* (12:7-12).

Since the fall of Adam and Eve, Satan had been able to stand before the throne of God and proclaim victory over mankind. With the crucifixion of Jesus, the Devil thought he had claimed the ultimate victory over God. There was one major flaw in his devious plan. With no sin, Jesus was not bound by the covenant of death and the grave could not hold him as it had every other person who had lived on the earth. With his atoning sacrifice he could now free all those who had been held captive by Satan since creation. The Devil was forever banished from heaven, never again able to stand before God and accuse his people of sin, because the blood of Jesus had removed sin forever.

Jesus came to destroy the Devil and his work. 1 John 3:8, *"He who does what is sinful is of the devil, because the devil has been sinning from the beginning. **The reason the Son of God appeared was to destroy the devil's work.**"* The writer of Hebrews said in chapter 2:14-15, *"Since the children have flesh and blood, he too shared in their humanity so that by his death he might destroy him who holds the power of death—that is, the devil— and free those who all their lives were held in slavery by their fear of death."* The Devil was hurled to the earth where he would continue his battle, but his time was limited.

> *"When the dragon saw that he had been hurled to the earth, he pursued the woman who had given birth to the male child. The woman was given the two wings of a great eagle, so that she might fly to the place prepared for her in the desert, where she would be taken care of for a time, times and half a time, out of the serpent's reach. Then from his mouth the serpent spewed water like a river, to overtake the woman and sweep her away with the torrent. But the earth helped the woman by opening its mouth and swallowing the river that the dragon had spewed out of his mouth. Then the dragon was enraged at the woman and went off to make war against the rest of her offspring—those who obey God's commandments and hold to the testimony of Jesus"* (12:13-17).

When the Devil was hurled to the earth, he first made war against the woman, the faithful of Israel, who had given birth to the male child, Jesus. The reference to time, times and half a time clearly identified the events John was revealing as the same prophesied by Daniel in chapters 7 and 12 of that Old Testament book.

> *"The fourth beast is a fourth kingdom that will appear on earth. It will be different from all the other kingdoms and will devour the whole earth, trampling it down and crushing it. The ten horns are ten kings who will come from this kingdom. After them another king will arise, different from the earlier ones; he will subdue*

three kings. He will speak against the Most High and oppress his saints and try to change the set times and the laws. The saints will be handed over to him for a ***time, times and half a time.***

But the court will sit, and his power will be taken away and completely destroyed forever. Then the sovereignty, power and greatness of the kingdoms under the whole heaven will be handed over to the saints, the people of the Most High. His kingdom will be an everlasting kingdom, and all rulers will worship and obey him" (Daniel 7:23-28).

"At that time Michael, the great prince who protects your people, will arise. There will be a time of distress such as has not happened from the beginning of nations until then. But at that time your people—everyone whose name is found written in the book—will be delivered. Multitudes who sleep in the dust of the earth will awake: some to everlasting life, others to shame and everlasting contempt. Those who are wise will shine like the brightness of the heavens, and those who lead many to righteousness, like the stars for ever and ever... Then I, Daniel, looked, and there before me stood two others, one on this bank of the river and one on the opposite bank. One of them said to the man clothed in linen, who was above the waters of the river, 'How long will it be before these astonishing things are fulfilled?'

The man clothed in linen, who was above the waters of the river, lifted his right hand and his left hand toward heaven, and I heard him swear by him who lives forever, saying, 'It will be for a ***time, times and half a time.*** *When the power of the holy people has been finally broken, all these things will be completed' "* (Daniel 12:1-7).

Daniel said this would happen when the nation that would rise to power following the Babylonians, Medes and Persians, and the Greeks would invade the Beautiful Land, the home of his people, and set up *"the abomination that causes desolation"* in the temple. He further described it as *"...a time of distress such as has not happened from the beginning of nations until then."* Jesus clearly identified these very same things as he explained to his disciples the signs that would precede the destruction of Jerusalem in his generation (Matthew 24, Mark 13, Luke 21). The invading nation was Rome; the time was A. D. 70.

The believers who listened to Jesus were given "wings of an eagle" to flee Jerusalem and escape its destruction. He had told them, *"...let those who are in Judea flee to the mountains. Let no one on the roof of his house go down to take anything out of the house. Let no one in the field go back to get his cloak. How dreadful it will be in those days for pregnant women and nursing mothers! Pray that your flight will not take place in winter or on the Sabbath. For then there will be great distress, unequaled from the beginning of the world until now—and never to be equaled again. If those days had not been cut short, no one would survive, but for the sake of the elect those days will be shortened"* (Matthew 24:16-22). This time also brought about a great persecution against "the rest of her offspring;" Christians who had believed in Jesus Christ and were obedient to God. The history of the Roman Empire during this time, especially the reign of Nero, confirms the truth and fulfillment of these prophesies.

Revelation 13

John continued to parallel and explain the prophesies of Daniel in his description of the Roman armies who would advance against Jerusalem and destroy the city and its beloved temple.

> *"And the dragon stood on the shore of the sea. And*
> *I saw a beast coming out of the sea. He had ten horns*

> *and seven heads, with ten crowns on his horns, and on each head a blasphemous name. The beast I saw resembled a leopard, but had feet like those of a bear and a mouth like that of a lion. The dragon gave the beast his power and his throne and great authority. One of the heads of the beast seemed to have had a fatal wound, but the fatal wound had been healed. The whole world was astonished and followed the beast. Men worshiped the dragon because he had given authority to the beast, and they also worshiped the beast and asked, 'Who is like the beast? Who can make war against him?'*
>
> *The beast was given a mouth to utter proud words and blasphemies and to exercise his authority for forty-two months. He opened his mouth to blaspheme God, and to slander his name and his dwelling place and those who live in heaven. He was given power to make war against the saints and to conquer them. And he was given authority over every tribe, people, language and nation. All inhabitants of the earth will worship the beast—all whose names have not been written in the book of life belonging to the Lamb that was slain from the creation of the world. He who has an ear, let him hear. If anyone is to go into captivity, into captivity he will go. If anyone is to be killed with the sword, with the sword he will be killed. This calls for patient endurance and faithfulness on the part of the saints"* (13:1-10).

The ten-horned beast in John's vision was the same ten-horned beast seen hundreds of years earlier by Daniel. Daniel clearly identified this beast as the Roman Empire. This beast was given its power by the dragon, who has already been identified as the Devil.

John said to worship the beast was also to worship the dragon, because they were working together. This is a critical point to understand. Emperor worship was also Devil worship. The Devil was empowering the Roman Empire to try to destroy the kingdom of heaven. The Devil himself is referred to in future verses of Revelation as the beast. It is also crucial to comprehend those whom John said were not worshipping the beast or the Devil. They were the ones whose names were written in the book of life who belonged to the Lamb that was slain **since the creation of the world**. The judgment that John was revealing was not only about the physical city of Jerusalem, but about all who had lived since creation. But there was another beast in John's vision.

> *"Then I saw another beast, coming out of the earth. He had two horns like a lamb, but he spoke like a dragon. He exercised all the authority of the first beast on his behalf, and made the earth and its inhabitants worship the first beast, whose fatal wound had been healed. And he performed great and miraculous signs, even causing fire to come down from heaven to earth in full view of men. Because of the signs he was given power to do on behalf of the first beast, he deceived the inhabitants of the earth. He ordered them to set up an image in honor of the beast who was wounded by the sword and yet lived. He was given power to give breath to the image of the first beast, so that it could speak and cause all who refused to worship the image to be killed. He also forced everyone, small and great, rich and poor, free and slave, to receive a mark on his right hand or on his forehead, so that no one could buy or sell unless he had the mark, which is the name of the beast or the number of his name. This calls for wisdom. If anyone has insight, let him calculate the number of the beast,*

> *for it is man's number. His number is 666"* (13:11-18).

This second beast looked like a lamb, yet exercised the same authority as the first beast. Remember, the authority of the first beast was the authority of the Devil. The second beast represented apostate Israel. It had two horns because Israel had been divided between the northern kingdom of Israel and the southern kingdom of Judah.

As was previously discussed regarding Paul's explanation of the "man of lawlessness" in 2 Thessalonians 2, John of Gischala was now in control of the Jewish resistance of the Roman invasion of Jerusalem. Instead of listening to Ananus or Josephus and making a truce with the Romans, he murdered the High Priest and set up his military defense in the temple, thus defying the law of God, and forced the Roman army to storm the temple. This false "savior" of Israel gained the following of the Jews in Jerusalem, and now Israel itself was exercising the authority of the first beast - the authority of the Devil. And even though savagely opposed to the Romans, they actually brought about the destruction of the temple by the Roman army. This second beast, apostate Israel, was actually more responsible for the destruction of the temple than Rome. They empowered the Romans to do what they otherwise would not have done.

What was the mark of the beast? The term is used several times in John's Revelation. Two times in chapter 13 it is used to refer to those who worship the beast, which John has already said was synonymous with worshipping the Devil. Specifically in this passage he was referring to the Jews who had remained in Jerusalem at the time of the Roman invasion. These Jews were forced to join John of Gischala. Anyone who refused, especially those who still tried to come to the temple to worship God, was slaughtered. As the apostle said, the beast was given power so that it could speak and cause all who refused to receive its mark to be killed. Normal life for anyone who refused to join the rebellion was impossible. Remember, the power and authority of this beast was the power and authority of the Devil.

But the mark of the beast does not only refer to Jews in Jerusalem at this time. In chapter 14:6-11 an angel with the gospel which was proclaimed to every nation on the entire earth went forth warning of the impending judgment. A following angel said, *"If anyone worships the beast and his image and receives his mark on the forehead or on the hand, he, too, will drink of the wine of God's fury, which has been poured full strength into the cup of his wrath. He will be tormented with burning sulfur in the presence of the holy angels and of the Lamb. And the smoke of their torment rises forever and ever. There is no rest day or night for those who worship the beast and his image, or for anyone who receives the mark of his name."* In this passage all those who lived on the earth, not just in Jerusalem, who had received the mark of the beast were condemned to eternal punishment.

In chapter 16:1-2, *"Then I heard a loud voice from the temple saying to the seven angels, 'Go, pour out the seven bowls of God's wrath on the earth.' The first angel went and poured out his bowl on the land, and ugly and painful sores broke out on the people who had the mark of the beast and worshiped his image."* As the seven angels began to pour out God's wrath on the entire earth, ugly sores broke out on all who had received the mark of the beast. This passage referred to those who had lived under the very first covenant God had established with Adam. Whatever the mark of the beast was, it had been around since Adam.

Chapter 19 describes the final judgment of all mankind. In this passage John was guided by the Holy Spirit to write, *"But the beast was captured, and with him the false prophet who had performed the miraculous signs on his behalf. With these signs he had deluded those who had received the mark of the beast and worshiped his image. The two of them were thrown alive into the fiery lake of burning sulfur."* Those who were deluded by the Devil were the ones who had the mark of the beast. Every person who had ever lived and was condemned to eternal punishment had this mark.

Finally in chapter 20:4 John saw, *"the souls of those who had been beheaded because of their testimony for Jesus and because of the word of God. They had not worshiped the beast or his image and had not received his mark on their foreheads or their hands."* The people who had believed the testimony of Jesus and were obedient to his will did not have the mark of the beast.

In Revelation the beast was the Devil, or a people empowered by and given the authority of the Devil. The work of those people was the work of the Devil. To worship the beast was to worship the Devil. The mark of the beast was the mark of the Devil. Whatever this mark was, it was the identifying characteristic that separated the saved from the lost, those who went to heaven from those who went to Hell. It was a mark that identified the unsaved from every generation since Adam. With this mark one was eternally separated from God, without this mark one was welcomed into his presence. The only people who did not have the mark were those who had believed the testimony of Jesus and obeyed his will. The only mark in all of human history that fits these consequences is SIN. John said if a person had enough insight he could calculate the number of the beast. He further said it is man's number. The original text does not indicate this was the number of an individual person, rather a number that described the condition of mankind. The NIV properly translates this, *"It is man's number."* The mark upon mankind that resulted in his separation from God was SIN. It can only be removed by the blood of Jesus. Those who believe and obey Jesus do not have the mark and are welcomed into the presence of God. Those who refuse to obey Jesus have the mark and are eternally separated from his presence. How the number 666 is calculated is a riddle.

Revelation 14

> *"Then I looked, and there before me was the Lamb, standing on Mount Zion, and with him 144,000 who had his name and his Father's name written on their foreheads. And I heard a sound from heaven like the roar of rushing waters and like a loud peal of thunder. The sound I heard was like that of harpists playing their harps. And they sang a new song before the throne and before the four living creatures and the elders. No one could learn the song except the 144,000 who had been redeemed from the earth. These are those who did not defile themselves with women, for they kept themselves pure. They follow the Lamb wherever he goes. They were purchased from among men and offered as firstfruits to God and the Lamb. No lie was found in their mouths; they are blameless"* (14:1-5).

John was shown the events that transpired on the great day of the Lord to accomplish the mystery of God. With the opening of the sixth seal in chapter six the question was asked, *"For the great day of their wrath has come, and who can stand"* (Revelation 6:17)? John saw this same 144,000 of Israel who had the seal of God on their foreheads (Revelation 7:1-8). As the judgment is described in chapters 14-20, John identifies the righteous Jews as the "firstfruits" to God and the Lamb. This is consistent with what the prophet said in Jeremiah 2:3, *"Israel was holy to the Lord, the firstfruits of his harvest; all who devoured her were held guilty, and disaster overtook them, declares the Lord."* The Apostle Paul used this same "firstfruits" analogy in explaining to Gentile Christians how Israel was the root of the tree into which they had been grafted. In Romans 11:16-18 he wrote, *"If the part of the dough offered as firstfruits is holy, then the whole batch is holy; if the root*

(Israel) is holy, so are the branches... You do not support the root, but the root supports you."

The prophet Joel spoke of this very time when he said in Joel 3:1-2, *"In those days and at that time, when I restore the fortunes of Judah and Jerusalem, I will gather all nations and bring them down to the Valley of Jehoshaphat. There I will enter into judgment against them concerning my inheritance, my people Israel, for they scattered my people among the nations and divided up my land. And God pronounced judgment against the enemies of Israel..."* Joel was speaking of the establishment of the church, the ultimate kingdom of Israel, during the first century. The Apostle Peter said, *"...this is that which was spoken by the prophet Joel"* in the first gospel sermon in Acts 2. Restoring the fortunes of Judah and Jerusalem was the ultimate fulfillment of God's promise to Abraham that *"...through you and your seed all nations will be blessed."*

In Joel 3:14-21 we read, *"Multitudes, multitudes in the valley of decision! For the day of the Lord is near in the valley of decision. The sun and moon will be darkened, and the stars no longer shine. The Lord will roar from Zion and thunder from Jerusalem; the earth and the sky will tremble. But the Lord will be a refuge for his people, a stronghold for the people of Israel... Then you will know that I, the Lord your God, dwell in Zion, my holy hill. Jerusalem will be holy; never again will foreigners invade her. In that day the mountains will drip new wine, and the hills will flow with milk; all the ravines of Judah will run with water. A fountain will flow out of the Lord's house and will water the valley of acacias. But Egypt will be desolate, Edom a desert waste, because of violence done to the people of Judah, in whose land they shed innocent blood. Judah will be inhabited forever and Jerusalem through all generations.* ***Their bloodguilt, which I have not pardoned, I will pardon.*** *The Lord dwells in Zion!"*

Pardon from the guilt of sin was only accomplished after Jesus died on the cross. Joel could have been prophesying about nothing other than the establishment of the spiritual kingdom where forgiveness would finally be available in Jesus. Even though the physical nation was headed for some terrible times and ultimately would be destroyed in what was called "that great day of the Lord," the new kingdom would be established as an eternal one in which all the faithful would receive a full pardon. This can only be the new Jerusalem, the heavenly Jerusalem, the City of the Living God, the church, which we read about in Hebrews 12 and Revelation 21. In the final judgment scene John first identified the saved of Israel.

> *"Then I saw another angel flying in midair, and he had the eternal gospel to proclaim to those who live on the earth—to every nation, tribe, language and people. He said in a loud voice, 'Fear God and give him glory, because the hour of his judgment has come. Worship him who made the heavens, the earth, the sea and the springs of water.'*
>
> *A second angel followed and said, 'Fallen! Fallen is Babylon the Great, which made all the nations drink the maddening wine of her adulteries.'*
>
> *A third angel followed them and said in a loud voice: 'If anyone worships the beast and his image and receives his mark on the forehead or on the hand, he, too, will drink of the wine of God's fury, which has been poured full strength into the cup of his wrath. He will be tormented with burning sulfur in the presence of the holy angels and of the Lamb. And the smoke of their torment rises for ever and ever. There is no rest day or night for those who worship the beast and his image, or for anyone who receives the mark of his name.' This calls for patient endurance on the part of the saints who obey God's commandments and remain faithful to Jesus.*
>
> *Then I heard a voice from heaven say, Write: Blessed*

> *are the dead who die in the Lord from now on. 'Yes,' says the Spirit, 'they will rest from their labor, for their deeds will follow them'* " (14:6-13).

Three angels appeared before John announcing this great event. The first proclaimed the hour of his judgment had come. The second angel announced the fall of the city of Jerusalem. The third angel exclaimed all those who had the mark of the beast were doomed to eternal torment away from the presence of God.

Remember what Daniel and Jesus said would happen at the "time of the end" when Jerusalem would be destroyed. *"Multitudes who sleep in the dust of the earth will awake: some to everlasting life, others to shame and everlasting contempt. Those who are wise will shine like the brightness of the heavens, and those who lead many to righteousness, like the stars forever and ever"* (Daniel 12:2-3).

Immediately following his triumphant entry into Jerusalem, just a week prior to his crucifixion, Jesus prayed for God to glorify his name. *"Then a voice came from heaven, 'I have glorified it, and will glorify it again.' The crowd that was there and heard it said it had thundered; others said an angel had spoken to him. Jesus said, 'This voice was for your benefit, not mine. Now is the time for judgment on this world; now the prince of this world will be driven out. But I, when I am lifted up from the earth, will draw all men to myself.' He said this to show the kind of death he was going to die"* (John 12:28-33). Jesus said "...***NOW is the time for judgment on this world.***"

If the judgment was not going to happen until after all people who would ever live on the earth died, there would be no need for patient endurance on the part of the saints. And in the very next verse, following the picture of the judgment scene, the inspired apostle heard a voice from heaven which said, *"Write: Blessed are the dead who die in the Lord from now on. 'Yes,' says the Spirit, 'they will rest from their labor, for their deeds will follow them.'* " People would still be "dying in the Lord" AFTER the judgment. This is consistent with Paul's explanation to the church in Thessalonica regarding those who died before the Lord's coming and those who would die after that event.

Judgment had to occur when the atonement sacrifice was complete. A future judgment would mean death still has its holding power and something other than the sacrifice of Jesus would have to break its power. In the beginning God pronounced judgment on all who sin. They would experience spiritual death, eternal separation from his presence. Under the divine plan of redemption (the mystery of the ages) the final judgment was placed in the hands of God's only Son. Jesus said in John 5:21, *"For just as the Father raises the dead and gives them life, even so the Son gives life to whom he is pleased to give it. Moreover, the Father judges no one,* ***but has entrusted all judgment to the Son****, that all may honor the Son just as they honor the Father. He who does not honor the Son does not honor the Father, who sent him."*

We learned from Hebrews that, because of sin, everyone would die and face God's judgment. *"Just as man is destined to die once, and after that to face judgment,* ***so Christ was sacrificed once to take away the sins of many people****; and he will appear a second time, not to bear sin, but to bring salvation to those who are waiting for him"* (Hebrews 9:27-28). Because we were destined to die and face God's judgment, Christ died for our sins. He took our sins and faced our judgment. His first "coming" was to bear our sins. His second "coming" (appearance) was to confirm God's acceptance of his blood sacrifice for our sin. There are only two groups of people in John's final judgment scene; those who stand with the Lamb and those who face God's wrath of judgment. If we accept his sacrifice we will never face God's judgment. All who stand in judgment are condemned. The only hope one has is to avoid God's judgment. The only way to do that is to accept Jesus as our Savior.

"I looked, and there before me was a white cloud, and seated on the cloud was one 'like a son of man' with a crown of gold on his head and a sharp sickle in his hand. Then another angel came out of the temple and called in a loud voice to him who was sitting on the cloud, 'Take your sickle and reap, because the time to reap has come, for the harvest of the earth is ripe.' So he who was seated on the cloud swung his sickle over the earth, and the earth was harvested.

Another angel came out of the temple in heaven, and he too had a sharp sickle. Still another angel, who had charge of the fire, came from the altar and called in a loud voice to him who had the sharp sickle, 'Take your sharp sickle and gather the clusters of grapes from the earth's vine, because its grapes are ripe.' The angel swung his sickle on the earth, gathered its grapes and threw them into the great winepress of God's wrath. They were trampled in the winepress outside the city, and blood flowed out of the press, rising as high as the horses' bridles for a distance of 1,600 stadia" (14:14-20).

The judgment was depicted as the "harvest of the earth." Jesus was seen sitting on a cloud with a sickle ready to harvest. An angel came out of the temple and told him the time had come. Then, assisted by the angels, he proceeded with the harvest. Jesus had explained to his apostles this would happen at the time the temple in Jerusalem was destroyed. In Mark 13:26-27 he said, *"At that time men will see the Son of Man coming in clouds with great power and glory. And he will send his angels and gather his elect from the four winds, from the ends of the earth to the ends of the heavens."* He further described this event as the separating of sheep and goats in

Matthew 25:31-33, *"When the Son of Man comes in his glory, and all the angels with him, he will sit on his throne in heavenly glory. All the nations will be gathered before him, and he will separate the people one from another as a shepherd separates the sheep from the goats. He will put the sheep on his right and the goats on his left."* Jesus said, *"…this generation will certainly not pass away until all these things have happened"* (Matthew 24:34). Jerusalem and its temple were destroyed in A.D. 70 by the Romans. Judgment had come.

Revelation 15

> *"I saw in heaven another great and marvelous sign: seven angels with the seven last plagues—last, because with them God's wrath is completed. And I saw what looked like a sea of glass mixed with fire and, standing beside the sea, those who had been victorious over the beast and his image and over the number of his name. They held harps given them by God and sang the song of Moses the servant of God and the song of the Lamb:*
>
> *'Great and marvelous are your deeds, Lord God Almighty. Just and true are your ways, King of the ages. Who will not fear you, O Lord, and bring glory to your name? For you alone are holy. All nations will come and worship before you, for your righteous acts have been revealed' "* (15:1-4).

The time for God's judgment had come. With the pouring out of the seven bowls of God's wrath it will be completed.

> *"After this I looked and in heaven the temple, that is, the tabernacle of the Testimony, was opened. Out of the temple came the seven angels with the seven*

> *plagues. They were dressed in clean, shining linen and wore golden sashes around their chests. Then one of the four living creatures gave to the seven angels seven golden bowls filled with the wrath of God, who lives for ever and ever. And the temple was filled with smoke from the glory of God and from his power, and no one could enter the temple until the seven plagues of the seven angels were completed"* (15:5-8).

As the angels prepared to pour out the wrath of God upon the nations, the temple was filled with smoke. Nobody could enter the temple until the seven plagues were completed. The purpose of the sacrifice of Jesus was to provide atonement for sin and provide a way for mankind to be restored to the presence of God. The place of his presence was represented on earth by the Holy of Holies in the temple. It is critical to understand when this access was made possible.

The writer of Hebrews carefully explained this in his comparison of the old covenant with the new covenant established by Jesus. In the earthly temple only the High Priest could enter the Holy of Holies. In Hebrews 9:7-8 he said, *"But only the high priest entered the inner room, and that only once a year, and never without blood, which he offered for himself and for the sins the people had committed in ignorance.* ***The Holy Spirit was showing by this that the way into the Most Holy Place had not yet been disclosed as long as the first tabernacle was still standing."*** According to Scripture, the Holy of Holies (presence of God) was not open for all mankind as long as the physical temple stood. This is a critical point in comprehending the completion of the atonement ritual of the High Priest.

In Hebrews 10:1-4 he said, *"The law is only a shadow of the good things that are coming—not the realities themselves. For this reason it can never, by the same sacrifices repeated endlessly year after year, make perfect those who draw near to worship. If it could, would they not have stopped being offered? For the worshipers would have been cleansed once for all, and would no longer have felt guilty for their sins. But those sacrifices are an annual reminder of sins, because it is impossible for the blood of bulls and goats to take away sins."* He went on to explain how Jesus, as our Great High Priest, had come to make that perfect sacrifice for sin whereby we can be truly forgiven.

He then encouraged the Christians, to whom he was writing, to persevere in their faith in anticipation of "the day" when the atonement would be complete and entrance into the Presence of God would be a reality. In 10:19-25 he said, *"Therefore, brothers, since we have confidence to enter the Most Holy Place by the blood of Jesus, by a new and living way opened for us through the curtain, that is, his body, and since we have a great priest over the house of God, let us draw near to God with a sincere heart in full assurance of faith, having our hearts sprinkled to cleanse us from a guilty conscience and having our bodies washed with pure water. Let us hold unswervingly to the hope we profess, for he who promised is faithful. And let us consider how we may spur one another on toward love and good deeds. Let us not give up meeting together, as some are in the habit of doing, but let us encourage one another—and all the more* ***as you see the Day approaching.****"* The day that was approaching was the day when Jesus would appear, indicating the atonement was complete and the Holy of Holies was now open. Remember, he had just explained in the previous chapter the way into the Most Holy Place had not yet been disclosed **as long as the first tabernacle was still standing.**

Then in Hebrews 10:35-39 he said, *"So do not throw away your confidence; it will be richly rewarded. You need to persevere so that when you have done the will of God,* ***you will receive what he has promised.*** *For in just a very little while* (literal translation; *"soon, very soon"*), ***He who is coming will come and will not delay.*** *But* *my righteous one will live by faith. And if he shrinks back, I will not be pleased with him. But we are not of those who shrink back and are destroyed, but of those who believe and are saved."* What had been promised was entrance into the Holy of Holies, the presence of God. It was contingent upon Jesus' second appearance, exactly like the second appearing of the earthly High Priest from behind the veil, indicating the atonement sacrifice for the people was accepted. He said that appearance was soon...very soon! The destruction of the earthly temple in A.D. 70 was the divinely orchestrated event that announced to the world the opening of the Holy of Holies in the eternal temple of God in heaven.

In Revelation John said no one could enter the temple until the seven plagues of the seven angels were completed. These seven plagues, or bowls of wrath, represent the final judgment of the earth. If the judgment has not yet occurred, we still do not have access to the temple of God and the Holy of Holies. We are still waiting for our redemption. John was revealing what the writer of Hebrews said was going to happen *very soon*. It happened, and we now have what was promised; confidence to enter the Most Holy Place by the blood of Jesus.

Revelation 16

> *"Then I heard a loud voice from the temple saying to the seven angels, 'Go, pour out the seven bowls of God's wrath on the earth.' The first angel went and poured out his bowl on the land, and ugly and painful sores broke out on the people who had the mark of the beast and worshiped his image"* (16:1-2).

As John saw the unfolding of the judgment, the seven bowls of God's wrath parallels the seven seals and seven trumpets. The first bowl of wrath was poured out on the land, and sores broke out on everyone who had the mark of the beast. This indicated the entrance of sin into the world during the time of Adam. All who remained unfaithful to God during this covenant time were judged according to their works.

> *"The second angel poured out his bowl on the sea, and it turned into blood like that of a dead man, and every living thing in the sea died"* (16:3).

The second bowl was poured out on the sea. This indicated God's judgment of all those who lived during the time of Noah.

> *"The third angel poured out his bowl on the rivers and springs of water, and they became blood. Then I heard the angel in charge of the waters say: 'You are just in these judgments, you who are and who were, the Holy One, because you have so judged; for they have shed the blood of your saints and prophets, and you have given them blood to drink as they deserve.' And I heard the altar respond: 'Yes, Lord God Almighty, true and just are your judgments' "* (16:4-7).

The third bowl, like the third trumpet, was directed at the rivers and springs of water. This scene, which was reminiscent of the Old Testament plague of water turning to blood, indicated God's judgment of all who lived from Abraham to Moses.

> *"The fourth angel poured out his bowl on the sun, and the sun was given power to scorch people with fire. They were seared by the intense heat and they cursed the name of God, who had control over these plagues, but they refused to repent and glorify him"* (16:8-9).

The fourth bowl of wrath, again like the fourth trumpet, was directed toward the sun. The covenant with Israel and the establishment of their kingdom was described in the Old Testament as the creation of a "heavens and earth." Prior judgments God had brought upon this nation were described as their sun being darkened and the moon not giving its light. But in Isaiah 9, following his prediction of Jesus in the familiar words, *"...unto us a child is born, unto us a Son is given,"* Isaiah also said of unrepentant Israel, *"By the wrath of the Lord Almighty the land will be scorched and the people will be fuel for the fire; no one will spare his brother."*

> *"The fifth angel poured out his bowl on the throne of the beast, and his kingdom was plunged into darkness. Men gnawed their tongues in agony and cursed the God of heaven because of their pains and their sores, but they refused to repent of what they had done"* (16:10-11).

The fifth bowl of wrath is poured out on the throne of the beast. The fifth seal that had to be loosed by the Lion of the Tribe of Judah was death. Hebrews 2:14-15, *"Since the children have flesh and blood, he too shared in their humanity so that by his death he might destroy him who holds the power of death—that is, the devil—and free those who all their lives were held in slavery by their fear of death."* Not only did Jesus free all the righteous who were held by the power of Satan until they could be redeemed, his death also ushered in the judgment of all the unrighteousness held by that same power. The righteous escaped God's wrath, but those who still had the mark of the beast were condemned along with the devil and his angels.

> *"The sixth angel poured out his bowl on the great river Euphrates, and its water was dried up to prepare the way for the kings from the East. Then I saw three evil spirits that looked like frogs; they came*

> *out of the mouth of the dragon, out of the mouth of the beast and out of the mouth of the false prophet. They are spirits of demons performing miraculous signs, and they go out to the kings of the whole world, to gather them for the battle on the great day of God Almighty. 'Behold, I come like a thief! Blessed is he who stays awake and keeps his clothes with him, so that he may not go naked and be shamefully exposed.' Then they gathered the kings together to the place that in Hebrew is called Armageddon"* (16:12-16).

Once death was destroyed, the grave could no longer hold its captives. This sixth bowl of wrath showed God's judgment against all the armies of the devil that were marshaled against the kingdom of heaven. This was a spiritual battle with everlasting results. Satan had great plans but, with the atonement of sin complete, he no longer had any power over the people of God. He was totally defeated. Jesus did exactly what he said he had come to do, destroy him who held the power of death and the grave.

Jesus said blessed is the person who stays awake and keeps his clothes with him, so that he may not go naked and be shamefully exposed. He is not speaking of physical nakedness, but rather not being clothed with the robe that had been made white by the blood of the Lamb. We saw this illustration in chapter seven. Those who had come out of the great tribulation of sin were wearing robes made white by the blood of the Lamb. The concept of sin making one shamefully naked before God originated in the Garden of Eden. When Adam and Eve sinned by eating the forbidden fruit, they hid from God because of their nakedness. Without sin we can stand in his presence without shame. The same concept was used here in Revelation. In keeping with its stated purpose, everything in this great book was written to reveal Jesus as the fulfillment of all Scripture. The historical timing of mankind's ultimate redemption coincides with the "battle of Armageddon" which is also mentioned in this passage. That time was clearly indicated in Jesus' statement, *"Behold, I come like a thief."*

In his discussion with the apostles about the events leading up to and including the destruction of Jerusalem, Jesus said in Matthew 24:42-44, *"Therefore keep watch, because you do not know on what day your Lord will come. But understand this: If the owner of the house had known at what time of night the thief was coming, he would have kept watch and would not have let his house be broken into. So you also must be ready, because the Son of Man will come at an hour when you do not expect him."*

In Luke's gospel, using a different figure of speech to express the same thought, he said the day would come unexpectedly, like the closing of a trap. *"Be careful, or your hearts will be weighed down with dissipation, drunkenness and the anxieties of life, and that day will close on you unexpectedly like a trap. For it will come upon all those who live on the face of the whole earth. Be always on the watch, and pray* ***that you may be able to escape all that is about to happen****, and that you may be able to stand before the Son of Man"* (Luke 21:34-36). The purpose of Jesus' admonition for them to watch for the signs of his coming was so they could escape the destruction that would befall Jerusalem. If he was predicting the end of the world, what he said would have made no sense as it would not have been possible to escape.

He had told them when they saw the signs to run to the hills. What would be the point if the entire physical creation was going to be destroyed? He compared this coming event to the flood of Noah's day. That flood brought God's judgment on the world because of sin. It did not destroy the physical creation, and people survived afterward. He also speaks in Matthew's account of some being taken and others left. If he was talking about the end of time, as we are commonly told, nobody would be left. Luke's account makes it plain that they were warned so they could escape the events that were soon to befall Jerusalem and its temple.

Several years later some of these same apostles wrote to Christians of that generation and reminded them of what the Lord had taught. Paul, in 1 Thessalonians 5:1-5 said, *"Now, brothers, about times and dates we do not need to write to you, for you know very well that* ***the day of the Lord will come like a thief in the night.*** *While people are saying, 'Peace and safety,' destruction will come on them suddenly, as labor pains on a pregnant woman, and they will not escape. But you, brothers, are not in darkness so that this day should surprise you like a thief. You are all sons of the light and sons of the day. We do not belong to the night or to the darkness."* This day would come like a thief ONLY to those who were not watching for the signs. Like a pregnant woman, nobody could know the exact day and hour of its demise, but by watching for signs they would know as it approached.

Peter used the same thief analogy in 2 Peter 3:10, *"But the day of the Lord will come like a thief. The heavens will disappear with a roar; the elements will be destroyed by fire, and the earth and everything in it will be laid bare."* This was to be the time of God's judgment on the world, not the ending of the physical universe. The subject was the "time of the end," not the "end of time." What was ending was the physical kingdom of Israel. What was being established was the eternal City of Jerusalem; the kingdom of heaven. This all happened in the generation in which Jesus and his apostles lived, just as he promised.

> *"The seventh angel poured out his bowl into the air, and out of the temple came a loud voice from the throne, saying, 'It is done!' Then there came flashes of lightning, rumblings, peals of thunder and a severe earthquake. No earthquake like it has ever occurred since man has been on earth, so tremendous was the quake. The great city split into three parts, and the*

> *cities of the nations collapsed. God remembered Babylon the Great and gave her the cup filled with the wine of the fury of his wrath. Every island fled away and the mountains could not be found. From the sky huge hailstones of about a hundred pounds each fell upon men. And they cursed God on account of the plague of hail, because the plague was so terrible"* (16:17-21).

Once again, the same symbolic language employed throughout the Old Testament prophesies to describe God's judgment on people and nations is used in the Revelation. The meaning of these graphic images will become clear as we look at the rest of the vision.

Revelation 17

> *"One of the seven angels who had the seven bowls came and said to me, 'Come, I will show you the punishment of the great prostitute, who sits on many waters. With her the kings of the earth committed adultery and the inhabitants of the earth were intoxicated with the wine of her adulteries.'*
>
> *Then the angel carried me away in the Spirit into a desert. There I saw a woman sitting on a scarlet beast that was covered with blasphemous names and had seven heads and ten horns. The woman was dressed in purple and scarlet, and was glittering with gold, precious stones and pearls. She held a golden cup in her hand, filled with abominable things and the filth of her adulteries. This title was written on her forehead:*
>
> *MYSTERY*

> *BABYLON THE GREAT*
> *THE MOTHER OF PROSTITUTES*
> *AND OF THE ABOMINATIONS OF THE EARTH.*
>
> *I saw that the woman was drunk with the blood of the saints, the blood of those who bore testimony to Jesus. When I saw her, I was greatly astonished. Then the angel said to me: 'Why are you astonished? I will explain to you the mystery of the woman and of the beast she rides, which has the seven heads and ten horns. The beast, which you saw, once was, now is not, and will come up out of the Abyss and go to his destruction. The inhabitants of the earth whose names have not been written in the book of life from the creation of the world will be astonished when they see the beast, because he once was, now is not, and yet will come' "* (17:1-8).

As mentioned in the last part of the former chapter, the judgment of God begins with "Babylon the Great." This city is described as an incredibly sinful adulterous woman sitting on a great beast. The beast in this vision is the same ten-horned beast already identified in chapters six and seven of John's Revelation. It was the Roman Empire. The woman sitting on the beast was drunk with the blood of the saints. Just as Daniel was "deeply troubled" in thought and his face turned pale when he realized the physical nation of Israel would ultimately be destroyed (Daniel 7:28), John was "greatly astonished" when he realized the identity of the adulterous woman. The fact that she is described as adulterous is key to our understanding. A person who commits adultery is one who is married, yet has an affair with someone to whom he or she is not married. One who is unmarried can commit fornication, but not adultery.

> *"This calls for a mind with wisdom. The seven heads are seven hills on which the woman sits. They are also seven kings. Five have fallen, one is, the other has not yet come; but when he does come, he must remain for a little while. The beast who once was, and now is not, is an eighth king. He belongs to the seven and is going to his destruction.*
>
> *The ten horns you saw are ten kings who have not yet received a kingdom, but who for one hour will receive authority as kings along with the beast. They have one purpose and will give their power and authority to the beast. They will make war against the Lamb, but the Lamb will overcome them because he is Lord of lords and King of kings—and with him will be his called, chosen and faithful followers.*
>
> *Then the angel said to me, 'The waters you saw, where the prostitute sits, are peoples, multitudes, nations and languages. The beast and the ten horns you saw will hate the prostitute. They will bring her to ruin and leave her naked; they will eat her flesh and burn her with fire. For God has put it into their hearts to accomplish his purpose by agreeing to give the beast their power to rule, until God's words are fulfilled. The woman you saw is the great city that rules over the kings of the earth' "* (17:9-18).

This adulterous woman would be hated by the beast. The beast would destroy her and burn her with fire. The woman here is called *"the great city that rules over the kings of the earth."*

Revelation 18

"After this I saw another angel coming down from heaven. He had great authority, and the earth was illuminated by his splendor. With a mighty voice he shouted: 'Fallen! Fallen is Babylon the Great! She has become a home for demons and a haunt for every evil spirit, a haunt for every unclean and detestable bird. For all the nations have drunk the maddening wine of her adulteries. The kings of the earth committed adultery with her, and the merchants of the earth grew rich from her excessive luxuries.'

Then I heard another voice from heaven say: 'Come out of her, my people, so that you will not share in her sins, so that you will not receive any of her plagues; for her sins are piled up to heaven, and God has remembered her crimes. Give back to her as she has given; pay her back double for what she has done. Mix her a double portion from her own cup. Give her as much torture and grief as the glory and luxury she gave herself. In her heart she boasts, I sit as queen; I am not a widow, and I will never mourn. Therefore in one day her plagues will overtake her: death, mourning and famine. She will be consumed by fire, for mighty is the Lord God who judges her' " (18:1-8).

In this passage the children of God are told to leave this city and not share in her sins, for they are piled up to heaven. God is going to unleash his judgment on her and she will be consumed by fire.

"When the kings of the earth who committed adultery with her and shared her luxury see the smoke

of her burning, they will weep and mourn over her. Terrified at her torment, they will stand far off and cry: 'Woe! Woe, O great city, O Babylon, city of power! In one hour your doom has come!' The merchants of the earth will weep and mourn over her because no one buys their cargoes any more— cargoes of gold, silver, precious stones and pearls; fine linen, purple, silk and scarlet cloth; every sort of citron wood, and articles of every kind made of ivory, costly wood, bronze, iron and marble; cargoes of cinnamon and spice, of incense, myrrh and frankincense, of wine and olive oil, of fine flour and wheat; cattle and sheep; horses and carriages; and bodies and souls of men.

They will say, 'The fruit you longed for is gone from you. All your riches and splendor have vanished, never to be recovered.' The merchants who sold these things and gained their wealth from her will stand far off, terrified at her torment. They will weep and mourn and cry out: 'Woe! Woe, O great city, dressed in fine linen, purple and scarlet, and glittering with gold, precious stones and pearls! In one hour such great wealth has been brought to ruin!' Every sea captain, and all who travel by ship, the sailors, and all who earn their living from the sea, will stand far off. When they see the smoke of her burning, they will exclaim, 'Was there ever a city like this great city?' They will throw dust on their heads, and with weeping and mourning cry out: 'Woe! Woe, O great city, where all who had ships on the sea became rich through her wealth! In one hour she has been brought to ruin' " (18:9-19)!

Some have suggested the city receiving God's judgment in this vision is Rome. However, Rome was the capital of the beast the woman was riding, not the woman.

> *"Rejoice over her, O heaven! Rejoice, saints and apostles and prophets! God has judged her for the way she treated you. Then a mighty angel picked up a boulder the size of a large millstone and threw it into the sea, and said: 'With such violence the great city of Babylon will be thrown down, never to be found again. The music of harpists and musicians, flute players and trumpeters, will never be heard in you again. No workman of any trade will ever be found in you again. The sound of a millstone will never be heard in you again. The light of a lamp will never shine in you again. The voice of bridegroom and bride will never be heard in you again. Your merchants were the world's great men. By your magic spell all the nations were led astray. In her was found the blood of prophets and of the saints, and of all who have been killed on the earth"* (18:20-24).

The adulterous woman was the city of Jerusalem. **Israel was the only nation ever betrothed to God.** No other nation and no other city could have been described in this way. Jeremiah 3:6-8, *"Have you seen what faithless Israel has done? She has gone up on every high hill and under every spreading tree and has committed adultery there. I thought that after she had done all this she would return to me but she did not, and her unfaithful sister Judah saw it. I gave faithless Israel her certificate of divorce and sent her away because of all her adulteries. Yet I saw that her unfaithful sister Judah had no fear; she also went out and committed adultery."*

The prophet Hosea was told by the Lord to marry an adulterous prostitute as a demonstration of how Israel had been unfaithful to God. Hosea 1:2, *"When the Lord began to speak through Hosea, the Lord said to him, 'Go, take to yourself an adulterous wife and children of unfaithfulness, because the land is guilty of the vilest adultery in departing from the Lord.' "*

Revelation 18:24 says, *"In her was found the blood of prophets and of the saints, and of all who have been killed on the earth."* In his discussion with the Pharisees Jesus said in Luke 11:47-51, *"Woe to you, because you build tombs for the prophets, and it was your forefathers who killed them. So you testify that you approve of what your forefathers did; they killed the prophets, and you build their tombs. Because of this, God in his wisdom said, 'I will send them prophets and apostles, some of whom they will kill and others they will persecute.' Therefore this generation will be held responsible for the blood of all the prophets that has been shed since the beginning of the world, from the blood of Abel to the blood of Zechariah, who was killed between the altar and the sanctuary. Yes, I tell you,* ***this generation will be held responsible for it all.****"* Jesus identified this adulterous city which would be held responsible for the blood of all the prophets and saints, Babylon the Great, as Jerusalem. And just as he did in his discussion with the apostles in Matthew 24, Mark 13, and Luke 21, Jesus said "this generation," the one in which he and the apostles were living, would be held responsible. John saw the destruction Jesus, and all the Old Testament prophets before him, had predicted. This "Babylon the Great" (Jerusalem) was destroyed by the beast she was riding (Roman Empire) in A.D. 70. God poured out his judgment on Jerusalem, but as we shall soon see, he was not finished.

Revelation 19

> *"After this I heard what sounded like the roar of a great multitude in heaven shouting: 'Hallelujah! Salvation and glory and power belong to our God, for*

> *true and just are his judgments. He has condemned the great prostitute who corrupted the earth by her adulteries. He has avenged on her the blood of his servants.' And again they shouted: 'Hallelujah! The smoke from her goes up for ever and ever.'*
>
> *The twenty-four elders and the four living creatures fell down and worshiped God, who was seated on the throne. And they cried: 'Amen, Hallelujah!' Then a voice came from the throne, saying: 'Praise our God, all you his servants, you who fear him, both small and great!' Then I heard what sounded like a great multitude, like the roar of rushing waters and like loud peals of thunder, shouting: 'Hallelujah! For our Lord God Almighty reigns. Let us rejoice and be glad and give him glory! For the wedding of the Lamb has come, and his bride has made herself ready. Fine linen, bright and clean, was given her to wear.' (Fine linen stands for the righteous acts of the saints.)*
>
> *Then the angel said to me, 'Write: Blessed are those who are invited to the wedding supper of the Lamb!' And he added, 'These are the true words of God.' At this I fell at his feet to worship him. But he said to me, 'Do not do it! I am a fellow servant with you and with your brothers who hold to the testimony of Jesus. Worship God! For the testimony of Jesus is the spirit of prophecy' "* (19:1-10).

Following the destruction of Jerusalem, that great prostitute who had corrupted the earth with her adulteries, the saints sang the praises of God and the Lamb. In chapter five they sang the praises of the Lamb who was able to open the seals of the scroll of God, *"You are worthy to take the scroll and to open its seals, because you were slain, and with your blood you purchased men for God from every tribe and language and people and nation. You have made them to be a kingdom and priests to serve our God, and they will reign on the earth."* In chapter six, with the opening of the fifth seal of death, the souls of those who had been slain because of the word of God cried out, ***"How long until you judge the inhabitants of the earth and avenge our blood?"*** With the destruction of the great city in chapter eighteen they were told, *"Rejoice over her, O heaven! Rejoice, saints and apostles and prophets!* ***God has judged her for the way she treated you."*** They had to wait no longer; they rejoiced!

The saints were also rejoicing because, once the atonement was complete and the old temple had been destroyed, the way into the Holy of Holies was now possible (Hebrews 9:8), the bride (church) was now ready, and the wedding of the Lamb had come. The concept of the church as the bride of Christ is confirmed throughout the New Testament. Jesus spoke in parables of the great wedding banquet in Matthew 22 and Luke 14. The Apostle Paul in Ephesians 5:25-32 said, *"Husbands, love your wives, just as Christ loved the church and gave himself up for her to make her holy, cleansing her by the washing with water through the word, and* ***to present her to himself as a radiant church, without stain or wrinkle or any other blemish, but holy and blameless.*** *In this same way, husbands ought to love their wives as their own bodies. He who loves his wife loves himself. After all, no one ever hated his own body, but he feeds and cares for it, just as Christ does the church— for we are members of his body. 'For this reason a man will leave his father and mother and be united to his wife, and the two will become one flesh.'* ***This is a profound mystery—but I am talking about Christ and the church."***

To fully comprehend the wedding of the Lamb that John saw, one needs to understand the Jewish marriage customs of the first century. The following description based on information from the

Concord Messianic Fellowship http://messianicfellowship.50webs.com clarifies this part of John's vision:

Shiddukhin refers to the first step in the marriage process; the arrangements preliminary to the legal betrothal. It was common in ancient Israel for the father of the groom to select a bride for his son. The next phase of this step was the Ketubah. Ketubah, written in Hebrew as "hbtk," means "written". The ketubah was, and still is today, the "marriage contract." The ketubah includes the provisions and conditions of the proposed marriage:

- The groom promises to support his wife-to-be.
- The bride stipulates the contents of her dowry indicating her financial status.

The Mohar, or bridal payment, was sometimes called the bride price. It is a gift paid by the groom to the bride's family, but ultimately belongs to the bride. It changed her status and set her free from her parent's household. We see this illustrated in two Biblical examples:

- Isaac and Rebecca - Gen. 24:53
- Jacob and his wives - Gen. 29:20,27

To prepare for betrothal, it was common for the bride and groom to separately take a ritual immersion. The ritual immersion, or mikveh (taken from the Hebrew "hwqm"), was prior to actually entering into the formal betrothal period, and was symbolic of spiritual cleansing.

The shiddukhin started with the father's selection of a bride for his beloved son. So too were we selected by the Father to be his Beloved Son's loving precious bride. Paul wrote in Ephesians 1:4, *"For he chose us in him before the creation of the world to be holy and blameless in his sight."* We also have a legal contract, a ketubah (hbtk), which is the new covenant itself in which:

- The groom promises love and care for his bride

and to give Himself for her. He also paid the proper price (Mohar) for his bride; his own life.

- The bride promises to pay her dowry. In our case this is not money, but a yielded life kept pure for him. 1 Corinthians 6:19-20, *"You are not your own; you were bought at a price. Therefore honor God with your body."*

Both bride and groom have undergone the waters of mikveh, or immersion; Jesus at the beginning of his ministry (Matthew 3:13-17) and we, his bride, when we are washed of our sin in the cleansing water of baptism. Acts 22:16, *"And now what are you waiting for? Get up, be baptized and wash your sins away, calling on his name."* Romans 6:1-7, *"What shall we say, then? Shall we go on sinning so that grace may increase? By no means! We died to sin; how can we live in it any longer? Or don't you know that all of us who were baptized into Christ Jesus were baptized into his death? We were therefore buried with him through baptism into death in order that, just as Christ was raised from the dead through the glory of the Father, we too may live a new life…For we know that our old self was crucified with him so that the body of sin might be done away with, that we should no longer be slaves to sin— because anyone who has died has been freed from sin."* 1 Corinthians 6:11, *"But you were washed, you were sanctified, you were justified in the name of the Lord Jesus Christ and by the Spirit of our God."*

Next came the Eyrusin, which means betrothal. The period is also called kiddushim, meaning "sanctification" or "set apart." This word truly defines the purpose of the betrothal period. It was a time in which the couple prepared themselves to enter into the covenant of marriage. The Jewish understanding of betrothal has always been much stronger than our modern understanding of an engagement. The betrothal was so binding that the couple would need a religious divorce in order to annul the contract. This option was only available to the husband, as the wife had no say in any divorce proceeding. This point is very important when we view the spiritual relationship we have with Jesus.

After the couple had undergone their Mikveh (hwqm-immersion), each separately, they would appear together under the Huppah, or canopy, and in public they would express their intention of becoming betrothed or engaged. From ancient times the wedding canopy has been a symbol of a new household being planned (Ps. 19:5; Joel 2:16). While under the Huppah the couple participated in a ceremony in which some items of value, such as rings, were exchanged and a cup of wine was shared to seal the betrothal vows. After the ceremony the couple was considered to have entered into the betrothal agreement. This period was to last for one year. During this time the couple was considered married, yet did not have sexual relations, and continued to live separately until the end of the betrothal. In sharing the wine of the last Passover meal with his disciples Jesus was looking forward to the coming marriage when he said, *"I tell you, I will not drink of this fruit of the vine from now on until that day when I drink it anew with you in my Father's kingdom"* (Matthew 26:29).

Following this betrothal ceremony the groom would return to his home to fulfill his obligations during the betrothal. But just prior to leaving he would give his wife to be a Matan (ntm), or bridal gift; a pledge of his love for her. Its purpose was to be a reminder to his bride during their days of separation of his love for her, that he was thinking of her, and that he would return to receive her as his wife. Jesus' bridal gift to his future bride was the Holy Spirit, given to comfort and guide them and guarantee their inheritance when he returned. Ephesians 1:13-14, *"And you also were included in Christ when you heard the word of truth, the gospel of your salvation. Having believed, you were marked in him with a seal, the promised Holy Spirit, who is a deposit guaranteeing our inheritance until the redemption of those who are God's possession—to the praise of his glory."*

During betrothal the groom's responsibility was to focus on preparing a new dwelling place for his bride and family. In Biblical times this was most often done, not by building a new home, but by simply adding additional rooms to the family's existing home. It was not the groom's duty to determine when the place he was preparing for the bride was ready. His father would make that determination and give the go ahead to receive his bride. John 14:1-4, *"Do not let your hearts be troubled. Trust in God; trust also in me. In my Father's house are many rooms; if it were not so, I would have told you. I am going there to prepare a place for you. And if I go and prepare a place for you, I will come back and take you to be with me that you also may be where I am. You know the way to the place where I am going."*

The bride also was to keep herself busy in preparation for the wedding day. During this period the bride would consecrate herself and prepare holy garments for the upcoming marriage. Paul puts this preparation in very clear terms in the passage already noted in Ephesians 5.

The culminating step in the process of the Jewish wedding was called Nissuin. The word comes from the Hebrew verb "hsn" (nasa), which means "to carry." This is a graphic description, as the bride would be waiting for her groom to come carry her off to her new home. The period of the betrothal was a time of great anticipation as the bride waited for the arrival of her betrothed. One of the unique features of the Biblical Jewish wedding was the time of the groom's arrival; it was to be a surprise. The bride took the betrothal seriously, expecting the bridegroom to come at the end of the period of the betrothal. She knew the approximate timing but the exact day and hour was uncertain. It was the father of the groom who would give the final approval for the marriage to begin. Speaking of his return, Jesus said in Matthew 24:36-42,

"No one knows about that day or hour, not even the angels in heaven, nor the Son, but only the Father. As it was in the days of Noah, so it will be at the coming of the Son of Man. For in the days before the flood, people were eating and drinking, marrying and giving in marriage, up to the day Noah entered the ark; and they knew nothing about what would happen until the flood came and took them all away. That is how it will be at the coming of the Son of Man... Therefore keep watch, because you do not know on what day your Lord will come." They knew the approximate time because Jesus had just told them, *"This generation will not pass away until all these things have happened"* (Matthew 24:34). But nobody but the Father knew the exact hour. The entire New Testament is filled with the anxious and excited anticipation of the Bridegroom's return.

Since the time of his arrival was a surprise the bride and her bridal party were always to be ready. This is the background of Jesus' parable in Matthew 25:1-13. It was customary for one of the groom's party to go ahead of the bridegroom, leading the way to the bride's house and shout, "Behold, the bridegroom comes." This would be followed by the sounding of the shofar. At the sounding of the shofar the entire wedding processional would go through the streets of the city to the bride's house. The groomsmen would again set up the huppah. Again the couple would say a blessing over the cup of wine. The ceremony finalized the promises and vows. The pinnacle of this joyful celebration was the marriage supper. It was much more than just a sit down dinner for all the guests. It included seven full days of food, music, dance and celebration. After the festivities the husband was free to bring his bride to their new home to live together as husband and wife in the full covenant of marriage.

Nothing could possibly illustrate more clearly the Revelation of Jesus Christ from the time of his personal ministry until his promised return to claim his bride than this picture of the Jewish marriage. No wonder the saints shouted, *"Hallelujah! For our Lord God Almighty reigns. Let us rejoice and be glad and give him glory! For the wedding of the Lamb has come, and his bride has made herself ready."* And the record goes on to say, *"Fine linen, bright and clean, was given her to wear.' (Fine linen stands for the righteous acts of the saints.)"* He came! We now are married to Christ and can proclaim to the world, as the angel said to John, *"Blessed are those who are invited to the wedding supper of the Lamb!"* If, as many today teach, we are still waiting for Jesus' return, we are not yet married, the church is not yet the bride of Christ. This concept is totally against all teaching of Scripture.

> *"I saw heaven standing open and there before me was a white horse, whose rider is called Faithful and True. With justice he judges and makes war. His eyes are like blazing fire, and on his head are many crowns. He has a name written on him that no one knows but he himself. He is dressed in a robe dipped in blood, and his name is the word of God. The armies of heaven were following him, riding on white horses and dressed in fine linen, white and clean. Out of his mouth comes a sharp sword with which to strike down the nations. 'He will rule them with an iron scepter.' He treads the winepress of the fury of the wrath of God Almighty. On his robe and on his thigh he has this name written:*
>
> *KING OF KINGS AND LORD OF LORDS"* (19:11-16).

In chapter 6:2, when the Lamb opened the first seal, John saw a white horse. *"Its rider held a bow, and he was given a crown, and he rode out as a conqueror bent on conquest."* The first seal was the covenant God made with Adam. The white horse was a symbol of the sin-free world over which Adam was made ruler. He was told to *"fill the earth and subdue it"* (Genesis 1:26-28). In Revelation we see him going forth to conquer, just as God had told him. Although Adam sinned and brought death into the world, he was the first prototype of Christ. In 1 Corinthians 15:45-49 the Apostle Paul wrote, *"So it is written: 'The first man Adam became a living being'; the last Adam, a life-giving spirit. The spiritual did not come first, but the natural, and after that the spiritual. The first man was of the dust of the earth, the second man from heaven. As was the earthly man, so are those who are of the earth; and as is the man from heaven, so also are those who are of heaven. And just as we have borne the likeness of the earthly man, so shall we bear the likeness of the man from heaven."* Everything that was lost by the first Adam was regained by the atonement sacrifice of the second one.

In John's vision the first Adam rode out alone. Jesus, the second Adam in chapter 19, came riding out with all the redeemed of the ages. They were also riding white horses and wearing white robes. They were, once again, sinless! They had reason to sing the praises of God and the Lamb.

> *"And I saw an angel standing in the sun, who cried in a loud voice to all the birds flying in midair, 'Come, gather together for the great supper of God, so that you may eat the flesh of kings, generals, and mighty men, of horses and their riders, and the flesh of all people, free and slave, small and great.'*
>
> *Then I saw the beast and the kings of the earth and their armies gathered together to make war against the rider on the horse and his army. But the beast was captured, and with him the false prophet who had performed the miraculous signs on his behalf. With these signs he had deluded those who had received the mark of the beast and worshiped his image. The two of them were thrown alive into the fiery lake of burning sulfur. The rest of them were*

> *killed with the sword that came out of the mouth of the rider on the horse, and all the birds gorged themselves on their flesh"* (19:17-21).

God had promised centuries before that he would one day redeem his people and avenge their enemies. The scene John saw was the fulfillment of this very specific promise made through the prophet Ezekiel. The exact same symbolic language is used so there can be no doubt that in the Revelation of Jesus Christ is found the fulfillment of what had been written in the Scroll. Once again we see how a thorough knowledge of the Old Testament prophesies is key to understanding John's writing.

> *"Son of man, this is what the Sovereign Lord says: Call out to every kind of bird and all the wild animals: 'Assemble and come together from all around to the sacrifice I am preparing for you, the great sacrifice on the mountains of Israel. There you will eat flesh and drink blood. You will eat the flesh of mighty men and drink the blood of the princes of the earth as if they were rams and lambs, goats and bulls—all of them fattened animals from Bashan. At the sacrifice I am preparing for you, you will eat fat till you are glutted and drink blood till you are drunk. At my table you will eat your fill of horses and riders, mighty men and soldiers of every kind,' declares the Sovereign Lord.*
>
> *I will display my glory among the nations, and all the nations will see the punishment I inflict and the hand I lay upon them. From that day forward the house of Israel will know that I am the Lord their God. And the nations will know that the people of Israel went into exile for their sin, because they were unfaithful to me. So I hid my face from them and*

handed them over to their enemies, and they all fell by the sword. I dealt with them according to their uncleanness and their offenses, and I hid my face from them.

Therefore this is what the Sovereign Lord says: I will now bring Jacob back from captivity and will have compassion on all the people of Israel, and I will be zealous for my holy name. They will forget their shame and all the unfaithfulness they showed toward me when they lived in safety in their land with no one to make them afraid. When I have brought them back from the nations and have gathered them from the countries of their enemies, I will show myself holy through them in the sight of many nations. Then they will know that I am the Lord their God, for though I sent them into exile among the nations, I will gather them to their own land, not leaving any behind. I will no longer hide my face from them, for I will pour out my Spirit on the house of Israel, declares the Sovereign Lord" (Ezekiel 39:17-29).

The prophet Joel had predicted that in the "last days" of Israel God would pour out his Spirit, redeem the righteous, and bring judgment on the ungodly. The Apostle Peter, preaching the very first Gospel sermon in Acts 2, said, *"This is that which was spoken by the prophet Joel…"* The Holy Spirit was poured out on the day of Pentecost. The "last days" ended with the return of the Bridegroom and the final destruction of the kingdom of Israel and its temple in A.D. 70 by the Roman army. God was faithful to his promise. The souls of those who were crying out under the alter in chapter six had to wait no longer! The "great day of the Lord" had come! Jesus returned in the clouds with power and great glory, exactly as and when he said he would in Matthew 24, Mark 13, and Luke 21. And just as he had told Peter, John lived until he returned to witness and record the events of the Revelation of Jesus Christ (John 21:20-22).

Revelation 20

> *"And I saw an angel coming down out of heaven, having the key to the Abyss and holding in his hand a great chain. He seized the dragon, that ancient serpent, who is the devil, or Satan, and bound him for a thousand years. He threw him into the Abyss, and locked and sealed it over him, to keep him from deceiving the nations anymore until the thousand years were ended. After that, he must be set free for a short time"* (20:1-3).

The Abyss has already been identified in chapters 9, 11, and 17 as the abode of Satan. The Gospel accounts of Jesus' ministry also reveal the same truth. In Matthew 8:29 the Legion of demons Jesus cast out asked him, *"What do you want with us, Son of God? Have you come here to torture us* ***before the appointed time?****"* Luke includes another request these demons had in Luke 8:31, *"And they begged him repeatedly not to order them to go into the Abyss."* The demons knew they were destined to the Abyss at "the appointed time." During Jesus' earthly ministry that time had not yet come. Jesus sent them into a herd of pigs. In John's Revelation, their time had come. Satan and his demonic messengers were thrown into the Abyss and sealed there for a thousand years.

When did Jesus bind the Devil in the Abyss? Speaking with the Pharisees about casting out demons in Matthew 12:29 he said, *"How can anyone enter a strong man's house and carry off his possessions unless he first ties up the strong man? Then he can rob his house."* 1 John 3:8 says, *"He who does what is sinful is of the devil, because the devil has been sinning from the beginning. The reason the Son of God appeared was to destroy the devil's work."* And in Hebrews 2:14-15, *"Since the children have flesh and blood, he too shared in their humanity so that* ***by his death*** *he might destroy him who holds the power of death—that is, the devil— and free those who all their lives were held in slavery by their fear of death."* When Jesus died he entered the Devil's house, destroying his power over death because death only had controlling power over one who had sinned. He bound Satan so that he could never again possess people against their will. As James 1:14-15 says, *"Each one is tempted when,* ***by his own evil desire****, he is dragged away and enticed. Then, after desire has conceived, it gives birth to sin; and sin, when it is full-grown, gives birth to death."* Sin is certainly still in the world today but, "The Devil made me do it" is no excuse. God even controls the amount of temptation we face. 1 Corinthians 10:13, *"No temptation has seized you except what is common to man. And God is faithful; he will not let you be tempted beyond what you can bear. But when you are tempted, he will also provide a way out so that you can stand up under it."*

> *"I saw thrones on which were seated those who had been given authority to judge. And I saw the souls of those who had been beheaded because of their testimony for Jesus and because of the word of God. They had not worshiped the beast or his image and had not received his mark on their foreheads or their hands. They came to life and reigned with Christ a thousand years. (The rest of the dead did not come to life until the thousand years were ended.) This is the first resurrection. Blessed and holy are those who have part in the first resurrection. The second death has no power over them, but they will be priests of God and of Christ and will reign with him for a thousand years"* (20:4-6).

To comprehend the thousand years, during which Satan was bound and the righteous dead came to life and reigned with Christ, one must first understand how the term is used in Scripture. This was not a literal one thousand years. The term "thousand years" is used figuratively throughout Scripture to denote the whole of something, all there is or from beginning to end, as the following passages demonstrate.

Deuteronomy 5:9-10, *"I, the Lord your God, am a jealous God, punishing the children for the sin of the fathers to the third and fourth generation of those who hate me, but showing love to a thousand generations of those who love me and keep my commandments."* God does not show his love for exactly one thousand generations and not one day longer. It is a term used in this context meaning forever.

Psalm 50:9-10, *"I have no need of a bull from your stall or of goats from your pens, for every animal of the forest is mine, and the cattle on a thousand hills."* Again, the Psalmist does not mean that God only owns the cattle on exactly one thousand hills. He owns them all.

Psalm 105:7-10, *"He is the Lord our God; his judgments are in all the earth. He remembers his covenant forever, the word he commanded, for a thousand generations, the covenant he made with Abraham, the oath he swore to Isaac."* God does not remember his covenant for exactly one thousand years, but forever.

Psalm 90:4, *"For a thousand years in your sight are like a day that has just gone by, or like a watch in the night."* The Apostle Peter, explaining to the first century Christians that Jesus would come in that generation as he had promised, quoted from this same Psalm in 2 Peter 3:8, *"But do not forget this one thing, dear friends: With the Lord a day is like a thousand years, and a thousand years are like a day."* These passages do not mean, as many today would suggest, that when God says something will happen in "this generation" he may mean a thousand generations. The point the Psalmist and

Peter made was that God can remember forever as easily as we can remember one day, and he will always be faithful to his promises. In the context of 2 Peter, Jesus promised he would return in that first generation. He did!

It is also important to understand the thousand years in these passages was the time between the resurrection of the righteous dead and the resurrection of the unrighteous ones, during which time Satan was bound. **It is NOT the duration of the reign of Christ.** His reign is forever. Isaiah 9:7, *"Of the increase of his government and peace there will be no end. He will reign on David's throne and over his kingdom, establishing and upholding it with justice and righteousness* ***from that time on and forever****. The zeal of the Lord Almighty will accomplish this."*

When Gabriel was explaining to Mary that she would give birth to the Son of God, he said in Luke 1:30-33, *"Do not be afraid, Mary, you have found favor with God. You will be with child and give birth to a son, and you are to give him the name Jesus. He will be great and will be called the Son of the Most High. The Lord God will give him the throne of his father David, and* ***he will reign over the house of Jacob forever; his kingdom will never end.****"* Nowhere does the Bible say Jesus will reign on a physical throne on a physical earth for one thousand years. The reign of Jesus as King of Kings and Lord of Lords is forever.

Predicting the resurrection of Jesus and the righteous dead, Psalm 68:17-19 says, *"The chariots of God are tens of thousands and thousands of thousands; the Lord has come from Sinai into his sanctuary. When you ascended on high, you led captives in your train; you received gifts from men, even from the rebellious— that you, O Lord God, might dwell there. Praise be to the Lord, to God our Savior, who daily bears our burdens."* The Apostle Paul, speaking of the fulfillment of this promise in Ephesians 4:7-10 wrote, *"But to each one of us grace has been given as Christ apportioned it. This is why it says: 'When he ascended on high, he led captives in his train and gave gifts to men.' (What does 'he ascended' mean except that he also descended to the lower, earthly regions? He who descended is the very one who ascended higher than all the heavens, in order to fill the whole universe.)"* When Jesus arose from the grave he loosed the righteous dead from the power of the grave and set the captives free.

Hebrews 2:14-17, *"Since the children have flesh and blood, he too shared in their humanity so that by his death he might destroy him who holds the power of death—that is, the devil— and free those who all their lives were held in slavery by their fear of death. For surely it is not angels he helps, but Abraham's descendants. For this reason he had to be made like his brothers in every way, in order that he might become a merciful and faithful high priest in service to God, and that he might make atonement for the sins of the people."* This was the first resurrection.

According to Matthew's Gospel account of the crucifixion, there were two graphic demonstrations of the spiritual significance of that holy death. Matthew 27:50-53, *"And when Jesus had cried out again in a loud voice, he gave up his spirit. At that moment the curtain of the temple was torn in two from top to bottom. The earth shook and the rocks split. The tombs broke open and the bodies of many holy people who had died were raised to life. They came out of the tombs, and* ***after Jesus' resurrection*** *they went into the holy city and appeared to many people."* The tearing of the physical veil in the temple signified that the barrier between people and the presence of God would be taken away. The physical opening of the graves of many righteous souls demonstrated the death of Jesus would result in the overcoming of death for all the righteous. It is important that these righteous souls were not seen alive by others until after Jesus' own resurrection. At the resurrection of Jesus all the righteous souls were freed from death to reign with Christ as victors over sin. A few of them were given physical bodies and went into Jerusalem to be seen as proof that death had been overcome.

The spiritual significance of the timing of the resurrection of the righteous dead cannot be overstated. The first resurrection occurred when the sins of the righteous were blotted out by the sacrifice of Jesus. We overcome death when we are baptized. When a person accepts the atonement of Jesus in obedient baptism he is raised from spiritual death in sin to new life in Christ. That is the first resurrection. 1 Peter 3:21 *"This water symbolizes baptism that now saves you also—not the removal of dirt from the body but the pledge of a good conscience toward God.* ***It saves you by the resurrection of Jesus Christ.*** *"* Romans 6:4, *"We were therefore buried with him through baptism into death in order that, just as Christ was raised from the dead through the glory of the Father, we too may live a new life." "Blessed and holy are those who have part in the first resurrection. The second death has no power over them."* Unlike the righteous, whose thousand year reign would be forever, the Devil and all his followers faced a far different fate…the second death.

When did the reign of Jesus begin? Paul wrote in Romans 1:2-4, Jesus *"…was a descendant of David, and was declared with power to be the Son of God by his resurrection from the dead."* The same writer said in Ephesians 1:19-23, *"That power is like the working of his mighty strength, which he exerted in Christ* ***when he raised him from the dead*** *and seated him at his right hand in the heavenly realms, far above all rule and authority, power and dominion, and every title that can be given, not only in the present age but also in the one to come. And God placed all things under his feet and appointed him to be head over everything for the church, which is his body, the fullness of him who fills everything in every way."* The apostle clearly taught that Jesus was declared with power to be the Son of God by his resurrection. He was anointed king over all authorities and powers after his resurrection, and the kingdom over which he was made king was the church. It is important to remember, however, that the kingdom (church) was not established at the time, or by the single act of his resurrection from the grave. Because he had no sin, death and the grave had no power over him. His resurrection proved his sinless life and made it possible for him to then make atonement by his own blood for the sins of mankind, thus overcoming death, Hell, and the grave for all the righteous.

Paul addressed this same subject in his letter to the Corinthian church. Discussing the resurrection of the dead, he wrote in 1 Corinthians 15:20-28, *"But Christ has indeed been raised from the dead, the firstfruits of those who have fallen asleep. For since death came through a man, the resurrection of the dead comes also through a man. For as in Adam all die, so in Christ all will be made alive. But each in his own turn: Christ, the firstfruits; then, when he comes, those who belong to him. Then the end will come, when he hands over the kingdom to God the Father after he has destroyed all dominion, authority and power. For he must reign until he has put all his enemies under his feet. The last enemy to be destroyed is death. For he 'has put everything under his feet.' Now when it says that 'everything' has been put under him, it is clear that this does not include God himself, who put everything under Christ. When he has done this, then the Son himself will be made subject to him who put everything under him, so that God may be all in all."*

From the above passage it is clear the following things happened, or would happen, each in its turn:

- The resurrection of Jesus
- The resurrection of the "firstfruits"
- Jesus' return
- The resurrection of the righteous dead
- The end will come
- All dominion, authority and power destroyed
- Jesus reigns until all enemies are subdued
- The last enemy to be destroyed is death
- Jesus delivers the kingdom of heaven to his Father

- Jesus made subject to the Father
- God is all in all

These are exactly the same events in the same order John saw in the Revelation of Jesus Christ. The Lion of the Tribe of Judah was able to open the seals of the Scroll because he had triumphed over death by the power of his resurrection (Revelation 5). At the death and resurrection of Jesus the graves were opened and those who had been held captive by Satan's power over death and the grave were set free. Many of them went into the city of Jerusalem as living proof that Jesus had overcome and *"led the captives in his train"* (Matthew 27:52-53, Ephesians 4:7-9, Hebrews 2:14-16). The faithful of Israel were the first to be offered to God as "firstfruits" of the harvest of the earth (Revelation 14). Once the atonement was complete in heaven and the time was fulfilled, Jesus returned in the clouds, all the righteous dead were raised, and the "time of the end" had come (Matthew 24, Mark 13, Luke 21, Daniel 8:16-18, 9:25-27, 11:34-36, 12, Habakkuk 2:2-4, Matthew 13:38-40, Hebrews 9:25-27). The "great day of the Lord" had come, the city of Jerusalem and its temple were destroyed, the remainder of the dead were raised, and the judgment of Almighty God was pronounced on all peoples and nations. Jesus had overcome all authorities, powers and dominions, death was destroyed forever, and the kingdom of heaven was now a reality. The "consummation (fulfillment) of the ages" had come (1 Corinthians 10:11, Hebrews 9:25-27). Jesus came into the world to destroy the Devil's stronghold (Hebrews 2:13-15, 1 John 3:7-9). He had succeeded in his mission and could now deliver the kingdom to his Father. The promise of God to redeem mankind was now complete and, with his Son now back at his side, he was truly "all in all." **MYSTERY ACCOMPLISHED!**

Many Christians today believe and teach that "the end" spoken of in Revelation and other Scriptures is the end of the physical universe and is still in our future. There is only one "end" prophesied in the Bible and it is the end of the physical kingdom of Israel which was replaced with the new Jerusalem, the church, the kingdom of heaven. That happened with the destruction of Jerusalem and its temple in A.D. 70. If Jesus has not yet returned, death has not yet been destroyed, the righteous dead are still held captive by the power of the grave, and the church has not yet been established. This is simply false doctrine.

As has been pointed out many times before, the confusion comes in our failure to understand the difference between physical and spiritual death and life. Jesus was not crucified and resurrected to overcome physical death, but spiritual death...eternal separation from God. He did not make atonement so we can have physical life, but eternal spiritual life with God. The church is a spiritual kingdom, not a physical one. 1 Corinthians 15:50-57, *"I declare to you, brothers, that* ***flesh and blood cannot inherit the kingdom of God, nor does the perishable inherit the imperishable.*** *Listen, I tell you a mystery: We will not all sleep, but we will all be changed— in a flash, in the twinkling of an eye, at the last trumpet. For the trumpet will sound, the dead will be raised imperishable, and* ***we will be changed.*** *For the perishable must clothe itself with the imperishable, and the mortal with immortality. When the perishable has been clothed with the imperishable, and the mortal with immortality, then the saying that is written will come true: 'Death has been swallowed up in victory.' Where, O death, is your victory? Where, O death, is your sting? The sting of death is sin, and the power of sin is the law. But thanks be to God! He gives us the victory through our Lord Jesus Christ."*

Paul said at the sounding of the last trumpet the dead would be raised and all who were still living would be changed. The perishable would be clothed with the imperishable, the mortal with immortality. He was not speaking of physical changes, but spiritual. He clearly said the physical (flesh and blood) cannot inherit the kingdom of God. The perishable (physical) cannot inherit the imperishable (spiritual). What brought about this change from physical to spiritual, from mortality to immortality? 2 Timothy 1:9-10, *"This grace was given us in Christ Jesus before the beginning of time, but it has* ***now been revealed*** *through the appearing of our Savior, Christ Jesus, who has* ***destroyed death and has brought life and immortality to light through the gospel****. And of this gospel I was appointed a herald and an apostle and a teacher."*

Life and immortality was the "good news" of the Gospel of Christ. It had been promised before the beginning of time, foretold by the prophets, and heralded since the day of Pentecost. But at the time of Paul's writing to the Corinthian church the last trumpet had not yet sounded. The angel in Revelation who introduced this seventh and final trumpet said, *"There will be no more delay! But in the days when the seventh angel is about to sound his trumpet,* ***the mystery of God will be accomplished****, just as he announced to his servants the prophets"* (Revelation 10:7).

The Apostle Paul explained the mystery of God in his letter to the church in Ephesus. Ephesians 1:9-10, *"And he made known to us the* ***mystery of his will*** *according to his good pleasure, which he purposed in Christ,* ***to be put into effect when the times will have reached their fulfillment****—to bring all things in heaven and on earth together under one head, even Christ."* Ephesians 3:6-12, *"This mystery is that* ***through the gospel the Gentiles are heirs together with Israel, members together of one body****, and sharers together in the promise in Christ Jesus...His intent was that now,* ***through the church****, the manifold wisdom of God should be made known to the rulers and authorities in the heavenly realms, according to his eternal purpose which he accomplished in Christ Jesus our Lord. In him and through faith in him we may approach God with freedom and confidence."* The mystery of God did not change between Ephesians and Revelation. The sounding of the seventh and final trumpet would signal the completion of this mystery. It would also signal that the times were fulfilled, the "time of the end" had come, the physical temple could be removed, opening up the way into the Holy of Holies so we may approach God with freedom and confidence.

We learned from Hebrews 9:8, *"The way into the Most Holy Place had not yet been disclosed* ***as long as the first tabernacle was still standing.****"* The first tabernacle stood until it was destroyed by the Roman invasion of A.D. 70. That was the final God-directed event Jesus had said would signify his "coming in the clouds." This "second appearing" of our Great High Priest proclaimed to all that the atonement blood was accepted by the Father and our sins were forgiven. The last trumpet had sounded. The physical temple was no longer the place of atonement, so it was forever destroyed. Animal sacrifices were no longer needed. The way into the Holy of Holies was open. The mystery of God was accomplished. The kingdom of heaven, the church, was complete. Gentiles and Jews were now members of one body. Death had been destroyed. The righteous dead were raised imperishable. Life and immortality were now a reality. The fate of all who were living, and all who would ever live, was instantly changed. The fulfillment, or consummation, of the ages had come. In the twinkling of an eye, everything had changed.

Victory in Jesus does not spare us from physical death. It spares us from spiritual death so we may live forever with God, here on earth and in heaven when we experience physical death. That is why Christians have no fear of physical death. It no longer has any power over our eternal destiny. Jesus has destroyed its power. If death has not been destroyed, the new covenant in Christ is not yet a reality, the mystery of God has still not been accomplished, and we are still living under the Law of Moses. Paul said in the above Corinthian passage the sting of death is sin and the power of sin was the law. If death has not been destroyed, sin still has its sting and we are still under its power...the law. That would mean the death and resurrection of Jesus failed to accomplish the very thing he came to do - destroy the Devil's power, overcome the sting of death, and bring life and immortality to fallen mankind.

The Devil's power and his kingdom have been destroyed. This brings us back to the "thousand years" during which the devil was bound and the righteous dead came to life and reigned with Christ.

> *"When the thousand years are over, Satan will be released from his prison and will go out to deceive the nations in the four corners of the earth—Gog and Magog—to gather them for battle. In number they are like the sand on the seashore. They marched across the breadth of the earth and surrounded the camp of God's people, the city he loves. But fire came down from heaven and devoured them. And the devil, who deceived them, was thrown into the lake of burning sulfur, where the beast and the false prophet had been thrown. They will be tormented day and night for ever and ever"* (20:7-10).

Satan was released at the end of the "thousand years." Again, the term is used to describe the period of time Satan was bound, not the duration of Jesus' reign. Revelation says the Devil would be bound for a thousand years. Nowhere in Revelation, or the entire Bible, does it say the reign of Christ would be limited to this same time period. Nowhere in Revelation, or the entire Bible, does it say the reign of Christ will ever end. There is no mention in Revelation, or the entire Bible, of a "thousand year reign of Christ." As a matter of fact, Revelation teaches just the opposite. There was a "thousand year reign of the righteous dead" *with Christ.* The Lion of the Tribe of Judah had prevailed. Satan's reign over death and the grave ended. His power over mankind was destroyed. Jesus was victorious. He had accomplished his mission to atone for sin and establish the eternal kingdom of heaven. When he finished his divine task he delivered the kingdom to the Father, and reigns with him forever. *"**The throne of God and of the Lamb** will be in the city, and his servants will serve him. They will see his face, and his name will be on their foreheads. There will be no more night. They will not need the light of a lamp or the light of the sun, for the Lord God will give them light. **And they will reign forever and ever**"* (22:3-5).

There was a thousand-year binding of Satan which began when Jesus was exalted to the throne in heaven after his resurrection. The Devil was loosed at the end of the thousand years and gathered all his demons, along with the unrighteous dead, to make one final attempt to overcome the Lamb of God. The time Satan was locked in the Abyss was called a thousand years. While the term was used in the usual figurative sense, meaning as long as *his time* lasted, his reign was not forever and the remainder of his time was relatively short. This "thousand years" was the entire time it took to finish the divine work of atonement at which time all the dead would be raised to face the eternal judgment of Almighty God. This time period began when Jesus overcame the power of the grave and the righteous dead were raised. That was when he arose from the dead. It ended at the "time of the end" on the "great day of the Lord" when he was loosed for a short time. He marshaled his forces for one final stand; the battle of Armageddon. God's judgment was pronounced and fire came from heaven and devoured them. Keep in mind that according to Scripture "the end" was the end of physical Israel, NOT the end of the world. The Bible speaks of "the time of the end," it NEVER speaks of the "end of time."

Like the return of Jesus, many Christians today also believe the judgment is still in our future. Again, this is simply not the case in Scripture. John 5:22-30, *"Moreover, the Father judges no one, but has entrusted all judgment to the Son, that all may honor the Son just as they honor the Father. He who does not honor the Son does not honor the Father, who sent him. I tell you the truth, whoever hears my word and believes him who sent me has eternal life and will not be condemned;* ***he has crossed over from death to life.*** *I tell you the truth, a time is coming and has now come when the dead will hear the voice of the Son of God and those who hear will live. For as the Father has life in himself, so he has granted the Son to have life in himself. And he has given him authority to judge because he is the Son of Man. Do not be amazed at this, for* ***a time is coming when all who are in their graves will hear his voice and come out—those who have done good will rise to live, and those who have done evil will rise to be condemned.*** *By myself I can do nothing; I judge only as I hear, and my judgment is just, for I seek not to please myself but him who sent me."* When Jesus overcame the power of the grave and completed the atonement ritual for sin, judgment had to occur. That is why Jesus, speaking of his own death, said in John 12:31, *"**Now** is the time for judgment on this world; **now** the prince of this world will be driven out."*

Satan was bound by the resurrection of Jesus. He was loosed when the atonement was complete and God was ready to judge the world on the "great day of the Lord." That was at the "time of the end" when the earthly kingdom was destroyed (A.D. 70), replaced by the eternal kingdom of heaven, the church. The thousand years was from the time he was bound until the "time of the end." It was the entire time Satan had left before his kingdom of death would be forever destroyed and his eternal fate, and the fate of all those who have his mark (sin), was sealed forever.

If one were to substitute "the time of the end" for "a thousand years," the verses in Revelation would read as follows:

> *"He seized the dragon, that ancient serpent, who is the devil, or Satan, and bound him* ***until the time of the end.*** *He threw him into the Abyss, and locked*

and sealed it over him to keep him from deceiving the nations anymore ***until the time of the end.*** *After that he must be set free for a short time"* (20:2-3).

"They came to life and reigned with Christ ***until the time of the end.*** *(The rest of the dead did not come to life* ***until the time of the end.****) Blessed and holy are those who have part in the first resurrection. The second death has no power over them, but they will be priests of God and of Christ and will reign with him* ***until the time of the end. At the time of the end,*** *Satan will be released from his prison and will go out to deceive the nations in the four corners of the earth—Gog and Magog—to gather them for battle"* (20:4-8).

Prophesies concerning Gog and Magog are found in Ezekiel chapters 38-39 and, like so many other Old Testament prophesies, were a physical foreshadowing of the final spiritual battle John saw in his Revelation. Ezekiel 38:14-16, *"Therefore, son of man, prophesy and say to Gog: 'This is what the Sovereign Lord says: In that day, when my people Israel are living in safety, will you not take notice of it? You will come from your place in the far north, you and many nations with you, all of them riding on horses, a great horde, a mighty army. You will advance against my people Israel like a cloud that covers the land. In days to come, O Gog, I will bring you against my land, so that the nations may know me when I show myself holy through you before their eyes."* This is one more example which shows how every prophecy concerning the future of Israel and the eternal kingdom was fulfilled in Christ. John was shown the Revelation of Jesus Christ and how the Lion of the Tribe of Judah opened the seals and fulfilled everything written in the Scroll.

"Then I saw a great white throne and him who was seated on it. Earth and sky fled from his presence,

> *and there was no place for them. And I saw the dead, great and small, standing before the throne, and books were opened. Another book was opened, which is the book of life. The dead were judged according to what they had done as recorded in the books. The sea gave up the dead that were in it, and death and Hades gave up the dead that were in them, and each person was judged according to what he had done. Then death and Hades were thrown into the lake of fire. The lake of fire is the second death. If anyone's name was not found written in the book of life, he was thrown into the lake of fire"* (20:11-15).

In this next scene John witnessed and recorded the judgment of the dead. These were the spiritually dead. The righteous had already come to life and were reigning with Christ. They were never judged because they had been cleansed by the blood of the Lamb. They did not have the mark of the beast (sin) and, therefore, had no accusation against them requiring judgment. With the sacrifice of Jesus, their sins had been removed. This was the first resurrection. The second death would have no power over them.

The dead (in sin) are the only people in John's Revelation who faced the judgment of Almighty God. The books were opened. There was a single volume, called the Lamb's Book of Life, and another set of books that could be called the Record of Works, in which were recorded the names and deeds of every person to be judged. It is critically important to understand:

- Every person's name was recorded in only one book.
- Only those whose names were in the "Record of Works" were judged.
- The dead (spiritually) were judged by their record.
- Not one single soul was saved by his or her works.

- All those judged according to the "Record of Works" were thrown into the Lake of Fire.
- Those whose names were in the Lamb's Book of Life were not judged because they were not in the "Record of Works."

Jesus made very clear the connection between the establishment of the kingdom of heaven and the judgment, and that they would both occur in that first generation. *"For the Son of Man is going to come in his Father's glory with his angels,* ***and then he will reward each person according to what he has done.*** *I tell you the truth,* ***some who are standing here will not taste death before they see the Son of Man coming in his kingdom****"* (Matthew 16:27-28). When Jesus completed the atonement, having destroyed death, judgment had to be rendered. Otherwise there would have to be another "holding place" for the dead, other than the grave while they wait for some imagined "end of time," neither of which are found in Scripture.

Every person, at some point in his or her life, chooses to eat of the forbidden fruit. The wages of sin is death...spiritual death; separation from the presence of God. This is the first death. Those who do not accept the atonement of Jesus for their sins will suffer eternal separation from God, which is the Lake of Fire, or the second death. Those who accept Jesus as Lord receive forgiveness from sin and are raised to life - eternal, spiritual life. This is the first resurrection. The second death has no power over them. The righteous who died prior to the coming of Jesus experienced the first resurrection when Jesus atoned for their sins. They came to life and reigned with him.

People today also experience the first resurrection when they accept Jesus' atonement for their sins. That is why baptism was the symbol chosen for our salvation. We die to sin, are buried in baptism by immersion, and raised sinless (first resurrection) to live a new life in Christ. *"We were therefore buried with him through baptism into death in order that, just as Christ was raised from the dead through the glory of the Father, we too may live a new life"* (Romans 6:4). Those who object to baptism as being necessary for salvation because they see it as a "work" of man simply do not understand the symbol. It is a physical demonstration of our willingness to die to self, to bury our old sin nature, to completely renounce any hope we have of saving ourselves, and trust fully and completely in the grace of God and the blood of Christ Jesus. We are not saved by *our* faith, but only by *his* grace. When we are baptized into Christ, we are clothed with him (Galatians 3:27) and our name is removed from the "Record of Works" and entered into the Lamb's Book of Life. Judgment for both sets of names has already been rendered and the sentence handed down. Our eternal destiny is determined by the choice we make while living on earth. When we die physically, if our name is in the Lamb's Book of Life, we go to be with the Lord forever in heaven. If our name is not in the Lamb's Book of Life, we experience the second death, eternal separation from the presence of God. Physical death has nothing to do with either, except that it brings to a close the time we have been given to make our choice. As Moses challenged the Israelites before entering the Promised Land (Deuteronomy 30:19), we have a choice between life and death. CHOOSE LIFE!

Revelation 21

> *"Then I saw a new heaven and a new earth, for the first heaven and the first earth had passed away, and there was no longer any sea. I saw the Holy City, the new Jerusalem, coming down out of heaven from God, prepared as a bride beautifully dressed for her husband. And I heard a loud voice from the throne*

> *saying, 'Now the dwelling of God is with men, and he will live with them. They will be his people, and God himself will be with them and be their God. He will wipe every tear from their eyes. There will be no more death or mourning or crying or pain, for the old order of things has passed away.'*
>
> *He who was seated on the throne said, 'I am making everything new!' Then he said, 'Write this down, for these words are trustworthy and true.' He said to me: 'It is done. I am the Alpha and the Omega, the Beginning and the End. To him who is thirsty I will give to drink without cost from the spring of the water of life. He who overcomes will inherit all this, and I will be his God and he will be my son. But the cowardly, the unbelieving, the vile, the murderers, the sexually immoral, those who practice magic arts, the idolaters and all liars—their place will be in the fiery lake of burning sulfur. This is the second death' "* (21:1-8).

Before we immediately jump to the conclusion that he is describing heaven after we die physically, let's examine what John said here in light of other passages of Scripture. Twice in this text John described the Holy City, the new Jerusalem, coming down out of heaven from God, prepared as a bride beautifully dressed for her husband.

Compare this with what the writer of Hebrews said concerning this same heavenly Jerusalem. In Hebrews 11:10, concerning the promise made to Abraham, *"For he was looking forward to the city with foundations, whose architect and builder is God."* In chapter 12:18-21 he first described the time Moses received the old covenant when God was setting up the physical kingdom of Israel which would serve as a pattern for the spiritual kingdom promised to Abraham. He said, *"You have not come to a mountain that can be touched and that is burning with fire; to darkness, gloom and storm; to a trumpet blast or to such a voice speaking words that those who heard it begged that no further word be spoken to them, because they could not bear what was commanded: 'If even an animal touches the mountain, it must be stoned.' The sight was so terrifying that Moses said, 'I am trembling with fear.' "*

Then comparing that physical kingdom to the much superior spiritual kingdom of Jesus Christ, in verses 22-29:

> *"But you have come to Mount Zion,* **to the heavenly Jerusalem, the city of the living God**. *You have come to thousands upon thousands of angels in joyful assembly, to* **the church** *of the firstborn, whose names are written in heaven. You have come to God, the judge of all men, to the spirits of righteous men made perfect, to Jesus the mediator of a new covenant, and to the sprinkled blood that speaks a better word than the blood of Abel.*
>
> *See to it that you do not refuse him who speaks. If they did not escape when they refused him who warned them on earth, how much less will we, if we turn away from him who warns us from heaven? At that time his voice shook the earth, but now he has promised, 'Once more I will shake not only the earth but also the heavens.' The words 'once more' indicate the removing of what can be shaken—that is, created things—so that what cannot be shaken may remain. Therefore, since we are receiving a kingdom that cannot be shaken, let us be thankful, and so worship God acceptably with reverence and awe, for our God is a consuming fire."*

The Hebrew writer clearly identified the heavenly Jerusalem as the church. He further stated that the old physical kingdom of Israel was passing away and, *"…we are receiving a kingdom that cannot be shaken."* John and the writer of Hebrews are referring to the same heavenly Jerusalem, the church. This is the city promised to Abraham whose builder was God. Jesus said, *"Upon this rock I will build my church, and the gates of Hell shall not prevail against it"* (Matthew 16:18).

The church is the "kingdom of heaven." In John 18:36 Jesus said, *"My kingdom is not of this world. If it were, my servants would fight to prevent my arrest by the Jews. But now my kingdom is from another place."* As the Apostle Paul said, our citizenship is in heaven. While we recognize the eternal, spiritual nature of this heavenly Jerusalem, the church, we are not waiting for the physical universe to be destroyed for it to be established by God. John was describing that eternal kingdom in which we enjoy citizenship now as well as throughout all eternity.

That John was not speaking of life with God in heaven after we die physically is further underscored by his wording when he said, *"Now the dwelling of God* ***is with men****, and* ***he will live with them****."* Jesus said in John 14:23, *"If anyone loves me, he will obey my teaching. My Father will love him, and we will come to him and* ***make our home with him.****"* Yes, we will live with God in heaven forever. In the meantime, he lives with us through his Holy Spirit, whom he gives to all who obey his will.

Some may say this cannot be a description of life in the church on the earth because John said, *"He will wipe every tear from their eyes. There will be no more death or mourning or crying or pain, for the old order of things has passed away."* He who was seated on the throne said, *"I am making everything new!"* As is the case from beginning to end of John's Revelation, he was explaining how Jesus fulfilled Scripture at the "consummation of the ages" when the "mystery of God" would finally be revealed. In this description of the "heavenly Jerusalem" identified in Scripture as the church, he was referring to Old Testament prophesies that were being fulfilled.

Isaiah 25:7-8, *"On this mountain he will destroy the shroud that enfolds all peoples, the sheet that covers all nations; he will swallow up death forever. The Sovereign Lord will wipe away the tears from all faces; he will remove the disgrace of his people from all the earth."* When did Jesus "swallow up death" and "remove the disgrace" (sin) of his people? Surely it was in his death, resurrection and atonement for sin.

Prophesying about the coming spiritual kingdom in Isaiah 35:8-10 the prophet said, *"And a highway will be there; it will be called the Way of Holiness. The unclean will not journey on it; it will be for those who walk in that Way; wicked fools will not go about on it. No lion will be there, nor will any ferocious beast get up on it; they will not be found there. But only the redeemed will walk there, and the ransomed of the Lord will return. They will enter Zion with singing; everlasting joy will crown their heads. Gladness and joy will overtake them, and* ***sorrow and sighing will flee away."***

And in Isaiah 65:17-19, *"Behold, I will create* ***new heavens and a new earth.*** *The former things will not be remembered, nor will they come to mind. But be glad and rejoice forever in what I will create, for I will create* ***Jerusalem*** *to be a delight and its people a joy. I will rejoice over Jerusalem and take delight in my people;* ***the sound of weeping and of crying will be heard in it no more.****"* In 2 Corinthians 5:17 the Apostle Paul said, *"Therefore, if anyone is in Christ, he is a new creation; the old has gone, the new has come!"*

Again, in Isaiah 49:8-10, *"This is what the Lord says: In the time of my favor I will answer you, and in the day of salvation I will help you; I will keep you and will make you to be a covenant for the people, to restore the land and to reassign its desolate inheritances, to say to the captives, 'Come out,' and to those in darkness, 'Be free!' They will feed beside the roads and find pasture on every barren hill.* ***They will neither hunger nor thirst, nor will the desert heat or the sun beat***

upon them. *He who has compassion on them will guide them and lead them beside springs of water."* In a typical "this is that" passage Paul quoted from this very same Scripture in Isaiah, indicating its fulfillment in the church, when he said in 2 Corinthians 6:2, *"For he says, 'In the time of my favor I heard you, and in the day of salvation I helped you.' I tell you, now is the time of God's favor, now is the day of salvation."* He said the prophet's message is fulfilled NOW.

All the above prophesies, and many more, clearly indicate that in the kingdom of heaven, the new Jerusalem, the church, there will be no more sorrow, hunger, death, crying, etc. This does not mean these things will literally disappear from the earth, nor are these Scriptures referring to heaven after we die. The comparison is between the physical kingdom of Israel and the spiritual kingdom of heaven. The physical kingdom was subject to all these physical problems; wars, captivity, calamities, sorrow, hunger and death. The spiritual kingdom of Jesus Christ is vulnerable to none of these things. Jesus said, *"I will build my church and the gates of Hell will not overcome it"* (Matthew 16:18). In John 5:24 he said, *"I tell you the truth, whoever hears my word and believes him who sent me has eternal life and will not be condemned; he has crossed over from death to life."* Again, in John 11:25-26, *"I am the resurrection and the life. He who believes in me will live, even though he dies; and* **whoever lives and believes in me will never die.** *Do you believe this?"* Paul, writing to Christians in Thessalonica said, *"We do not want you to be ignorant about those who fall asleep, or to grieve like the rest of men, who have no hope"* (1 Thessalonians 4:13). The concept of "no tears, no sorrow, no death" relates to the spiritual nature of the kingdom of heaven as compared with the former physical kingdom. The former things have passed away, all things have become new.

"One of the seven angels who had the seven bowls
full of the seven last plagues came and said to me,

'Come, I will show you the bride, the wife of the Lamb.' And he carried me away in the Spirit to a mountain great and high, and showed me the Holy City, Jerusalem, coming down out of heaven from God. It shone with the glory of God, and its brilliance was like that of a very precious jewel, like a jasper, clear as crystal. It had a great, high wall with twelve gates, and with twelve angels at the gates. On the gates were written the names of the twelve tribes of Israel. There were three gates on the east, three on the north, three on the south and three on the west. The wall of the city had twelve foundations, and on them were the names of the twelve apostles of the Lamb.

The angel who talked with me had a measuring rod of gold to measure the city, its gates and its walls. The city was laid out like a square, as long as it was wide. He measured the city with the rod and found it to be 12,000 stadia in length, and as wide and high as it is long. He measured its wall and it was 144 cubits thick, by man's measurement, which the angel was using. The wall was made of jasper, and the city of pure gold, as pure as glass. The foundations of the city walls were decorated with every kind of precious stone. The first foundation was jasper, the second sapphire, the third chalcedony, the fourth emerald, the fifth sardonyx, the sixth carnelian, the seventh chrysolite, the eighth beryl, the ninth topaz, the tenth chrysoprase, the eleventh jacinth, and the twelfth amethyst. The twelve gates were twelve pearls, each gate made of a single pearl. The great street of the city was of pure gold, like transparent glass" (21:9-21).

There is no question that John here was describing the church. In Ephesians 5:25-27 the Apostle Paul wrote, *"Husbands, love your wives, just as Christ loved the church and gave himself up for her to make her holy, cleansing her by the washing with water through the word, and to present her to himself as a radiant church, without stain or wrinkle or any other blemish, but holy and blameless."* The church is the bride of Christ. It is also the heavenly Jerusalem. Hebrews 12:22-23, *"But you have come to Mount Zion, to the heavenly Jerusalem, the city of the living God. You have come to thousands upon thousands of angels in joyful assembly, to the church of the firstborn, whose names are written in heaven."* It is also God's household, built on the foundation of the apostles and prophets, with Christ Jesus himself as the chief cornerstone (Ephesians 2:19-20).

> *"I did not see a temple in the city, because the Lord God Almighty and the Lamb are its temple. The city does not need the sun or the moon to shine on it, for the glory of God gives it light, and the Lamb is its lamp. The nations will walk by its light, and the kings of the earth will bring their splendor into it. On no day will its gates ever be shut, for there will be no night there. The glory and honor of the nations will be brought into it. Nothing impure will ever enter it, nor will anyone who does what is shameful or deceitful, but only those whose names are written in the Lamb's book of life"* (21:22-27).

The temple in Jerusalem was built to house the Ark of the Covenant in the Holy of Holies. That is where the High Priest would go to make the annual atonement sacrifice for the sins of the people. It represented God's presence with the kingdom of Israel and was a prototype of heaven itself. There is no need for a physical temple in heaven since that is God's dwelling place. He and the Lamb are the temple. The gates into the kingdom of heaven are always open to anyone who will submit to the king.

We become citizens of the kingdom of heaven when we obey the Gospel message. As was the case with the Jews on, and following, the Day of Pentecost, the Lord adds to the church all who are saved (Acts 2). He writes their names in the Lamb's Book of Life. Eternal life begins the moment a person is cleansed of his or her sins by the blood of Jesus. We live in victory for the duration of our days on earth, then, when we die physically, we simply go to be with the Lord forever in heaven.

Revelation 22

> *"Then the angel showed me the river of the water of life, as clear as crystal, flowing from the throne of God and of the Lamb down the middle of the great street of the city. On each side of the river stood the tree of life, bearing twelve crops of fruit, yielding its fruit every month. And the leaves of the tree are for the healing of the nations. No longer will there be any curse. The throne of God and of the Lamb will be in the city, and his servants will serve him. They will see his face, and his name will be on their foreheads. There will be no more night. They will not need the light of a lamp or the light of the sun, for the Lord God will give them light. And they will reign for ever and ever. The angel said to me, 'These words are trustworthy and true. The Lord, the God of the spirits of the prophets, sent his angel to show his servants the things that must soon take place' "* (22:1-6).

Jesus said to the woman at the well in John 4:10, *"If you knew the gift of God and who it is that asks you for a drink, you would have asked him and he would have given you living water."* Jesus was speaking of the water of life, pictured here in Revelation flowing from the throne of God. This is a continuation of the description of the church, the kingdom of heaven.

> *"Behold, I am coming soon! Blessed is he who keeps the words of the prophecy in this book. I, John, am the one who heard and saw these things. And when I had heard and seen them, I fell down to worship at the feet of the angel who had been showing them to me. But he said to me, 'Do not do it! I am a fellow servant with you and with your brothers the prophets and of all who keep the words of this book. Worship God!'*
>
> *Then he told me, 'Do not seal up the words of the prophecy of this book, because the time is near. Let him who does wrong continue to do wrong; let him who is vile continue to be vile; let him who does right continue to do right; and let him who is holy continue to be holy.'*
>
> *Behold, I am coming soon! My reward is with me, and I will give to everyone according to what he has done. I am the Alpha and the Omega, the First and the Last, the Beginning and the End. Blessed are those who wash their robes, that they may have the right to the tree of life and may go through the gates into the city. Outside are the dogs, those who practice magic arts, the sexually immoral, the murderers, the idolaters and everyone who loves and practices falsehood. I, Jesus, have sent my angel to give you this testimony for the churches. I am the Root and the Offspring of David, and the bright Morning Star.'*
>
> *The Spirit and the bride say, 'Come!' And let him who hears say, 'Come!' Whoever is thirsty, let him come; and whoever wishes, let him take the free gift of the water of life. I warn everyone who hears the words*

of the prophecy of this book: If anyone adds anything to them, God will add to him the plagues described in this book. And if anyone takes words away from this book of prophecy, God will take away from him his share in the tree of life and in the holy city, which are described in this book.

He who testifies to these things says, 'Yes, I am coming soon.' Amen. Come, Lord Jesus. The grace of the Lord Jesus be with God's people. Amen" (22:7-21).

The identity of the servant who showed John this vision of the church is not revealed, but his message should not be missed. Worship God!

To make sure nobody misses the point made in the beginning of the Revelation and misunderstands the time frame for the events described in this book, the Spirit directs John to repeat FIVE TIMES in the closing verses these things were going to happen SOON.

> Revelation 22:6 *"The angel said to me, 'These words are trustworthy and true. The Lord, the God of the spirits of the prophets, sent his angel* ***to show his servants the things that must soon take place.'"***

> Revelation 22:7, *"Behold,* ***I am coming soon!*** *Blessed is he who keeps the words of the prophecy in this book."*

> Revelation 22:10, *"Then he told me, 'Do not seal up the words of the prophecy of this book, because* ***the time is near.'"***

> Revelation 22:12-13, *"Behold,* ***I am coming***

> **soon!** *My reward is with me, and I will give to everyone according to what he has done. I am the Alpha and the Omega, the First and the Last, the Beginning and the End."*
>
> Revelation 22:20, *"He who testifies to these things says,* **'Yes, I am coming soon.'** *Amen. Come, Lord Jesus."*

In Daniel 8:26 the Bible says, *"The vision of the evenings and mornings that has been given you is true, but seal up the vision, for it concerns the distant future."* John was told, *"Do not seal up the words of the prophecy of this book, because the time is near"* (Rev. 22:10). How can 490 years be the "distant future" and two centuries and counting be "very soon," "at hand," "at the door," "what must soon take place," "near?" We do not need to explain God's time statements in these passages any more than when John the Baptist said, *"Repent for the kingdom of heaven is at hand."* The meaning did not change, and we have no Scriptural authority to change it now. What is confusing people today are all the modern "philosophies of men" concerning the "end of time," of which the Bible does not speak.

The Revelation of Jesus Christ as revealed to the Apostle John is not to be taken lightly. It contains a sobering warning. *"I warn everyone who hears the words of the prophecy of this book: If anyone adds anything to them, God will add to him the plagues described in this book. And if anyone takes words away from this book of prophecy, God will take away from him his share in the tree of life and in the holy city, which are described in this book"* (Revelation 22:18-19).

One final thought about John's writing seems appropriate. If the coming of the Lord is to destroy the earth and bring to an end the possibility of one more sinner hearing the gospel and being saved, why would Christians want to hasten his coming? If, on the other hand, the Lord's coming was to usher in the spiritual kingdom, to proclaim the completion of the atonement sacrifice of Jesus for sin, to destroy death and Hades, to reveal the mystery of God's redemptive plan so that every sinner might hear the gospel message of reconciliation and have the opportunity for salvation, then by all means...AMEN! COME LORD JESUS!

He came! ***MYSTERY ACCOMPLISHED!***

CONCLUSION

The Hope of the World

When presented with the concept that the Scriptures have been fulfilled, especially the idea that Jesus has already made his second appearance, many Christians want to know where that leaves us today. If the Lord has already come, what is left? They feel empty, as if there is nothing left for which to live. Where is our hope?

This line of thinking underscores just how pervasive termination theology has been over the past few decades and how it has confused the Christian world about the resurrection. Those who espouse a future end-time philosophy reason that the second coming of Jesus will bring about the resurrection; therefore, teaching that he has already come denies the resurrection, since people are still dying. This is a complete misunderstanding of what Scripture teaches about resurrection life, which is our hope.

In Genesis 3:15 God pronounced future judgment on the Serpent when he said, *"He* (Jesus) *will crush your head and you will strike his heel."* Jesus did indeed deal the fatal blow to the Devil when he overcame death by his triumphant resurrection from the grave. 1 John 3:8, *"He who does what is sinful is of the devil, because the devil has been sinning from the beginning. The reason the Son of God appeared was to destroy the devil's work."*

Hebrews 2:14-15, *"Since the children have flesh and blood, he too shared in their humanity so that by his death he might destroy him who holds the power of death—that is, the devil—and free those who all their lives were held in slavery by their fear of death."* The result of sin was death, spiritual death, and eternal separation from the presence of God. The day Adam and Eve ate the forbidden fruit they suffered this fate. They were expelled from the Garden and from the presence of their heavenly Father.

Also in the Garden of Eden God introduced the hope of all mankind. That hope was redemption that would come through the death, burial, and resurrection of Jesus Christ. The hope of man had nothing to do with some distant, future destruction of the universe. It was, is, and always will be redemption from the curse of sin. The curse was spiritual death, separation from God. Redemption results in spiritual life, being granted access once again into God's presence, the Holy of Holies.

In his covenant with Abraham God promised, *"In you and your seed all nations of the earth will be blessed."* The hope of the Patriarchs was in the same promised Redeemer through whom people of all nations would find salvation. The writer of Hebrews said through faith, *"He (Abraham) looked for a city whose builder and maker was God."* The city of Abraham's hopes and dreams was the church.

Paul said in Ephesians 3:10-12, *"His intent was that now, through the church, the manifold wisdom of God should be made known to the rulers and authorities in the heavenly realms, according to his eternal purpose which he accomplished in Christ Jesus our Lord. In him and through faith in him we may approach God with freedom and confidence."* The church is *"...the heavenly Jerusalem, the city of the living God"* (Hebrews 12:22). It is made up of all those who are "called out" from the bondage of sin and redeemed by the blood of Jesus. This is the city for which Abraham longed. His hope was in the promise of God to one day redeem the world, not destroy it. The prophets all had the same hope.

They all spoke of the coming Redeemer, the hope of Israel. That hope has always been based in the resurrection of Jesus from the grave. David said in Psalm 16:9-10, *"Therefore my heart is glad and my tongue rejoices; my body also will rest secure, because you will not abandon me to the grave, nor will you let your Holy One see decay."* David was not speaking of himself.

Acts 2:29-33, *"Seeing what was ahead, he spoke of the resurrection of the Christ, that he was not abandoned to the grave, nor did his body see decay. God has raised this Jesus to life, and we are all witnesses of the fact. Exalted to the right hand of God, he has received from the Father the promised Holy Spirit and has poured out what you now see and hear."* David's hope was in the resurrection of Jesus.

No proper understanding of Scripture can ever deny the resurrection of the dead or eternal life with God in heaven. That is the hope of the world. The confusion comes from a failure to distinguish between the physical and the spiritual. There is physical life and death and there is spiritual life and death. Animals have physical life; they do not have spiritual life. Animals experience physical death; they do not experience spiritual death.

The true consequence of sin was not loss of physical life, but loss of spiritual life with God. Resurrection from the dead is spiritual resurrection resulting in the elimination, not of physical death, but the eternal consequence of sin. Spiritual resurrection is the redemption of the soul so one can live forever in the kingdom of heaven with God.

Consider what Jesus said in John 5:24, *"I tell you the truth; whoever hears my word and believes him who sent me has eternal life and will not be condemned; he has crossed over from death to life."* Jesus was not saying those who believed in him would not die physically. Again in John 8:51 Jesus said, *"I tell you the truth, if anyone keeps my word, he will never see death."* Do Christians experience death? Jesus said they do not. If one is not dead, how can he possibly be resurrected?

The truth is we were all dead in sin. When we accept the atonement blood of Jesus for our sin we are raised from the dead so that we may truly have a "new life" (Romans 6:4). **That is the resurrection from death.** If we are alive in Jesus Christ, we will never die. Eternal life is in Jesus Christ.

This also explains why, when the atonement sacrifice had been completed, all those who were in the grave had to be resurrected to eternal life (or eternal death). Death no longer ruled. The sign that it was complete was the return of Jesus to destroy the physical temple where "prototypes" of the atonement sacrifice had been formerly offered.

Look again at the context of what Jesus taught in John 5.

> *"I tell you the truth; whoever hears my word and believes him who sent me has eternal life and will not be condemned; he has crossed over from death to life. I tell you the truth, a time is coming and has now come when the dead will hear the voice of the Son of God and those who hear will live. For as the Father has life in himself, so he has granted the Son to have life in himself. And he has given him authority to judge because he is the Son of Man.*
>
> *Do not be amazed at this, for a time is coming when all who are in their graves will hear his voice and come out—those who have done good will rise to live, and those who have done evil will rise to be condemned. By myself I can do nothing; I judge only as I hear, and my judgment is just, for I seek not to please myself but him who sent me"* (John 5:24-30).

This is completely consistent with what the writer said in comparing the sacrifice of Jesus to the sacrifices made by the earthly High Priests. First in Hebrews 6:17-20, *"Because God wanted to make the unchanging nature of his purpose very clear to the heirs of what was promised, he confirmed it with an oath. God did this so that, by two unchangeable things in which it is impossible for*

God to lie, we who have fled to take hold of the hope offered to us may be greatly encouraged. We have this hope as an anchor for the soul, firm and secure. It enters the inner sanctuary behind the curtain, where Jesus, who went before us, has entered on our behalf. He has become a high priest forever, in the order of Melchizedek."

And in chapter 9:24-28, *"For Christ did not enter a man-made sanctuary that was only a copy of the true one; he entered heaven itself, now to appear for us in God's presence. Nor did he enter heaven to offer himself again and again, the way the high priest enters the Most Holy Place every year with blood that is not his own. Then Christ would have had to suffer many times since the creation of the world. But now he has appeared once for all at the end of the ages to do away with sin by the sacrifice of himself. Just as man is destined to die once, and after that to face judgment, so Christ was sacrificed once to take away the sins of many people; and he will appear a second time, not to bear sin, but to bring salvation to those who are waiting for him."* If he has not returned, we do not yet have salvation!

Another reason given for a future coming of Jesus is the judgment. If he has already come, how does one explain the judgment day? Although opinions differ greatly among those who teach a future coming of the Lord, most include a mass gathering of all who have ever lived standing before Almighty God to be judged. What does the Bible say?

The first judgment day happened in the Garden of Eden. The Apostle Paul wrote in Romans 5:16, *"Again, the gift of God is not like the result of the one man's sin: The judgment followed one sin and brought condemnation, but the gift followed many trespasses and brought justification."* Adam and Eve lived for a time sin-free in the presence of God. They had but one rule; *"Do not eat of the tree of knowledge of good and evil."* They ate, the court was convened, the case presented, witnesses questioned, sentence pronounced, and they were expelled from his presence. As Paul said, judgment followed one sin and brought condemnation. This became the destiny of every human, since we all sin. Hence the Hebrew writer said, *"...man is destined to die and after that the judgment."*

It is important to understand the concept of judgment. Prior to Adam and Eve's sin there was no judgment because there was no accusation of wrongdoing. A person who has committed no offense does not go to court. Only those accused of breaking the law appear before a judge.

Jesus definitely spoke of another judgment day (Matthew 10:15, 11:22-24, 12:36-43). Because all people sin, every person who ever lived, or who would ever live, stood accused and condemned before God. The entire Bible is about a plan of redemption whereby we might escape this judgment.

Immediately following his triumphant entry into Jerusalem, just a week prior to his crucifixion, Jesus was teaching and prayed for God to glorify his name. *"Then a voice came from heaven, 'I have glorified it, and will glorify it again.' The crowd that was there and heard it said it had thundered; others said an angel had spoken to him. Jesus said, 'This voice was for your benefit, not mine. Now is the time for judgment on this world; now the prince of this world will be driven out. But I, when I am lifted up from the earth, will draw all men to myself.' He said this to show the kind of death he was going to die"* (John 12:28-33). Jesus said, *"NOW is the time for judgment on this world."* The judgment of the world is inextricably linked to the atonement of Jesus on the cross. The two cannot be separated.

Remember what Daniel and Jesus said would happen at the "time of the end" when Jerusalem would be destroyed. *"Multitudes who sleep in the dust of the earth will awake: some to everlasting life, others to shame and everlasting contempt. Those who are wise will shine like the brightness of the heavens, and those who lead many to righteousness, like the stars forever and ever"* (Daniel 12:2-3).

In the beginning God pronounced judgment on all who are guilty of sin. They shall experience spiritual death, eternal separation from his presence. Under the divine plan of redemption (the mystery of the ages) there was only one way whereby an appeal could be made. This second judgment would be placed in the hands of his only Son. Jesus said in John 5:21, *"For just as the Father raises the dead and gives them life, even so the Son gives life to whom he is pleased to give it. Moreover, the Father judges no one, but has entrusted all judgment to the Son, that all may honor the Son just as they honor the Father. He who does not honor the Son does not honor the Father, who sent him."*

Remember, it had already been appointed that all who sin would die and face God's judgment. The only hope anyone would ever have for salvation would to somehow be able to stand before God *without sin*. That is why the Hebrew writer did not stop when he mentioned man's destiny. The verse says, *"Just as man is destined to die once, and after that to face judgment,* ***so Christ was sacrificed once to take away the sins of many people;*** *and he will appear a second time, not to bear sin, but to bring salvation to those who are waiting for him."* Because we were destined to die and face God's judgment, Christ died for our sins. He took away our sins so we do not have to face judgment. Hallelujah!!

His first "coming" was to bear our sins. His second "coming" (appearance) was to confirm God's acceptance of his blood sacrifice for our sin. If we accept his sacrifice, we will never face God's judgment. All who stand in judgment are condemned. The only hope one has is to avoid God's judgment. The only way to do that is to accept Jesus as our Savior.

Paul makes essentially the same point in Romans 14:10 and in 2 Corinthians 5 when he says, *"So we make it our goal to please him, whether we are at home in the body or away from it. For we must all appear before the judgment seat of Christ, that each one may receive what is due him for the things done while in the body, whether good or bad."* Again, the destiny of every person is to stand before God and be judged by what we do. As clearly seen in John's vision of the judgment in Revelation 20, those who are judged by their works are all condemned. There is nothing we can do to earn our own salvation because we cannot atone for our own sins. The teaching of Scripture is that we will stand before God and be judged by what we do, or accept the atonement of Jesus. We will either be judged by our works (and lose) or we will not be judged at all because we no longer stand accused. Jesus took our place at the judgment. So we *"…make it our goal to please him."*

In Revelation 14 there is a magnificent picture of the judgment day. Three angels appear before John announcing this great event. The first one had the gospel to proclaim to the whole earth and said in a loud voice, *"Fear God and give him glory, because the hour of his judgment has come. Worship him who made the heavens, the earth, the sea and the springs of water"* (Verse 7).

In the following verse another angel appears and announced the fall of the city of Jerusalem. *"Fallen! Fallen is Babylon the Great, which made all the nations drink the maddening wine of her adulteries."* Babylon is used in Revelation as a prototype of adulterous Jerusalem and is identified as such.

> *"A third angel followed them and said in a loud voice: 'If anyone worships the beast and his image and receives his mark on the forehead or on the hand, he, too, will drink of the wine of God's fury, which has been poured full strength into the cup of his wrath. He will be tormented with burning sulfur in the presence of the holy angels and of the Lamb. And the smoke of their torment rises forever and ever. There is no rest day or night for those who worship the beast and his image, or for anyone who receives the mark of his name.' This calls for patient endurance on the part of the saints who obey God's commandments and remain faithful to Jesus"* (Verses 9-12).

If the judgment was not going to happen until after all people had died there would be no need for patient endurance on the part of the Saints. And in the very next verse, following the picture of the judgment scene, the inspired apostle heard a voice from heaven which said, *"Write: Blessed are the dead who die in the Lord from now on. 'Yes,' says the Spirit, 'they will rest from their labor, for their deeds will follow them.' "* People are still going to be "dying in the Lord" AFTER the judgment. This is consistent with Paul's explanation to the church in Thessalonica regarding those who died before the Lord's coming and those who would die after that.

Judgment had to occur when the atonement sacrifice was complete. A future judgment means death still has its holding power and something other than the sacrifice of Jesus is needed to break its bond. That is precisely why Jesus, just prior to his crucifixion, said, *"NOW is the time for judgment of the world."* In addition, if our sin is truly washed away by the blood of Jesus, what is the basis for our appearing before a judge? We no longer stand accused. We are forgiven! That is the hope of the world.

The condemnation of those who refuse to obey God (past and present) is described in John's revelation as the "second death" (Revelation 2:11, 20:6, 20:14, 21:8). Those who refuse to accept the atonement of Jesus for sin still stand accused before God and will face his wrath. The court has convened, sentence has been pronounced. Accept Jesus and live eternally, reject him and die…eternally.

The end-time prophets of today are right about one thing. If Jesus has not yet appeared a second time, the resurrection is still not a reality, and the judgment is still in our future. However, if this is true, we are also still waiting for him to finish the atonement, destroy the power of death, overcome the grave, and bring salvation to mankind…and we still do not know the outcome of God's judgment. That is a message that steals the Christian hope!

The hope of the world has always been the death, burial,

resurrection, and appearing of Jesus. As a result of Jesus' resurrection, every man and woman from Adam and Eve forward can have resurrection life. They can be resurrected from eternal death, the result of sin, and live eternally with the Father. That life begins the moment one receives forgiveness from sin and continues forever in eternity. Eternal life is possible because of the finished atonement sacrifice of Jesus. This is the blessed hope, the hope of the world, the hope of eternal life, and the anchor of the soul.

Even those who espouse a future end-time theology do not deny that we receive salvation and eternal life the moment we accept, through obedient faith, Jesus' sacrifice for our sin. If, as this doctrine proposes, the world is still waiting for Jesus' return to "rapture" the saints, judge the world, and destroy the universe, that second coming would still NOT be the basis or the goal of our hope. The only basis for real hope is Jesus' sacrifice on the cross and subsequent resurrection. The goal of our hope is eternal life with God.

It is easy to understand the hope the Israelites had of a promised Messiah, the Great Redeemer who would come. It is easy to understand their excitement and hope as they awaited the second appearing of the High Priest to emerge from behind the veil of the Holy of Holies signifying God's acceptance of their atonement sacrifice. It is also easy to understand the anticipation of the apostles and first century Christians as they awaited the coming of Jesus as the Great High Priest proclaiming the ultimate atonement had been accepted in heaven for the sins of all. What is difficult to understand is how a future coming to "rapture" the church and end civilization has replaced the atonement for sin as the "hope of the world." Fulfilled prophecy does not deny the resurrection. It simply centers that hope on the resurrection of Jesus, which is where the Bible says he overcame death.

Another point that should be considered is the negative effect decades of failed prophesies based on faulty theology has had, not only on the credibility of the church in the world, but on the faith of Christians. Solomon said in Proverbs 13:12, *"Hope deferred makes the heart sick, but a longing fulfilled is a tree of life."* Most of us who have lived any length of time on this earth understand all too well this proverb. We have been promised something would happen, we get excited about it and wait in anxious anticipation, yet it never happens. This is very disheartening. The greater the promise the more discouraging it is when it is not realized.

This is perhaps the most insidious and damaging result of the failed prophesies concerning the second coming as taught by the futurist doctrine. In revealing the prophecy to Daniel, God was careful to clearly explain to him that he would not see it in his lifetime. *"As for you, go your way till the end. You will rest* (die), *and then at the end of the days you will rise to receive your allotted inheritance"* (Daniel 12:13).

The New Testament reveals that with the coming of Jesus and his sacrifice on the cross, the "time of the end" prophesied by Daniel had come. Jesus said all those events would happen in that generation. Nine times in his Revelation John said the time was *at hand, near, soon.* To defer this hope for thousands of years is, to use Solomon's analogy, a sickening doctrine. With every prediction of Jesus' future coming has come the disappointment in its non-occurrence. To understand God has kept all his promises and all the prophesies have been fulfilled exactly as he said they would be, and at the exact time he decreed, is a "tree of life."

One could cite hundreds of examples of people who have been deluded by the "deferred hope" of a second coming and have made life changing decisions with devastating results to themselves, their families, and the church. Most Christians are familiar with the song *It Is Well with My Soul.* The words were written in 1873 by Horatio G. Spafford. Mr. Spafford lived in Chicago and, though a lawyer by profession, was deeply interested in the Scriptures, active in his home church, and very involved in evangelism.

Despite the loss of a son and having the Great Chicago Fire of 1871 destroy most of his real estate holdings, in 1873 Spafford planned a trip to Europe to assist Moody and Sankey in one of their evangelistic campaigns in Great Britain. The day he, his wife, and four daughters were to leave he had a situation arise that required him to take a later ship. He sent his family on ahead, planning to join them in a few days. On November 22 the first ship collided with another vessel and sank in minutes. Only his wife was saved. As he traveled to meet her in Europe he wrote the words to the song.

When peace, like a river, attendeth my way,
When sorrows like sea billows roll;
Whatever my lot, Thou has taught me to say,
It is well, it is well, with my soul.

Though Satan should buffet, though trials should come,
Let this blest assurance control,
That Christ has regarded my helpless estate,
And hath shed his own blood for my soul.

The third stanza contains some of the most poignant words ever penned.

My sin, oh, the bliss of this glorious thought!
My sin, not in part but the whole,
Is nailed to the cross, and I bear it no more,
Praise the Lord, praise the Lord, O my soul!

What an incredible message of hope to a lost and dying world. But it is the last two verses that express his growing interest in the theory of the future second coming of Jesus.

But, Lord, 'tis for Thee, for Thy coming we wait,
The sky, not the grave, is our goal;
Oh trump of the angel! Oh voice of the Lord!
Blessed hope, blessed rest of my soul!

And Lord, haste the day when my faith shall be sight,
The clouds be rolled back as a scroll;
The trump shall resound, and the Lord shall descend,
Even so, it is well with my soul.

Mr. Spafford became so committed to the futurist theology of the second coming he later moved to Jerusalem with his wife and one daughter (who had been born after the sea tragedy) and started a small utopian community to wait for the coming of the Lord. No longer was he active in a neighborhood church or involved in missions. The hope of salvation for the lost had been replaced with the hope of the Lord's second coming. He died waiting, as did the next two generations of his followers. The community was finally dispersed in the 1950's. Who knows how many lost souls might have heard the Gospel if Mr. Spafford had stayed with the Gospel message of his first three stanzas?

Well over a century and hundreds more failed prophesies later, the modern church still sings the same message of hope deferred. The world desperately needs the church to get over its fascination with the end of time and begin eagerly and earnestly sharing the true hope of the world, the gospel of Jesus Christ. The continual stream of false prophesies over the past decades has done nothing but derail the church from its mission, distort its message, and undermine its credibility in the world.

Sadly, this teaching has virtually replaced redemption from sin as the modern "Christian hope." Most Christians today are much more excited about the soon coming of the Lord than about winning a lost soul. It is extremely difficult to understand a Christian's "hope" to be that the Lord will descend from heaven and destroy everything, thus ending anyone's chance of accepting him and being saved. This is misplaced hope, at best.

Some Christians today view the teaching of fulfilled prophecy as explained herein as bordering on outright heresy.

Please consider the ultimate beliefs that are common regardless of one's view of eschatology:

1. Jesus is the Son of God who died for the sins of the world.
2. All who accept his Lordship and surrender in obedient faith are saved.
3. All who are saved will experience the resurrection from death.
4. All believers will go to heaven and spend eternity with God.

Understanding that prophecy has been fulfilled denies none of these beliefs. It simply recognizes God's time frame for the fulfillment of his eternal plan for redemption upon which all of the above are based.

The hope of the world has always been Jesus Christ's death, burial, and resurrection to atone for sin. Redemption was the hope of Adam, the hope of Abraham, the hope of Israel and continues to be the hope of every person who lives today or in the future. The fact that Jesus returned to fulfill his promises and take away the Old temple in Jerusalem does not diminish the Christian hope. Just the opposite is true. His removal of the temple proved for all time we are no longer living under the Law, but under the grace of Jesus Christ. It is even more evidence that our hope for redemption and eternity in God's presence is assured. "My hope is built on nothing less than Jesus blood and righteousness," not "Jesus is coming soon, morning or night or noon." Thank God for this blessed hope!

Perhaps it is too much to expect all Christians to come to agreement on many issues concerning eschatology. Regardless of one's view, the message of the church to the lost should be the death, burial, and resurrection of Jesus Christ which provided the atoning blood for sin and guaranteed our hope of eternal life with God. What must one do to be saved? *"Repent and be baptized in the name of Jesus Christ!"* Nothing more…nothing less. One does not have to understand anything about the second coming to be baptized and have fellowship in the Lord's kingdom.

What one should reasonably expect is that the study of these issues be a vibrant part of every maturing Christian's effort to learn more about the Father and come to a more complete understanding of his word, not part of the fundamental message of the Gospel one must believe and obey to become a child of God and enjoy fellowship with his saints. We need to get the distractions off the television programs and out of our pulpits and return to the clear, simple message of the gospel. That is the only hope the world has. As a preacher friend said in a conversation about the millennial reign of Christ, "I am a Pan-Millennialist…in the end it will all pan out." Of that we can be certain.

May God bless your growth as you enjoy his everlasting presence!

About the Author

Jim Reeves was the youngest of six children. Growing up on a dairy farm in rural Northwest Arkansas shaped his approach to life. His mother was a deeply religious, gentle lady who had an insatiable desire to know and understand the Bible. Her influence made a deep impression on her children and Jim has spent a lifetime following a similar quest.

He graduated from York College with honors and then attended David Lipscomb University in Tennessee where he continued his studies in Bible and music. He also holds a BA in Organizational Management from Concordia University. Jim had a successful career in the oil and gas industry, and has always been actively involved in a local church, having preached, led worship, and taught Bible classes for churches in Arkansas, Indiana, Colorado, and Texas. He married his wife, Donna, in 1967 and they have two grown children.

His professional career took him to several countries, the most life-changing being almost four years in Lagos, Nigeria on two assignments. It was during this time he decided to put on paper what he believes to be the simple Biblical truth concerning the end times and the Revelation of Jesus Christ; Mystery Accomplished!

He can be contacted via email at jdr.reeves@gmail.com and is always willing to answer questions or study the Scriptures with anyone who is interested.

www.ingramcontent.com/pod-product-compliance
Lightning Source LLC
Chambersburg PA
CBHW021038090426
42738CB00006B/136

* 9 7 8 1 5 0 6 9 1 2 3 1 8 *